Indians in American History

To the memory of

LAWRENCE W. TOWNER

and

ALFONSO ORTIZ

Indians in American History

An Introduction
Second Edition

Edited by
Frederick E. Hoxie
Vice President
for Research and Education
The Newberry Library
&

Peter Iverson
Professor of History
Arizona State University

Harlan Davidson, Inc.
Wheeling, Illinois
60090-6000

Indians in American History: an introduction / edited by Frederick E. Hoxie
  & Peter Iverson. — 2nd. ed.
      p.   cm.
   Includes bibliographical references and index.
   ISBN 0-88295-939-5
   1. Indians of North America—Historiography. 2. Indians of North America—History—Study and teaching. 3. United States—Historiography— 4. Indians of North America—History. 5. United States—History—Study and teaching.   I. Hoxie, Frederick E., 1947–. II. Iverson, Peter.
E76.8I57   1998
973'.0497'0072—dc21   97-37468
                                                                  CIP

Cover painting: "Buffalo Dance" by Tonita Peña (San Ildefonso), c. 1920. Courtesy, The Newberry Library
Cover design by DePinto Graphic Design.

Manufactured in the United States of America
00 99 98 1 2 3 MG

Contents

Contributors

James A. Brown is Professor of Anthropology at Northwestern University. He is the author of *Pre-Columbian Shell Engraving From the Craig Mound at Spiro, Oklahoma* (1975) and joint author of *Ancient Art of the Woodland Indians* (1985).

Henry F. Dobyns is an anthropologist and author whose works include *Native American Historical Demography* (1976) and *Their Number Become Thinned: Native American Population Dynamics in Eastern North America* (1983).

R. David Edmunds (Cherokee) is Professor of History at Indiana University and author of *The Potawatomis: Keepers of the Fire* (1979), *The Shawnee Prophet* (1983), *Tecumseh and the Quest for Indian Leadership* (1984), and coauthor of *The Fox Wars*.

Kevin Gover (Pawnee) practices law in Albuquerque with the firm of Gover, Stetson, and Williams, and was nominated by President Clinton as assistant secretary of the interior for Indian affairs.

William T. Hagan retired from the State University of New York College at Fredonia and from the University of Oklahoma. His many publications include *American Indians* (1961), *United States-Comanche Relations: The Reservation Years* (1976), and *Theodore Roosevelt and Six Friends of the Indians* (1997).

Paivi Hoikkala received her Ph.D. in history from Arizona State University and currently teaches history at Santa Monica College and the California State Polytechnic University at Pomona. Her other publications include "Mothers and Community Builders: Salt River Pima and Maricopa Women in Community Action" in *Negotiators of Change,* edited by Nancy Shoemaker (1995).

Frederick E. Hoxie is Vice President for Research and Education at the Newberry Library, Chicago. He has written *The Final Promise: The Campaign to Assimilate the Indians, 1880–1920* (1984) and *Parading Through History: The Making of the Crow Nation in America, 1805–1935* (1995) and is editor of *The Encyclopedia of North American Indians* (1996).

Peter Iverson (editor) is Professor of History at Arizona State University. His most recent book is *"We Are Still Here": American Indians in the Twentieth Century* (1998).

Alvin M. Josephy, Jr. was founding chairman of the board of trustees of The National Museum of the American Indian. Editor of *The American Heritage Book of Indians* (1964) and *America in 1492* (1991), he has also written *The Patriot Chiefs* (1961), *The Nez Perces and the Opening of the Northwest* (1965), *After the Buffalo's Gone* (1984), *500 Nations* (1994) and numerous other books and magazine articles.

Kenneth M. Morrison is the author of *The Embattled Northeast: The Elusive Ideal of Alliance in Abenaki-Euramerican Relations* (1984). Professor Morrison teaches religious studies at Arizona State University.

Alfonso Ortiz (San Juan Tewa) served as a member of the National Advisory Council of the D'Arcy McNickle Center for the History of the American Indian from its inception in 1972 until his death in January 1997; he chaired the group after 1977. Professor of Anthropology at the University of New Mexico, he authored *The Tewa World: Space Time, Being, and Becoming in a Pueblo Society* (1969), and edited volumes 9 and 10 of the *Smithsonian Institution's Handbook of North American Indians*.

Theda Perdue is Professor of History at the University of Kentucky. Her most recent work is *Cherokee Women: Gender and Culture Change, 1700–1835* (1998).

Neal Salisbury is Professor of History at Smith College. He is the author of *Manitou and Providence: Indians, Europeans, and the Making of New England, 1500–1643* (1982), coauthor of *The Enduring Vision: A History of the American People* (3rd ed., 1998), and editor of *Mary Rowlandson's "The Sovereignty and Goodness of God" and Related Documents* (1997).

Mark N. Trahant (Shoshone-Bannock) is a journalist who has covered Indian Country for two decades. He is editor and publisher of the *Moscow-Pullman Daily News* in Moscow, Idaho, and author of *Pictures of Our Nobler Selves* (1995), a history of Native American contributions to the news media.

W. Richard West, Jr. (Cheyenne/Arapaho) is Director of the National Museum of the American Indian, Smithsonian Institution.

Charles F. Wilkinson is Professor of Law at the University of Colorado and the author of *American Indians, Time and the Law: Native Societies in Modern Constitutional Democracy* (1987).

Preface

A s its title suggests, *Indians in American History* seeks to bring Native histories and cultures more fully into the study of the American past. Although not a conventional American Indian history text, it also attempts to provide a useful presentation of subjects and themes central to that history. The volume thus yields new ways to understand, for example, the American Revolution, the U.S. Constitution, southern history, and national expansion. In addition, it reflects the breadth and complexity of American Indian history.

This second edition features three new chapters. Neal Salisbury examines the dynamics of the colonial period. Mark Trahant furnishes a probing discussion of the recent Native past, while Paivi Hoikkala reviews the challenges faced and leadership demonstrated by American Indian women in the twentieth century. Theda Perdue has also incorporated significant new material into her chapter on Indians in southern history. All the chapters conclude with updated, revised lists for further reading. Finally, the material in the appendix has also been revised to incorporate recent developments.

The first edition was edited by Fred Hoxie, former director of the D'Arcy McNickle Center for American Indian History at the Newberry Library. After Fred assumed new responsibilities at the Newberry, Peter Iverson served as acting director of the McNickle Center until a permanent director could be selected. During that interim period, planning began for the second edition, and Peter agreed to take on primary responsibility for necessary alterations and additions. We would like to acknowledge again those individuals who assisted in the preparation of the first edition: Richard H. Brown, the late Harlan Davidson, Sr., Maureen Hewitt, Colin Calloway, Rose Summers, John Aubrey, Jeff Auld, Rose Marie White, and Marilyn DeBerry. For the second edition, Arizona State University graduate student Shawn Kline provided valuable editorial assistance. Maureen Hewitt helped us initiate the project and Andrew Davidson made sure we finished it. To all, many thanks.

Most of the illustrations in this book are from the collections of the Newberry Library. Many of them are reprints from first editions of books that have been out of print for decades. Others, including the cover, are from original art that is being published here for the first time. James Bier drew the maps for this book from information provided by Fred Hoxie and (for chapter 3) Henry F. Dobyns. Jane Domier drew an additional new map. Bob Easton kindly allowed us to reproduce his drawings in the legend to the map on Indian house types in chapter 1. Caleb Christopher, Neal Salisbury, and Mark Trahant all helped locate new illustrations for this edition.

The second edition of *Indians in American History* is dedicated to the memory of Lawrence W. Towner and to the memory of Alfonso Ortiz. Bill Towner served for twenty-four years as president and librarian at the Newberry, retiring in 1986. During his administration, the D'Arcy McNickle Center for American Indian History was established, and, in no small part because of his enthusiastic support, began to flourish. From the inception of the Center in the fall of 1972 until his death in January 1997, Alfonso Ortiz was a member of its national advisory council. For nearly all of that period, he served as its chair. A professor of anthropology at the University of New Mexico, a San Juan Tewa, and a mentor for countless colleagues, he provided the kind of vision and wisdom that guided the evolution of the Center to its present, ongoing status as a meeting ground for all who share a common interest in the Indian past, present, and future. Under its current director, Craig Howe, the McNickle Center will continue to build upon the legacy of Bill Towner and Alfonso Ortiz.

FREDERICK E. HOXIE
Vice President for Research
and Education
The Newberry Library

PETER IVERSON
Professor of History
Arizona State University

Preface to the First Edition

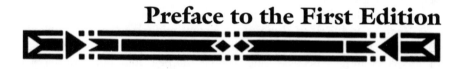

*T*he unruliness of American educational life is one of the sources of its genius. Rooted in a tradition of local control, accountable to social and political pressures from myriad interest groups, and stretched across a vast and various landscape, "education" is difficult to summarize, control, or change. While there are periodic efforts to "open" classrooms or return to "basics," there are always countertrends in evidence, and reformers are almost always frustrated in their efforts to transform the schools. Our diversity and size keep our system responsive, innovative.

But unruliness can also be a terrible liability. It can stifle changes that are generally acceptable, and it can place a brake on progress. Technical improvements and curricular innovations can be held up by educators who want to keep doing things their own way.

Since 1972 the D'Arcy McNickle Center for the History of the American Indian has been both pleased and frustrated by the unruliness of the American educational system. As a center committed to improving the quality of what is taught and written about American Indian history, it has benefited from the exploding interest in the subject in our schools and colleges. Teachers, professors, tribal historians, and others have come to the Newberry Library to write books, prepare classroom materials, and gather copies of our holdings for tribal archives and cultural centers. At the same time, the Center has felt the frustration of watching a body of scholarly literature develop that has not seemed to alter the way American history is taught. The size and diversity of the American educational enterprise has limited the "new" Indian history's impact on classroom discourse. This volume represents the McNickle Center's effort to alleviate that frustration and to bridge the distance between specialized scholarship and the world of teachers and students.

Ten of the essays in this book were originally presented at a series of McNickle Center conferences. Each conference addressed the theme of "The Impact of Indian History on the Teaching of U.S. History," with lectures and discussions on the Indian component of familiar topics in the American past. Supported by the National Endowment for the Humanities and the Lloyd A.

Fry Foundation, these gatherings attracted a total of 250 college teachers and generated a great deal of enthusiasm for the task of integrating Native American materials into the conventional U.S. history curriculum. All of the conferees expressed a need for better materials, particularly publications that students could use to supplement or correct what they learned in their textbooks. This volume is a response to that need.

Indians in American History is not a conventional textbook. It contains chronologically arranged essays by thirteen authors who speak from a variety of disciplines and perspectives. The chapters can be read together or in conjunction with a survey text. They are intended to provide an introduction to the Indian side of the usual narrative. The topics will be familiar to most readers—the Revolution, the Constitution, the Twentieth Century—but the content will probably be new. It will provide an opening lesson in the breadth and complexity of American Indian history. And the suggestions following each chapter will direct readers further into the scholarly literature. However the book is read, we hope it will infect its readers with some of the excitement inherent in the rapidly expanding field, and that it will contribute to a fuller appreciation of American history.

A great many people have assisted in preparing this volume. Richard H. Brown helped spark the original idea for the "impact" conferences and brought the Newberry Library squarely behind the project at several critical points. The late Harlan Davidson, Sr., first invited the Center to develop an introductory Indian history volume for students and was an eager sponsor of the project. Maureen Hewitt, editor-in-chief at Harlan Davidson, Inc., carried that sponsorship forward with great patience and skill. Others at the Newberry provided a range of valuable services. Colin Calloway assisted in editing and proofreading the essays, Rose Summers helped with proofreading and communicating with authors, and John Aubrey made a number of valuable suggestions regarding illustrations. Finally, the excellent word processing department of Jeff Auld, Rose Marie White, and Marilyn DeBerry was a vital source of clean copy following what must have seemed like an endless series of revisions.

Most of the illustrations in this book are from the collections of the Newberry Library. Many of them are reprints from first editions of books that have been out of print for decades. Others, including the cover, are from original art that is being published here for the first time. James Bier drew the maps for this book from information provided by myself and (for chapter 3) Henry F. Dobyns. Bob Easton kindly allowed us to reproduce his drawings in the legend to the map on Indian house types in chapter 1. Together, the visual material in the volume should suggest again the richness and freshness of this aspect of American history.

Finally, this book is dedicated to Lawrence W. Towner on the occasion of his retirement. During his twenty-four years as president and librarian at the Newberry, Bill Towner pursued a simple, yet eloquent objective: making the matchless collections of this institution more accessible to serious students and scholars. The McNickle Center, founded to bring people from universities, schools, Indian communities and the general public into greater contact with the library and its holdings, is a part of his legacy. Whatever contributions the Center and its projects might make to a new vision of the American past should also be credited to Dr. Towner's energy and commitment.

FREDERICK E. HOXIE
The Newberry Library

Introduction

Indian / White Relations: A View from the Other Side of the "Frontier"

Alfonso Ortiz

> So we went to school to copy, to imitate; not to exchange language and ideas, and not to develop the best traits that had come out of uncountable experiences of hundreds and thousands of years living upon this continent. Our annals, all happenings of human import, were stored in our song and dance rituals, our history differing in that it was not stored in books, but in the living memory. So, while the white people had much to teach us, we had much to teach them, and what a school could have been established upon that idea!
>
> LUTHER STANDING BEAR,
> *LAND OF THE SPOTTED EAGLE* (1933)

*M*ore than half a century after it was first proposed, this idea is as sound and exciting as it was then, and only a little closer to realization. Nevertheless, if we can introduce Standing Bear's suggestion to students and teachers, perhaps we can move it onto the nation's agenda in the years ahead. If Standing Bear's school is to be realized in the future something must be brought into being that, for the most part, does not exist today—a balanced and honest history of interactions between Indians and whites. The kind of history of which I speak is one that recognizes that Indian people have always been multidimensional and fully sentient human beings. It is also a history that would take up the Indian people's side of the historical encounter and tell their story fully. In the process, this new Indian history would lay to rest

Above: Detail from print. See page 7.

1

enduring stereotypes about Indians that have existed in the old history, and lay to rest as well even more enduring assumptions about the proper way to "do" history. This new Indian history would have to acknowledge Indians as teachers. It would frame questions and inquiries using terms and categories that reflect Indian realities and are important to Indians.*

Before progress can be made toward the ideal of a new Indian history, we have to ask why it has not come about before now. What kept it from emerging in the past? To answer this question we have to examine critically the concepts that historians of Indian/white relations have used in their efforts to interpret Indian experiences. There are eight of these notions, and together they form a stick with which we can flay the old way of doing history. Once these eight concepts are identified, we can examine the implications and consequences of the old way of historical conceptualization and suggest both correctives for the present and challenges for the future.

The first notion, that of Western civilization, is important to understand for anyone wanting to do Indian history, because it provides the context for previous histories of Indian/white relations. To those who celebrate Western culture alone, it is "civilization" that entered and advanced across America and either assimilated or destroyed everything in its path. Indian people and their communities have more often been destroyed rather than assimilated, but the push for assimilation of the survivors has been unrelenting, and it continues. The celebration of Western civilization, with its roots in the ancient Near East and its traditions running back to Egypt, Greece, Rome, Western Europe, and the Americas, has bred a relentless linearity of thought and, sometimes, cultural arrogance. Most historians have been both proponents of and participants in Western civilization, so the histories they have written have served the interest of their culture. This is the largest backdrop against which the historical enterprise must be viewed, as it is the assumptions and foundations of Western civilization that must be questioned if lasting changes are to be made in how history is done.

Thus, from the perspective of Western civilization, the history of Indian/white relations in the United States is the story of white people's attempts to assimilate the Indian past into the terms of their own history, their own internal dialogue. In this view, we shouldn't worry about what actual Indian peoples' own wishes and experiences might be. This kind of historical enterprise is, I submit, like a machine that devours or destroys everything in

---

*I should like at the outset to introduce a distinction between tribal histories and the more general process of writing about Indian/white relations through time. Despite a general reluctance on the part of historians of tribal histories to begin with the given tribe's own accounts of their origins and early migrations, specific tribal histories are on the right track in faithfully presenting histories of their encounters and relations with whites. The history of Indian/white relations as viewed from the white side of the frontier is another matter altogether, and it is this kind of history and only this kind of history that I am criticizing in this essay.

Cory, Laso, and Pok in Hopi race kilts, 1980. Photo by Victor Masayesva, Jr.

its path. Even the peoples who are destroyed are not left in peace, for this kind of "history" returns later to pick over their bones. Indeed, the evidence indicates that cultures are easier to deal with historically after they are dead.

Yet, any Indian person can look at the notion of Western civilization and say that, like the "moral majority" of our times, it is neither. It is a long-playing idea, Western civilization, but to the cause of a meaningful Indian history it has simply been, and remains, the enemy. No fully sentient Indian person I have known has ever wanted to be initiated into the terms and conditions of Western civilization or its history. That it happens so much to the Indian past is not their fault.

A related notion, that of the frontier, has been much more actively harmful to the cause of Indian survival and to the writing of meaningful histories of Indian/white relations, let alone of Indian tribes themselves. As long as the white frontier was alive and well, Indian people had to fight a desperate rearguard action to survive its advance, so they had neither the time nor the means to tell their stories, to relate their own experiences. The notion of the frontier has fallen into disfavor as both an assumption and a research tool, so I will avoid flaying it yet again. However, because it has been around so long and is so pervasive in our lives and language, it may be a long time, if ever, before the concept of frontier is expunged from our everyday consciousness. In any case, we must remind each new generation that one culture's frontier may be another culture's backwater or backyard. I shall return to the concept of frontier presently, with concrete examples. Suffice it to state here that I do not know of any Indian tribe that had a concept remotely comparable to "frontier" as part of its indigenous heritage.

A third notion, that of wilderness, is also very, very old in Euro-American cultural consciousness. It played itself out on the American earth by having European colonists define Indians as part of the American wilderness, as something that had to be expurgated or pushed back. This strain of thought continues in the American mind in the sense that many white Americans still think of the Indian as part of nature, if they think of the Indian at all. Again, I know of no Indian culture that has or had a notion comparable to "wilderness." In *Land of the Spotted Eagle*, Luther Standing Bear places this concept in a good Indian perspective:

> Only to the White man was nature a "wilderness" and only to him was the land "infested" with "wild" animals and savage people. To us it was tame. Earth was bountiful and we were surrounded with the blessings of the Great Mystery. Not until the hairy man from the east came and with brutal frenzy heaped injustices upon us and the families we loved was it "wild" for us. When the very animals of the forest began fleeing from his approach, then it was that for us the "Wild West" began.

Related to the notion of wilderness is the civilization/savagism dichotomy, which has also had such long-standing favor in American history, both as it was defined by whites and as it was written by historians. Of course, Indians were defined as savages through most of American history and, of course again, they were almost always on the other side of the frontier. The turn-of-the-century Greek poet C. P. Cavafy makes interesting commentary on the subject of barbarians, and we might as easily substitute savages for his barbarians. The poem is entitled "Waiting for the Barbarians," and it is set in decadent Rome:

What are we waiting for, assembled in the forum?

The barbarians are due here today.

Why isn't anything going on in the senate?
Why are the senators sitting there without legislating?

Because the barbarians are coming today.
What's the point of senators making laws now?
Once the barbarians are here, they'll do the legislating.

Why don't our distinguished orators turn up as usual
to make their speeches, say what they have to say?

Because the barbarians are coming today
and they're bored by rhetoric and public speaking.

Why this sudden bewilderment, this confusion?
(How serious people's faces have become.)
Why are the streets and squares emptying so rapidly,
everyone going home lost in thought?

Because night has fallen and the barbarians haven't come.
And some of our men just in from the border say
there are no barbarians any longer.

Now what's going to happen to us without barbarians?
Those people were a kind of solution.

Cavafy's last question is one we are going to have to ask and answer honestly if we are to find our way to a new Indian history, as the savages of America, like the barbarians for Imperial Rome, "were a kind of solution." Now, because the peoples on both sides of the American "frontier" have redefined and remade themselves over and over again in the course of 500 years, each in response to the other, we are finding that the old concepts and categories just will not do anymore. We shall have to find new ones.

Because civilization and Christianity were but flip sides of the same coin through most of American history, one cannot speak of the one without the other. Christianity was always presented to Indian people as an unquestionable good. It was not merely better than what was there before; on the contrary, Indian religions were denounced as idolatry and devil-worship, and the people themselves were pronounced as godless. The intolerance bred by this view in its always extreme manifestations resulted in the suppression and destruction of much that was suited to the Indian people in their diverse circumstances, much that was beautiful in its own right. The Hopi people asked the first American missionaries who came among them whether Jesus Christ could help them grow corn better in their oasis environment than their beloved kachinas. When the missionaries could put forth no proof that Christ could deliver any more moisture than the kachinas, the Hopis turned their backs on the missionaries. Yet, Indian people never, to my knowledge, had any objections to the ideals of Christianity nor to the teachings of Christ. What they objected to was the behavior of alleged Christians on the "frontier"—ruffians who would rob, steal, and defraud them, all in the name of Christianity.

John Woodenlegs, a Northern Cheyenne elder and religious leader who passed away a few years ago, liked to relate the story of how the Cheyenne Council had to go into an all-night session to try to explain the devil and the concept of hell to the Cheyenne people. This was at a time when they were being bedeviled by missionaries, so these questions were at the forefront of Cheyenne minds. After extended discussion, the council sent word out to the people that the devil was a fellow who came over on the boat with Columbus. Further, they were not to worry about hell, as that was a place only for white people, not Cheyennes.

Just as Indians were usually regarded as beyond the pale of civilization and God, so also were they regarded as without any law or government worthy of the name. Just how frontier barbarians from Europe, people who ignored their own laws and governments when dealing with Indian people, could so label Indians boggles the mind. But they did, and the lawless Indian stereotype has been one of the longest playing shows in American cultural history. It moved from captivity narratives and sermons to books and articles on the Wild West to films at the turn of this century, and its run has lasted into our own time. To cite one example of this phenomenon, "The Virginian," an immensely popular television series of the 1960s, placed Sitting Bull on the Arizona deserts and Geronimo somewhere near Dodge City, Kansas. So durable and flexible was the myth of bringing law and order to the Wild West that these historic figures could appear anywhere. People who had resisted the white man's trek across the continent had been reduced to simple props on a movable stage.

The notion of Manifest Destiny, that it was the American nation's sacred duty not only to bring law and order to the Wild West but to secure its borders from sea to shining sea, brought in its wake the Indian Wars and the final removal of Indian people to reservations away from the white man's civilization. When we ponder just how much they had endured by this time with the white man's history of colonization and conquest, it is a wonder that

This illustration from Ridpath's History of the United States *(1897) shows Columbus dreaming of his voyages. It illustrates the romantic belief that the Italian explorer was divinely inspired to bring Western civilization and Christianity to the American wilderness. Courtesy, The Newberry Library.*

any Indian people were left after Manifest Destiny had run its course. But they are still here and growing in numbers. These facts make it both imperative and urgent that we discard old historical baggage and find new concepts to account for Indian people and to deal with them in such a way as to understand their resiliency and cultural tenacity.

Finally, it should come as no surprise, in light of what I have discussed so far, that in viewing American history from the other side of the frontier I find all the names for the various periods to be patently self-serving. The names for the various periods of American history that historians have erected come entirely from their colonial and national experiences rather than from the nature and duration of their encounters and experiences with particular Indian peoples in particular times and places. I would ask, rhetorically, why we should not redefine periods in our common past in terms of the tribe or confederacy most prominent in Indian/white relations? In this scenario, the colonial period would be divided between the Coastal Algonkians and the Six Nations; the Early Republic would be renamed for the Shawnee; the Jacksonian era would be renamed the Cherokee; and the Gilded Age, the Lakota/Dakota. And so on.

The renaming of the periods of American history to include references to Indians will of course never happen, as the names were erected to tell the white people's story of their life on this continent. That is what history has overwhelmingly been. Those names also reinforce the old, imperious concepts I have discussed above: frontier, civilization, and manifest destiny.

The point to all of these objections to standard historical concepts and categories, of course, is that they are all self-serving, because what you get depends on who is in charge of defining these terms. As terms, they have always been defined by persons from the East, facing westward. And of course these people defining the terms have always put themselves on the civilized, Christian, and law-abiding side of the line. Indeed, when we contemplate how Indian people have been defined in American history, as uncouth, devilworshipping savages who had no proper notions of law or government and who, moreover, kept putting themselves on the wrong side of the frontier, one has to wonder just how they managed to survive during the thousands of years before Europeans came over to rescue them from their miserable condition. Once again, Luther Standing Bear addresses the issue eloquently:

> But all of the years of calling the Indian a savage has never made him one; all of the denial of his virtues has never taken them from him; and the very resistance he has made to save the things inalienably his has been his saving strength—that which will stand him in need when justice does make its belated appearance and he undertakes rehabilitation.

The terms and concepts under discussion also present other problems. They assume that civilization and culture are dispensed from the East and only from the East. This of course is purely an Anglo-American model of history, and it immediately runs into problems when we consider the prehistory and colonial history of the Spanish Southwest. Here, for centuries reaching into millennia, we have had advanced ideas and inventions—such as in astronomical and architectural knowledge, the knowledge of pottery-making, and corn agriculture—come up from the South.

I would propose that we dispense with the notion of frontier altogether when talking about historical encounters between peoples, both for the reasons I have already indicated and because it is possible to make so much mischief with this notion. Besides, we on earth may one day get our comeuppance if we encounter superior beings in outer space one day, beings who will look upon us as the backwash of their frontier and their history. In our everyday life, the concept of frontier is too deeply entrenched for there to be any hope of expunging it soon; but since historians put it there to begin with, historians and their students should work to root it out. It is too easy and tempting for keepers of texts to hide on one side of the idea and define everything on the other side as bad.

In view of all this, it is no wonder that historical documents enshrine the worst images ever visited on Indian peoples. In this sense, our written history has been the handmaiden of conquest and assimilation. (A romantic view of Indians has long lived in literature and the arts, but that is not my concern here except to note that it is no more realistic than the negative image of history.) Conventional history is so at odds with the facts that Indians often simply ignore it. Ironically, many tribes regard history as more acceptable to them than ethnography because they believe history has nothing to do with what they consider important to their identity as Indians. That is to say, they do not fear or worry about historians because history does not usually deal with what they really value about their native cultures: their languages, religions, oral traditions, arts, and kin networks. History is so distorted it is irrelevant.

To illustrate with a personal example: for many years I have been asked by Indian leaders to write a history of the eight northern Pueblos of New Mexico because so many white Americans visit among these communities as tourists and ask for a history to purchase and read. Pueblo officials quite obviously see the possibilities for making some money here.

I have not taken on the task, but if I were to embark on an in-depth community study of any *one* of the Pueblos, the people there would not cooperate; I would be getting too close to what they want to protect from prying eyes. What is striking is that in the Pueblo readers' view, if the whites want history, give it to them so that we Indians can continue to dance and tell our stories unmolested. Pueblo people do not think of history as revealing anything really important about themselves.

Some day, when historians start to frame questions Indians are interested in, to voice concerns Indians consider important and enduring about their lives, then the historians will be telling Indian peoples' stories and not merely extending their own. At that point the Pueblo leaders will find history more meaningful, even if it might also be less profitable and more trouble-some to write.

Most of us also know that history compartmentalizes experience in dangerous ways. One looks at politics, subsistence, environmental relations, federal policy, with Indians pushed through a prism not of their making—and certainly not to their liking. As a result they appear flat, one dimensional (or, in Marxist terms, historically opaque). This opacity is another one of the things we must confront, conquer, and move beyond. It has been too long a self-serving device of history to deal non-Westerners out of the process of participating in and shaping that history. The Indian-perceived past is all too often defined as "tradition," and then dropped, if it is dealt with at all.

To be concrete: in the many histories written of Indian/white relations in the Eastern Woodlands, I have rarely read about Indians who are believable as Indians or even, sometimes, as human beings. They are not presented as fully sentient and multidimensional beings. By contrast, their white counter-parts are usually fully fleshed out, and one can understand their values, their motivations, and their self-interests. I mention the Eastern Woodlands be-cause that represents the arena of longest encounter between Indians and whites in the English-speaking "New World." Hence, if we cannot present plausible Indian actors there, where can we? The record must be corrected from the beginning of the encounter. The further back we go, in fact, the more likely it is that Native Americans, as people, are very much submerged in favor of that European invention and abstraction—Indians.

There are other problems in conventional histories of Indian/white re-lations over which I shall pass briefly. One is the continuing failure of so many historians to understand and to deal with the importance of place to Indian people, the sense of belonging to and being at one with the land. So very often Indian people extend kinship to all living things in their environment, sometimes even to the sun, moon, and stars in the heavens. One can cite a large anthropological literature on this general subject, but I shall confine myself to one especially poignant example. It is a statement put out by the people of Taos Pueblo in New Mexico in 1968, when they were appealing for help from the American people to regain title to their sacred Blue Lake area.

> Our tribal government is responsible to this land and to the people. We have lived upon this land from days beyond history's records, far past any living memory deep into the time of legend. The story of my people and the story of this place are one single story. No man can think of us with-out also thinking of this place. We are always joined together.

When historians can understand and deal with this view of self in relation to the land, then they will begin to understand the Indian spirit of place.

Time is another misunderstood concept. The kind of time considered most important by Indian peoples who live in unbroken communities is cyclical and repetitive, rather than irreversible and linear. Since the beginnings of anthropology among Indian peoples, individual anthropologists have been surprised to find, on returning to particular reservations after an absence of several years, that they are treated by their hosts as if they had never left. From the Indian perspective, the years intervening since the last encounter need not be accounted for. What matters is that a friend has returned. The relationship and cyclical passage of time take precedence over a Western sense of linear chronology. Thus, once a person is taken into their cultural frame of reference, the passage of time between encounters does not much matter, for, as the Navajo refrain goes, "Anthropologists are like rain. They come every summer."

So, time as rhythm and repetition, rather than just irreversible linearity, is something historians still, for the most part, have to learn and appreciate about Indian cultures. All of this is not to suggest that Indian peoples are not aware of history and linear time; they just do not regard it as highly as cyclical time.

In many tribal communities, time and history can even be reenacted so as to minimize the disruptive influences of unexpected events. This phenomenon can be observed frequently in Pueblo communities on religious and festive occasions. Pueblo dramatizations, performed in their native languages, serve to transform what might have been unique and disruptive historical events into a part of the ongoing, internal, cultural dialogue of the people. They depict the first arrival of the Spaniards and encounters with government bureaucrats, missionaries, anthropologists, and others with whom they have recurrent encounters. What all of these depictions have in common is that they make fun of the outsiders, thereby reinforcing the community's own sense of self-worth and cultural continuity.

The Pueblo festivals also provide a much needed corrective to the idea that Indian cultures are uniform and homogeneous. To witness, in one relatively small area, a variety of Native communities commenting theatrically in a variety of ways on a variety of historical events is to see once again the diversity and creativity of Native cultures.

Historians also fail to see the religious meanings and motivations that Indian people brought to the historical encounter and its consequences. That is to say, Indian peoples have been much more motivated to preserve what they can of their traditional religions in their reactions to missionaries than has been appreciated heretofore. Histories that reveal a subtle grasp of the Indian religious motivation in the historical encounter are still too few and far between. It remains largely a challenge for the future for historians of Indian/white relations to understand Indian religions well enough to place them in their rightful, central place in the Indian system of values and motivations.

The general absence of proper orientation and sense of proportion in the writing of histories of Indian/white relations is also reflected in the kinds of Native biographies available. Until the 1970s, most biographies were of colorful and heroic war chiefs or artists. Biographies of Tecumseh, Crazy Horse, Sitting Bull, Cochise, and Geronimo have long been available, but only in recent years have biographies appeared of less colorful but equally effective leaders such as Ohiyesa (the Santee physician), Ella Deloria (the Sioux anthropologist), Carlos Montezuma (the Yavapai reformer), and Tecumseh's brother, the holy man Tenskwatawa, or The Prophet. We still need many more biographies of religious leaders, peace chiefs, and other people noteworthy through Indian eyes.

As well, there is a difference between writing about a period and getting lost in it. Too many historians of Indian/white relations fall into this trap and are overcome by a moral myopia, a failure to see the modern applications and implications of their findings from the past. Specifically, a lack of awareness that past lessons apply to their own times is reflected in historians' failure to see and note the continuing victimization of modern Indian peoples by the same attitudes and institutions of American society that operated in the past. One widely publicized modern example is provided by the Hopi/Navajo dispute over the relocation of several thousand Navajo people from Hopi land. The real problems, as so often in the past, are the federal government and greedy businesspeople, but those who could draw proper historical parallels with other Indian removals of the past fail to come forth to do so. Numerous examples in any generation of the American past could be cited, and they would all point toward an indictment of historians of Indian/white relations for failing to take moral stances when they are the best informed people in American society to do so.

Finally we need to address the problem of why Europeans view American society as being so violent. Richard Slotkin may not have been the first scholar to note that Americans have tended to experience "regeneration through violence," but he has been the first to brilliantly dissect that habit through to its roots. The focus on violence in the historical encounter has long been trained on Indian peoples, but we need to understand the violence of non-Indian Americans to have a more accurate view of Indian/white relations. To Slotkin's book, *Regeneration Through Violence* (Middletown, Conn., 1973), I can only add, rhetorically, how can it be otherwise in a society that is still burdened by so many frontier fears; that maintains a picture of the wilderness as a fearsome, untamed place; and whose citizens still worship law and order more than the accomplishments of the human spirit?

An introduction should properly be celebratory rather than critical, and a brief celebration is appropriate here, for the essays in this volume represent the outlines of a new history of Indian/white relations. They carry us through the standard chronology of the nation's past with one eye cocked to the horizon. What is the Indian component of American history? What has been the

Indian experience of familiar historical events? As the following essays explore these questions, they will make several points clear.

First, it will be clear that there is a special futility in trying to deal with abstract Indians or Indianness. It makes more sense to deal with particular tribes, confederacies, and bands. If that occurs, the history of Indian/white relations is a problem that will increasingly take care of itself. The way to a better history leads through a thick tangle of particular facts about particular peoples; there is no other way to go. The alternative is a choice between old stereotypes and new ones. We cannot find the correctives we need by just fine-tuning the machine we have now. We need a new machine, a new conceptual framework that will have to come from and be forged at the points of meeting of Indian and white at particular times in particular places. Any conceptual framework that remains wholly outside the experiences of actual Indian people is not going to represent them honestly or serve their interests. It is not going to suddenly become relevant, no matter how adroit the mental acrobatics to make it seem relevant. Together, these essays challenge our old framework.

Second, it will be evident that we must develop more respect within the historical profession for oral traditions, for there is much to be gained from tribes' own accounts of their origins, early migrations, and statements of how they came to where they are. I do not advocate a wholesale return to swapping stories around campfires—although that would be good for much of what ails us in our modern, fast-paced existence—but, rather, a new recovery of the past, a new way of showing how oral literature is a part of the present.

Navajo cartoonist, Vincent Craig, pokes fun at persisting Indian stereotypes. Courtesy, The Newberry Library.

Spoken traditions may not explain the distant past with the accuracy of careful historical research, if relevant documentation is available, but they do present meaningful, comforting, and useful windows to the past for Indian people. More historians should learn why Indian people cling stubbornly to their oral traditions, and profit, as historians, from this knowledge. It can only add a new and valuable dimension to scholarly research.

Third, the ideas presented in this volume should persuade us that there is a need to train more Indian people from Indian cultural backgrounds, and especially those who speak a Native language, to explore and write their history. Just by virtue of their backgrounds, such people would bring an important new perspective to the writing and teaching of American history. Some may even produce living histories in which the past and present are brought together to bear portents of and guides to the future, as do the best of the oral traditions. It just depends on how one uses the evidence.

Fourth, and as a logical extension, we can also consider accepting Indian cultural productions other than writing as history. I mean that we should take up Standing Bear's suggestion that we imagine a new school. If we do, we must believe that much history is bound up in tribal songs and dances as well as in the oral traditions. To these we can now add family photographs, records of transactions, and even sound and video recordings, which Indian people throughout North America are increasingly fond of making. As eloquent as the book may be, it should inspire us to look beyond books to a wide variety of methods for recording and presenting history.

Fifth and finally, as we reflect on these essays and consider the Columbus voyages of 500 years ago, we have a challenge and an opportunity in the decades ahead to explore, gather, and bring forth some real *Indian* history, some views from the other side of the white man's frontier. Historians and Americans in general are fond of commemorations for they provide a time to pause, reflect, reassess, and chart new directions. If we do not do more to tell the Indian peoples' stories as they would tell them, the task will remain—and grow more difficult—for future generations. In addition, we need to assess the impact the New World has had on the Old over 500 years of continuous contact. We need to go beyond books like Alfred Crosby's *The Columbian Exchange* (Westport, Conn., 1972) and focus our attention instead on the many ways America has affected Europe and the rest of the world. That exploration should examine in particular the nonmaterial realms of exchange, as they are not well known.

This volume provides but a sketch, an invitation to reconsider our past and to reexamine our historical assumptions. If we accept that invitation and carry the task forward, then we can expect not only to reformulate our understanding of Indian/white relations but to develop a sharper view of Indian history itself. To achieve these objectives would make a positive contribution to American culture and bring Luther Standing Bear's school closer to reality.

Chapter One

America Before Columbus

James A. Brown

*M*odern experience has dulled our appreciation of the diversity of ancient American cultures. The media bombard us with so many images of the Indian of Western fiction that we begin to think that all Native Americans wore feather bonnets and buckskin clothes, rode horses, and lived in tepees. Such images erode past diversity on this continent, and compel us to begin our description of America before Columbus by emphasizing the tremendous variety of lifeways that formerly existed on this continent.

Some of the diversity of pre-1492 Native Americans has survived and been incorporated into our popular culture. Eskimos, for example, are commonly portrayed as clothed in parkas and mukluks, living in igloos, and transported on dogsleds in the winter and in kayaks in the summer. The very words that encapsulate various features of Native lifeways in the arctic—*igloo, mukluk,* and *kayak*—are drawn from Native words in the Eskimo language. Similarly, modern cosmopolitan America has incorporated Native-derived words, such as *moccasin, tipi,* and *wigwam,* that were distinctive features of life in other parts of the hemisphere. We have implicitly recognized the diversity of Native Americans by retaining words that characterize the differing lifeways of the people who inhabited the distinct geographic regions of North America. Thus, we speak of the dome-shaped wigwam of the Eastern Woodlands, the collapsible tepees of the nomadic Plains Indians, the wooden-plank houses of the Northwest Coast Indians, and the stone-walled apartment buildings of the Pueblo Indians of the Southwest.

Two general points of view have influenced our understanding of Native American cultures. Products of nineteenth-century European thought,

Above: Detail from Chasse Générale. *See page 20.*

An early twentieth-century photograph shows a California Maidu woman using a traditional seed beater for gathering food. Courtesy, The Field Museum, #1835, Chicago.

these ideas have each led to false impressions and a naive understanding of precontact Native American life. The first point of view held that North America before European colonization was inhabited by peoples without civilization. For some this condition has amounted to a shortcoming that has justified applying the pejorative label "primitive" to Native American cultures, thereby denying them the respect their cultural achievements deserve. The second point of view stressed that the absence of "civilization" denoted a noble human condition in which Natives were unspoiled by the corrupting influences of Euro-American urban life. Unfortunately, these views are derived more from the virtues and prejudices of European thought than from a careful measure of Indian cultural attainments. Current investigations into the early cultures of North America reveal a very different picture. Present history and anthropological research has generated a data base that forces us to reject the naive notion that Americans before Columbus were either "primitive" or noble savages. Instead, this research has revealed a rich diversity of Native lifeways, each far more complex than was believed a century ago.

In general, America's distinct lifeways are associated with specific geographic regions on the continent—areas carrying both limitations and advantages to human occupation. The permanently frozen ground of the Arctic Circle and the aridity of the western deserts represent major constraints on human occupation and cultural development. Conversely, the marine fish resources of the oceans, the relative warmth of the southern latitudes, and the moisture of the eastern sections of the continent provided ample resources that may have enhanced cultural development in these areas.

Within these major geographic regions, distinct and diverse lifeways developed, each with its own set of attitudes, beliefs, and postures towards self, society, and nature. Technologies were developed that tapped locally available energy and provided necessary sustenance and shelter. Techniques were elaborated to exploit the unique resources available in each region. The cultures of each region show distinctive histories reaching back many thousands of years. The major features of these histories are the subject of this chapter.

One of the most telling indications of America's cultural diversity is the sheer number of distinct languages spoken as recently as 150 years ago. More than 170 North American languages are known, excluding those within the area of Mexican civilization. Relatively few are closely related, most are more dissimilar than modern Greek and English; and, like the latter, they shared common but distant ancestral languages. Eight different ancient groupings are known, of which an even more ancient three (two of which are identified mainly with the Eskimo and the Athapaskans, respectively; the third takes in the remainder of languages) testify to a linguistic diversity that probably reaches back to the initial beginnings of New World colonization.

Current anthropological research suggests that, in general, with the passage of each century Native American lifeways became increasingly complex and more diverse. However, with the colonization of the New World, this diversity became reduced by the influences of Europeans, first by their initial trading and exploration contacts and, second, by programs of colonization. Yet changes in cultural diversity cannot be attributed solely to European contact. Archaeological research indicates that changes in cultural diversity among Native Americans had begun prior to Euro-American contact. Increased popu-

0   500   1000
miles

Northwest
Coast

A r c t i c
S u b a r c t i c

Far West

Plains

Cahokia

Mesa
Verde

Eastern
Woodlands

Southwest

Poverty
Point

Casas
Grandes

Major Geographic Regions of North America

lation, increased inter- and intraregional communication, and changes in technology are three examples of other processes that could have resulted in the
changes we see in the cultural diversity of Native Americans at the time of
contact. For example, in our century the effects of industrialization have made
almost everyone dependent upon wage labor or a salary of some sort. Since
everyone now participates in a single economic system, the lifeways of all
Americans (Native Americans included) have become progressively more similar
and homogeneous.

The cultural diversity of Native Americans prior to European contact is
best understood by studying the human populations that inhabited the distinct geographic regions of North America. These include the Arctic, the Subarctic, the Northwest Coast, the Far West, the Southwest, the Plains, and the
Eastern Woodlands. These regions of the North American continent have
only recently been inhabited by human beings. The earliest occupation of the
New World began with the movement of people from western Asia into present-
day Alaska and northwest Canada.

Just when man first ventured into North America is not known with any certainty. It is widely believed that the migration was very ancient. The best estimate from various lines of indirect evidence places this event approximately 16,000 years ago; however, the oldest cultural remains with completely accepted dates occur toward the close of the last Ice Age, about 14,000 years ago. More ancient dates have been claimed, but scientific support for them is weak. So far, none has withstood close critical examination for any length of time. Many are hastily drawn conclusions from inadequate information or mistakenly drawn interpretations of equivocal evidence. Nonetheless, the quest to determine the earliest date of man's entry into the New World continues at an increasing pace.

One conclusion is certain. The earliest immigrants entered across the Bering Strait, which separates Siberia from Alaska. These people were hunters and gatherers pursuing the large Ice Age mammals—mammoths, ground sloths, and giant bison—that were common in the Far North but are now extinct. The first foothold was in present-day Alaska, which during the height of the Ice Age was connected to Siberia by a thousand-mile-wide "land bridge" that had resulted from the lowered sea levels brought on by glaciation. Major climatic changes characterized by decreased temperatures and altered precipitation produced the phenomenon that we call glaciation. Glaciation is marked by cool episodes of glacial advance and warm episodes of glacial retreat. Cool periods produced massive ice sheets that blocked entrance south and east into the North American continent. During warm periods, an ice-free corridor was created that enabled early man to move into the interior of North America, probably in the course of following the large game animals that had a long history of migration north to south through this corridor.

The early migrants were basically of a single stock drawn from the same populations that live today in eastern Siberia. Some idea of who the early migrants were can be readily established from their descendants. In terms of the physical diversity of humans around the world, the American Indians are a particular kind of Mongoloid.

When compared with other racial stocks around the world, the New World peoples show an overall physical similarity that denotes a relatively recent entrance into North America. Estimates place the splitting off of New World migrants from the parental Asian stock at between 20,000 and 16,000 years ago. Although of considerable antiquity, this split is relatively recent in the history of modern *Homo sapiens*. All other inhabited continents, including Australia, were colonized by modern man well before the North American continents. Eastern Siberia had been occupied long before the migration to the New World. Recent though the migration may be, however, the immigrants managed to disperse quickly and populate every habitable region of the continent in a short period of time after the end of the Ice Age. Following initial occupation of all the geographic regions mentioned, adaptations to specific regional conditions began.

The entry of humans into the New World is thought to have coincided with the development of a stone-tool technology oriented towards the exploitation of large mammals. The earliest well-documented occupants of the New World possessed a unique technology distinguished by chipped-stone spear tips with flutes on both faces of the points. These points have been found in association with large Ice Age mammals.

The rest of the story is one of increasing cultural separation over time. Languages themselves participated in this diversification by proliferating, many of them relatively recently. This trend towards distinct regionally based lifeways presents quite a contrast to the underlying similarity of biology that links all Native Americans.

The earth's climate began to warm significantly approximately 10,000 years ago, with the result that the huge ice sheets that covered most of Canada gradually shrank. Out of these far-reaching changes the modern geographic regions of the continent arose. By 7,000 years ago, the roving big-game hunter way of life had begun to change. Populations began to exploit specific regional resources, producing a series of distinct social, cultural, and economic lifeways characteristic of each of the various regions.

Native Americans developed a variety of hunting tools and techniques. This illustration from Antoine Simon Le Page du Pratz, Histoire de la Louisiane, *first published in 1758, indicates how Indians in the lower Mississippi Valley surrounded deer before dispatching them with bows and arrows. Courtesy, The Newberry Library.*

We should not leave the subject of ancient migration without making an additional observation. The people encountered by Columbus and other early European travelers were part of cultural traditions at least as old as those in the Old World. Thus, the Native Americans in 1492 were no more immigrants to the New World than John Smith was an immigrant to England or Jacques Cartier was an immigrant to France. In fact, all Indian groups have creation myths that stress the indigenous origins of their people.

Geographic Regions

The Arctic Area

Bordering the Arctic waters along the shores of present-day Alaska, Canada, and Greenland and the tip of Siberia live the Yupiks, Inupiats, and Inuits (previously called Eskimos) who have led a distinctive lifeway ever since they colonized the far north after the last Ice Age. Distinct in language and biology, they held to a lifeway mainly dependent upon fishing and sea-mammal hunting. Only a few Yupik, Inupiat, and Inuit groups engaged in hunting caribou in the interior regions. Of all the Native peoples, they had to depend almost exclusively on animal flesh because of the virtual nonexistence of edible plants in their habitat. Despite the many thousands of miles over which these peoples ranged, they maintained basically a single language. This uniformity of language was symptomatic of their recent spread along the Arctic coasts. Yupiks, Inupiats, and Inuits represent the last of the Native adaptations to evolve in North America.

Peoples of the Arctic evolved an elaborate technology for life in a region that presents many obstacles. Highly mobile in the winter, they developed dogsled transportation to traverse the vast regions of frozen ice. In the summer, they changed to kayak and umiak travel. Typically, they were very adept, switching from one focus of hunting to another when circumstances demanded. As a result, they were open to technological innovations. Their settlements ranged in number and permanence in accordance with the reliability of sea-mammal hunting. In Alaska, large runs of whale and other large sea mammals fostered the growth of large permanent villages with a rich social and religious ceremonial life. In the east, seal hunting was not as rewarding and allowed only small settlements of fluid composition and size. Typically, the household was the basic economic unit with a personnel composition that changed from year to year, often dramatically in response to population attrition.

The Subarctic

South of and inland from this region lies a broad belt of northern coniferous forest. This cold zone of rocks, trees, and water is not very bountiful, particularly along the northern edge, which borders the Arctic tundra. The southern border, along the more bountiful deciduous forest, has many more resources (such as nuts and sap—i.e., maple syrup) for both humans and animals. The numerous lakes and rivers in this region are not very rich in fish; therefore, subsistence practices centered upon the exploitation of the migratory caribou in the north and the moose in the south.

As a result of the migratory patterns of those large mammals, peoples in the subarctic maintained highly mobile residences. They lived in small groups and were accustomed to travel over large distances in quest of food. Shelters were impermanent and easily set up and dismantled, being either conical, hide-covered tents or small structures made of bent saplings covered with bark, woven mats, or hides.

Societies were organized around individual households and clans—social groups comprising a number of households, the heads of which claimed descent from a common ancestor and acknowledged headman. For example, in the western portion of the region, households were connected through membership in clans whose descent is traced through the mother's line. Each of these clans had a totemic animal that had religious and symbolic significance to the group and to the individual members of the clan.

The Northwest Coast

Along the Pacific Coast from southern Alaska to north of the Columbia River is a strip of moist woodland rich in riverine and off-coast marine resources. On the basis of the food potential of fish that included the migratory salmon returning to their spawning grounds up the rivers flowing from the Rockies, the Northwest Coast peoples were able to sustain permanent villages with an elaborate social and ceremonial life. An extremely rich cultural inventory was developed on the basis of this stable fishing economy, which was supplemented by hunting small mammals and gathering wild plants. The Northwest Coast cultures gave us the expressive art known so well from wood carvings, particularly the tall totem poles used to honor the dead, to commemorate events, and to mark the ownership of the large plank houses typical of the region. The totem pole complex developed from the widespread practice of erecting a pole at or near the grave. These poles were decorated and festooned with ornaments.

The extraordinary accomplishment of these cultures was the complex elaboration of a way of life on an economic foundation of hunting and fishing without the resources of corn agriculture. However, one of the consequences of intense utilization of the natural environment was competition over the best and most reliable of these resources. Not only was warfare rife among the competing villages of the various tribes, but when not fighting with arms, villagers practiced a competitive feasting through the potlatch.

Occupation of this region began with the penetration of the area by big-game hunters. Although marine resources were part of the subsistence pattern by 6,000 years ago, the complex culture of the level known in historic times emerged only by A.D. 1. These cultures were characterized by large settlements and the abundant use of woodworking tools which were so important in the development of complex woodcraft industries. Distinctions of social rank among these people were marked by control of wealth that presaged the class distinctions of the historic period. Wealth, here as elsewhere in the New World, was represented by carefully crafted marine-shell artifacts, objects of beaten native (uncast) copper, and large and carefully polished implements of exotic stones.

The Far West

This vast area of relatively dry country with temperate climate extends south and west from the northwest coastal zone south of the mouth of the Columbia River and includes the present-day states of Washington and Oregon (the Plateau subregion), most of California (the Coastal subregion), and Nevada

Principal Subsistence Patterns in Precontact North America

0   500   1000
miles

Principal Basis of
Subsistence

Fish, shellfish and
sea mammals

Agricultural
products

Seeds, nuts, roots
and small game

Large game

and Utah (the Great Basin subregion). American Indians who occupied these subregions all shared a common adaptation to hunting and gathering.

The earliest occupants of this region were highly mobile hunter-gatherers who possessed few distinguishing cultural differences. However, approximately 6,000 years ago changes took place in these hunter-gatherer cultures that were indicative of a shift toward greater permanence of habitation. In the Coastal subregion, particularly, this shift was characterized by permanent villages, some with densities exceeding ten or more persons per square mile. Population densities of this magnitude were unparalleled elsewhere in North America at this time. As a consequence, human groups in the Coastal subregion became significantly wealthier and their cultures more complex than those of the other parts of the region. The diversity and abundance of food resources found along this coastal zone easily supported dense populations and appear to have been primarily responsible for the development of a rich cultural life.

In the Coastal subregion, local subsistence economies were based on salmon fishing; inland, acorn harvesting and deer hunting assumed greater importance. The basic political unit was a village community, called a triblet, that was more circumscribed than areas with common language, culture, and history (customarily termed *tribes*). Most of these communities, particularly those in the northern section of the Coastal subregion, showed little social organization above the level of the triblet. However, in the present-day Santa Barbara area, the Chumash were united into political confederations cemented by sophisticated alliances. An important part of these alliances was intergroup trade facilitated by trade beads crafted from different kinds of seashells. In keeping with the pattern of local-level autonomy in northern California, social groups were organized more through residence patterns than along lines of kinship. Throughout California those societies that occupied permanent villages were divided into social classes, which maintained the possession of wealth and prestige through the control of important specializations in religion and craft production. Chiefs, shamans, council members, and various craft specialists tended to be associated with the upper class. Beneath them were the commoners and, lastly, the lower classes and the slaves.

By contrast to the complex Coastal cultures of California, the cultures of inland peoples of the Great Basin remained relatively simple. As in the Arctic and Subarctic regions to the north, population densities here were low. The Great Basin subregion today is characterized by arid deserts with sparse food resources. However, at one time the area was bountiful, containing sixty-eight lakes—all but a handful of which have dried up in recent times. The most prominent still in existence is the Great Salt Lake. Food resources available to the Native Americans living in this subregion included piñon nuts, rabbits, ducks, and locally available wild seeds. These resources were not plentiful and varied greatly in abundance according to the unpredictable local climates. As a result of the scarcity and unpredictable nature of food resources, human groups were organized into bands of fluid size and composition. Although occupants of the Great Basin were basically nomadic peoples divided into many self-contained groups, semipermanent habitations were common for those populations living in areas rich in natural resources. Cultural cooperation and interaction above the local group were short lived and impermanent.

The Plateau is a high-altitude subregion whose resource base is similar to the Northwest Coast in fishing and gathering. Culturally, in many respects,

Major North American House Types

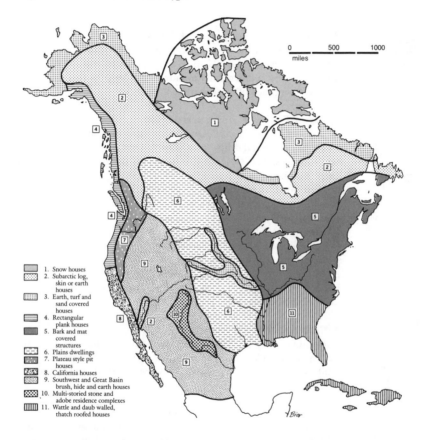

1. Snow houses
2. Subarctic log, skin or earth houses
3. Earth, turf and sand covered houses
4. Rectangular plank houses
5. Bark and mat covered structures
6. Plains dwellings
7. Plateau style pit houses
8. California houses
9. Southwest and Great Basin brush, hide and earth houses
10. Multi-storied stone and adobe residence complexes
11. Wattle and daub walled, thatch roofed houses

[Note: Readers should understand that this map does not cover ceremonial dwellings, temporary shelters, or the many seasonal structures erected for hunting, fishing, and ritual activities. In addition, the map's boundaries are arbitrary; different house types could appear in the same region as Native people adapted to variations in local resources and environments. Information for this map was drawn largely from *America's Architectural Roots,* edited by Dell Upton (Washington, D.C.: The Preservation Press, 1986). The section of this book dealing with Native Americans was written by Peter Nabokov.]

Major North American House Types (continued)

1. Snow Houses

In the central Arctic, Native people alternated between winter snow houses and summer tents. Snow houses provided homes for one or two families. They could be erected by two people, who would cut two-by-three-foot blocks from the snow bank and lay them in a spiral to form a dome. Six-inch-thick walls were often lined with skins to provide effective protection in a harsh and treeless environment. Summer tents were similar to those elsewhere in the region: seal, caribou, or walrus skins were stitched together and stretched over a frame of poles.

2. Subarctic Log, Skin, or Earth Houses

During the winter months, Subarctic peoples lived in hide- or earth-covered shelters that were 12 to 15 feet in diameter and approximately 5 feet high. In summer, families moved into lean-tos that were often erected facing each other with a fire in between.

3. Earth, Turf, and Sand Covered Houses

Arctic: In this region, small, semisubterranean dwellings were framed with whale bone and driftwood and roofed with turf. These were winter residences. The *tupik,* or hide tent, was the summer home. The latter was pitched near favored fishing locations.

Missouri and Platte River Areas: Here Plains farmers erected large earth- or sod-covered lodges on a frame of cottonwood timbers. Such structures provided a home village from which tribesmen would fan out in the spring and fall to hunt buffalo and live in hide tepees.

Lower Colorado River: The Yuman peoples of this area framed lodges with heavy mesquite timbers and covered their roofs with sand. These multifamily dwellings provided an anchor for these agricultural peoples, but residents of the area often moved to brush arbors and shades during the summer months.

4. Rectangular Plank Houses

These multifamily dwellings were built with cedar posts and covered with split cedar planks. With ceilings 12 to 18 feet high, and up to 2,000 square feet of living space, plank houses could house dozens of kinsmen.

5. Bark and Mat Covered Structures

Great Lakes: Here winter dwellings were small conical and domical wigwams; in summer people moved to gable-roofed structures which allowed greater ventilation. In both types, frames of saplings were lashed together with fiber cords and covered with bark (birch, elm, or chestnut) or mats made from grass or reeds.

Northeast: Barrel-roofed longhouses provided year-round shelter for the people of New York and much of the St. Lawrence valley. Central to both political and social life, these bark-covered buildings stretched up to 300 feet in length. They were in towns and protected by extensive palisades.

Southern Subarctic: Along the northern border of the Great Lakes and Northeast areas stretched a broad band of people who lived in small, birch-covered wigwams. These were often built on a frame of fir poles.

Middle Atlantic: Here John White's sixteenth-century drawings of North Carolina (see page 35) provide a vivid portrait of the variety of bark structures which could occur in a single area. Middle Atlantic peoples alternated between multifamily longhouses, similar to those of the Northeast, and smaller, mat-covered homes. The former were grouped in protected villages, while the latter appear to have been erected in a more dispersed fashion.

6. Plains

While tipis existed on the Plains at the time of European contact, they were not the only form of habitation. In the South, farming communities erected cottonwood framing and covered it with grass thatching. The result was a large, beehive-shaped structure which could house several families. Along the northern Platte and Missouri rivers, similar lodges were covered with earth. During the summer, most Plains peoples preferred the portable tipi. This most famous of Native dwellings consisted of hides stretched over a pole frame. With its sides rolled up, the tepee could be cool in the summer; banked with moss and earth, it provided a snug winter home for the hunting peoples of the region.

7. Plateau Style Pit Houses

These dwellings were semisubterranean. Round floors, rarely more than twenty feet in diameter, were excavated. Roof supports were buried in the earth and tied together at the peak smoke hole. The latter also served as an entrance. Individuals climbed in and out of the pit houses by using notched-log ladders.

8. California Houses

California contained a variety of Indian house types. In the north there were large plank houses built with cedar and redwood. Here residents slept in wood-lined pits arranged around a central hearth. The northern coast and the northern portion of the central valley also contained pit houses similar to those described in number seven. Along the central coast, domical lodges were erected and covered with thatch. In the drier areas of the south, similar dwellings consisted entirely of grass thatching. These were complimented by extensive, open-air brush arbors and shades.

9. Southwest and Great Basin Brush, Hide, and Earth Houses

Ranging from log-framed and earth-covered Navajo hogans to desert brush houses, dwellings in this area provided shelter for family groups. These shelters occurred in an area with a wide climate variation and few available building materials.

10. Multistoried Stone and Adobe Residence Complexes

Along the Rio Grande and stretching east into the Hopi country of central Arizona, the pueblos formed a center for agricultural production, religious rituals, and social cohesion. Pueblo dwellings were up to five stories high and were entered by ladders projecting from the roofs of individual apartments. These roofs consisted of frameworks of poles covered with brush and finished with adobe.

11. Wattle and Daub Buildings

While generally alternating between a round, conical-roofed winter house and a rectangular summer house, Southeastern Indians had a uniform allegiance to wattle and daub walls. These walls were built by weaving oak or other saplings in and out of vertical posts and covering the exterior surface with a mixture of clay and grass. The result was sturdy and provided effective insulation. Winter houses were 15 to 30 feet in diameter. The rectangular summer dwellings were of a similar length; however, they were frequently open-sided and joined by shades and arbors. (In Florida and the Caribbean, most houses were completely open.) Roofs consisted of palmetto or grass thatching or bark.

peoples of this subregion may be regarded as transitional between the Northwest Coast and the Great Basin. For instance, after the introduction of the horse during the Spanish period, some groups living in the Plateau borrowed many of the customs of the Great Plains populations, specifically those involving the incorporation of the horse into their cultural inventory. However, prior to this cultural change, Plateau peoples lived in earth lodges in the winter and gabled arbors in the summer. Occupants of the Columbia River drainage benefited most from the bounty of salmon. They organized their life around the seasonal salmon spawning runs. By 6,000 to 7,000 years ago, a seasonally settled life based on these runs was established in the best fishing areas of the major river valleys. But this mode of subsistence was not generally common outside of the most important fisheries until approximately 3,000 years ago. This seasonal pattern consisted of a rotation between the stable settlements of the summertime fishing stations and the less active winter camps. The balance of the year was spent hunting and gathering in the territories surrounding the major river valleys.

The three subareas reveal the degree to which the relative natural bounty of readily available and reliable food resources influenced population density, the scale of social development, and the variety and richness of culture. None of these societies rested on an agricultural economy. Hence, they benefited from increased efficiency in the cultural exploitations of the natural environment.

The Southwest

In the arid region now encompassing the southwestern states of Arizona and New Mexico and the southern parts of Utah and Colorado, cultural evolution resulted in a sedentary farming lifeway. Herding became important here in historic times, but the potential for successful agriculture of corn and other plants was the principal factor that set it off from the rest of western North America in the era before Columbus. Despite the high altitude of some areas and the frequent lack of rainfall in others, the Southwest has long held the environmental and ecological ingredients for the development of complex cultural life based on a settled existence.

Initial settlement took place around 8,000 years ago and was characterized by localized adaptations to specific environments. Although cultural innovations initially were conservative in nature in the Southwest, major cultural changes were decisively affected by the appearance of domesticated plants from central Mexico. The incorporation of corn agriculture, particularly, set the stage for a significantly expanded economic base that supported and produced a major demographic expansion within the region.

The initial stages of this expansion, between A.D. 150 and 700, saw the emergence of clearly defined regional cultural traditions—the Hohokam, Mogollon, and Anasazi. Settled villages were highly nucleated and consisted of small clusters of substantial living structures called pit houses. Sophisticated technologies of pottery making and weaving in cotton with a true loom also were developed.

Continued expansion of the economy was fed by intensified agriculture that included irrigation in selected areas. Up to A.D. 1100, steady population growth coincided with changes in housing architecture, the scale of communities, the intensity of trade, craft production, and ceremonial life. Farming communities spread widely into both mountain and valley canyons. Over time, dwellings changed from pit houses to surface structures constructed of stone or adobe. Frequently, these structures were constructed in large apartment blocks that we know today as pueblos. Large town-sized settlements developed as the result of the consolidation of groups in a few localities. One of the most important was centered in Chaco Canyon, where populations concentrated on a scale unknown up to this time. The Chaco center supported a complex, and probably stratified, society that was connected to most of the region through a variety of sophisticated trade networks. A system of roadways radiating from Chaco provides us with indications of the more important linkages.

Subsequent developments were characterized by fewer, but larger, settlements with the abandonment of formerly occupied territory. This consolidation led to the construction within the region of many of the great pueblos, such as Mesa Verde and Casa Grande. However, for reasons not clearly understood, major trade centers shifted to the south. An example of this shift is the settlement of Casas Grandes (in Mexico). The vacuum created by these shifts of population produced isolated, poorly defended areas and marginally productive lands. Small, mobile groups of northern hunter-gatherers migrated into these abandoned geographic zones. These populations were the ancestors of the present-day Apaches, Navajos, and Utes.

Periodic droughts began to plague the Southwest from the end of the thirteenth century to the present. People were driven from the areas most greatly affected by the drought, with the gradual effect that over the centuries the center of population in the Southwest gravitated into the Rio Grande valley, where most Pueblo peoples live today. The floodplain of the Rio Grande provided a more stable environment for agricultural practices. The modern Hopi are the only Indian group that has retained the traditional farming practices of the past—a technique that does not foster dependence on permanent reservoirs of water.

Pueblo societies were characterized by cohesive groups organized into clans. Group cohesion was maintained by an elaborate ceremonial cycle. Sponsored under the guidance of male organizations headquartered in ritual buildings called *kivas*, these societies were essentially egalitarian. Centralized leadership was not strongly developed despite the density of settlement and the obvious degree of mutual cooperation necessary to maintain social life in these pueblos.

The Great Plains

In 1492, the center of the continent was occupied by grasslands and scrub extending from southern Canada to northeastern Mexico. Although food resources were sparsely distributed, the area was home to millions of bison. As a result, the animals popularly called buffalos dominated all food quests in the area.

The basic cultural pattern for Plains peoples was nomadic bison hunting; this changed little for thousands of years until the onset of European colonization. Generally, populations were organized into small bands whose composition was fluid. Plains populations were mobile; dwellings were portable (the tipi); and technology was oriented towards hunting.

Intrusive into this basic Plains nomadic-hunter lifeway was the sedentary lifeway of the Eastern Woodlands, a lifeway based on corn agriculture. These "intruders" settled in clusters of permanent earth lodges—large timbered buildings set partially in the ground and covered with earth. These settlements often were surrounded by a defensive wall and ditch. The large and often dispersed villages were loosely linked, politically and socially. In general, however, the villages were politically independent. Ceremonial life centered around the rituals of individual clans and lodge organizations.

By A.D. 1000, semisedentary foragers and part-time agriculturists occupying the Missouri River valley were replaced by, or developed into, fully sedentary agriculturists. These settled farmers were the antecedents of the Plains sedentary, earth-lodge-dwelling peoples such as the Pawnees, Mandans, and Hidatsas. The nomadic, bison-hunting lifeway to the west was unaffected by these developments until the arrival of the horse in the early eighteenth

A Pawnee family in front of their earth lodge on the Loup River in Nebraska. Earth lodges were the principal house type for Plains agriculturalists. Courtesy, The Newberry Library.

century. This event so transformed the economic advantages of hunting bison that even the settled agriculturists abandoned their villages at times to engage in long-range hunting. The attraction of the bison was so great that, once mounted on horses, farmers—such as the Cheyennes and others from neighboring regions of the Eastern Woodlands, the Subarctic, and the Far West—migrated onto the Plains to live off the vast herds.

The Eastern Woodlands

This region stretches from the upper edge of the Great Lakes to the Gulf Coast, and from Kansas City, Missouri, to the Atlantic Coast. Because of its relatively warm, moist climate, the region has the greatest food potential of all the North American regions. Fertile lands, rivers, and lakes generally are rich in a variety of resources. Deer and various kinds of fowl are abundant; furthermore, the plant and animal resources of the Eastern Woodlands are unexcelled.

The Eastern Woodlands, for our purposes, can be divided roughly into northern and southern subregions by the Mason-Dixon line. The northern subregion shares many features of the social and cultural lifeways of the Subarctic groups to the north. Although the northern subregion is not as harsh for humans as the Arctic or Subarctic, the climate is so variable as to limit the impact of agriculture on settled life. Most economies were a mixture of hunting, gathering, and agriculture. Settlement was seasonally sedentary, and housing tended to be impermanent dwellings. Just prior to Euro-American contact there developed in present-day upstate New York one of the most complex societies in the northern subregion—the Iroquois Confederation.

The southern subregion, with its significantly milder climates, was the homeland of settled agricultural peoples. The agricultural subsistence economy that characterized these societies supported substantial populations, some of which were organized into compact towns of mud-walled, thatched-roof dwellings. Social agencies were large, and the component households were organized by descent groups that, in some instances, were stratified. These descent groups commonly traced inheritance through the female line. The southern subregion contained numerous elaborate forms of social and political organization.

As early as 7,000 or 8,000 years ago, climatic warming appears to have contributed to a shift from nomadic lifeways to seasonal, settled life in the most favorable habitats. By 5,000 years ago, native annual plants began to be heavily exploited, and tentative human cultivation began. At the same time, networks of trade in crafted seashells, native copper, and valued stones extended from the Great Lakes to the Gulf of Mexico. Centers of distribution

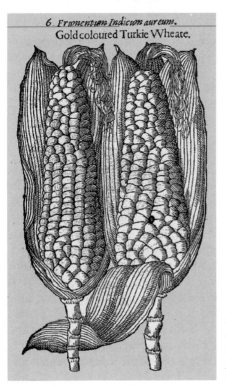

6. *Frumentum Indicum aureum.*
Gold coloured Turkie Wheate.

An early illustration of North American corn from John Gerard's Herbal History of Plants, *first published in London in 1597. Courtesy, The Newberry Library.*

for trade goods also arose, the earliest of which was at Poverty Point in Louisiana. By the beginning of the Christian Era, the center of distribution had shifted to the Ohio River valley. The famous Ohio Hopewell earthworks mark the apogee of this large-scale trade network. A slow but persistent rise in population contributed to the establishment of permanently settled villages that were concentrated in the rich river floodplains.

Population growth was gradual in this subregion until corn was incorporated into the agricultural repertoire around A.D. 900. In the following two centuries, increased population growth and the aggregation of small, scattered populations resulted in much larger settlements in this subregion. One of these major centers was Cahokia—a strategically located village in the expansive floodplain of the Mississippi River near the confluence of the Illinois and Missouri rivers. This large, sprawling center, covering over six square miles, consisted of more than 100 mounds of different sizes and shapes, including the largest earthen mound north of the Valley of Mexico.

The expansionist phase of agricultural societies tapered off by A.D. 1200 and was followed by a period of population consolidation within defensively planned towns. These town-dwelling peoples were organized into political hierarchies and divided into social strata based upon descent. Specialized priesthoods held important functions. Social advancement was accompanied mainly by military service to chiefs and, secondarily, by the control of supernatural powers. Intergroup trade and military struggle characterize the period prior to European contact.

The stress of this continued power struggle began to unravel the stability of southern tribes by the fifteenth century, with the consequence that food suppliers were jeopardized by the loss of social and political control over these resources. As a result, the Indian population declined; large areas became deserted; and northern tribes slowly moved south, filling these voids. By the time Europeans entered the Eastern Woodlands, the cultures of the southern subregion had changed dramatically. Cultures in the northern subregion were less affected by political and social stresses. In the Lower Great Lakes area, for example, the Iroquois Confederacy was more willing to incorporate the new and fascinating items presented to them by the Europeans than were most southern tribes.

European culture introduced more than technological innovations and trade goods to the Native North Americans. Wherever Europeans intruded, they inadvertently introduced diseases that were commonplace in the Old World but highly destructive among immunologically defenseless New World peoples. The result was an extreme population loss that was particularly damaging as it spread among compact, nucleated towns. The viability of these towns became completely undermined in the succeeding centuries with the consequence that they disappeared through death by disease, conquest, or voluntary dispersal.

Native North American Cultural Development

Cultural lifeways in North America before Columbus were regionally diverse. Anthropological and archaeological investigations, however, have revealed that several themes marked cultural development in all geographic regions.

The first major theme in Native American cultural development is a movement toward the fixity of community residence—sedentism. Sedentism is characterized by a gradual rise in the proportion of the year spent in one location instead of shifting locations to exploit seasonally available resources. Approximately 7,000 years ago, semisedentary ways of life had become established in certain regions of North America. By the beginning of the Christian Era, these sedentary lifeways were well established in all regions of North America. Coinciding with this movement towards sedentism came an increase in population growth, the development of social and cultural complexity, and a growing dependence upon a limited number of locally available plants and animals.

The second major theme of cultural development that we have seen in our examination of Native North America is the gradual domestication of plants and animals. For example, in the Eastern Woodlands, early subsistence economies focused on the cultivation of seed plants, nut trees, and fruit-bearing plants, some of which became domesticates. Of these native cultivated plants, the best known is the sunflower. Recent investigations in the Eastern Woodlands indicate that several other native seed plants were exploited extensively. These include goosefoot, knotweed, maygrass, little barley, and sumpweed. Squash and pumpkins also were common domesticates throughout North America.

In contrast to the richness of potentially domesticable plants in the New World, the number of animals in North America with characteristics conducive to domestication was limited. The domestic dog universally was part of Native life from very early times, and it is even possible that these animals came to North America with the earliest migrants. The only documented example of the domestication of a native North American animal is the turkey, which was kept in cages by Southwestern peoples. Domestication of other native North American animals is unknown.

Related to the trend of more productive and reliable food sources was a trend of population growth. While changes in climate, migration, and warfare decimated particular groups and regions from time to time, the general tendency through history was toward an even larger Native American population. Estimates of the North American population at the time of the Columbus voyages vary widely, but most scholars agree that the 1 million figure, which was uniformly accepted until the 1960s, is far too small. New evidence of the sophistication of both hunter-gatherers and horticulturalists, as well as improved knowledge of the impact of European diseases on New World

Village life in the Eastern Woodlands was captured by Englishman John White in a series of illustrations made near the North Carolina coast in July 1585. One of White's drawings, which was the basis for this engraving by the Flemish engraver and publisher Theodor DeBry, was of the village of "Secota." It shows the Indians cultivating three varieties of corn (indicated by the gardens of the newly sprouted, young, and mature plants to the right), squash (bottom center), and tobacco (top center) and living in a village of longhouses. Indians hunting in the nearby woods also illustrate how the practice of burning off forest underbrush encouraged game animals to graze in the resulting park lands. Courtesy, The Newberry Library.

peoples, has caused modern anthropologists and historians to conclude that the population in North America in 1492 was probably 3–5 million. Whatever the exact figure, it is clear that Native Americans—like other people elsewhere in the world—experienced an increase in population in conjunction with the increased sophistication of their subsistence strategies.

A third and final trend we find in Native American societies is a persistent increase in cultural and social complexity. Anthropologists generally agree that this trend is a product of increased sedentism and domestication of plants and animals. In short, as part of the trend toward sedentism and domestication came the development of more elaborate social customs and an increase in the richness of cultural expression. All of the elaborate expressions of Native life in the Eastern Woodlands, the Southwest, southern California, the Northwest Coast, and western Alaska came after the localization of villages and an increased specialization in food production.

With the rise of more complex social lifeways came the elaboration of significant cultural interchange between regions. The interchange between Eastern Woodlands, the Great Plains, and the Southwest is the best known. It is one that developed early and increased steadily to historic times. This complex trade network included a host of tribes that coalesced seasonally at specific rendezvous points to exchange a wide variety of products.

Increased cultural complexity brought with it its own problems, however. Although scholars are somewhat undecided about the chain of causation, complexity seems to stretch a community's capacity for sustaining its social and economic development. Thus, peoples of the Southwest, Plains, and Eastern Woodlands often experienced periods of population decline, territorial shrinkage, and social stress even as they expanded and traded with one another. At one time it was standard for scholars to dismiss periods of perceived "cultural decline" as either inevitable consequences of Native ways or the mechanical response to the vicissitudes of environment. This is tantamount to saying that Native Americans could not help themselves or rise above their

Large earthworks, such as these at Cahokia (across the Mississippi from modern St. Louis), attest to the size and complexity of precontact lifeways in the Midwest. The Mississippian cultures were at their peak during Europe's Middle Ages, but were in decline by 1492. This 1841 engraving by J. C. Wild also reflects our continuing fascination with the "mound builders." Courtesy, The Newberry Library.

condition. More thoughtful reflection on the subject has brought many scholars to realize that other forces have operated through time.

The capacity for taking innovative action has been ever present among all peoples and was surely a part of Native American cultures. We also know that environments change and affect cultural development. Clearly, then, the rise and fall of regional societies is part of all cultural development that was truncated at various periods in Native American history by a host of factors— European intervention being the most recent expression.

What would have developed in the absence of European intervention is speculation, but it is certain that Europeans benefited greatly by the timing of their discovery and colonization. They entered the Southeast at a time of cultural decline, and in the Northeast they were able to ally themselves with their largest potential adversary—the Iroquois—through trade. In the Southwest their progress was hampered by both Native resistance and an unfamiliar environment, but here too they were fortunate that they came on the scene after the disintegration of the great Anasazi towns. Add to the European's good fortune the silent ally of Old World diseases and it is easy to understand that Native "helplessness" had less to do with the character of their cultures than it had to do with situations beyond their control. It is not difficult to imagine a different and more complicated postdiscovery history if disease had not paved the way for colonization or if Native American cultural development had been—like the Europeans—in an expansionist phase.

For Further Reading

A general overview of North American scholarship is provided in J. D. Jennings, ed., *Ancient North Americans* (San Francisco, 1983). R. F. Spencer and J. D. Jennings, et al., *The Native Americans* (New York, 1977) presents a solid anthropological treatment. Alvin M. Josephy, Jr., ed., *America in 1492* (New York, 1991) provides surveys of Native life in the era prior to European incursion. Edward H. Spicer, ed., *Perspectives in American Indian Culture Change* (Chicago, 1961) examines and summarizes cultural change and adaptation in six North American Indian tribes. *The Handbook of North American Indians*, still in progress, is an invaluable reference work.

There are several excellent regional summaries. For the northeastern United States, see Dean R. Snow's *The Archaeology of New England* (New York, 1980). Charles M. Hudson's *The Southeastern Indians* (Knoxville, 1976), Linda S. Cordell's *Prehistory of the Southwest* (Orlando, 1984), and Ronald J. Mason's *Great Lakes Archaeology* (Orlando, 1981) give thorough overviews of their areas. Linda S. Cordell and George J. Gumerman, eds., *Dynamics of Southwestern Prehistory* (Washington, D.C., 1989) is also very useful, while the first two volumes of D. H. Thomas, ed., *Columbian Consequences* (Washington, D.C., 1989 and 1990) yield additional details on the archaeology of the Spanish borderlands region. L. S. Cressman introduces the *Prehistory of* the *Far West* (Salt Lake City, 1977), and Erna Gunther surveys *Indian Life of the Northwest Coast of North America* (Chicago, 1972) as seen through the eyes of eighteenth-century Euro-American observers. W. Raymond Wood and Margot Liberty provide an overview of the Plains region in their *Anthropology in the Great Plains* (Lincoln, 1980).

The major studies in revising traditional estimates of aboriginal population are Henry S. Dobyns, *Native American Historical Demography* (Bloomington, 1976) and *Their Number Became Thinned: Native American Population Dynamics in Eastern North America* (Knoxville, 1983), as well as W. M. Denevan, ed., *The Native Population of the Americas in 1492* (Madison, 1976), and Russell Thornton, *American Indian Holocaust and Survival: A Population History Since 1492* (Norman, 1987). Alfred W. Crosby, Jr., *The Columbian Exchange* (Westport, Conn., 1972) presents a broad consideration of the biological and cultural consequences of 1492.

Finally, several scholars have attempted to depict precontact North America in fiction. Among the best examples of this genre are Kathleen King, *Cricket Sings* (Athens, Ohio, 1983) on Cahokia, and Adolf Bandelier's study of early pueblo life, *The Delightmakers* (originally published in 1890 and most recently reissued in 1971).

Chapter Two

The Indians' Old World:
Native Americans and
the Coming of Europeans

Neal Salisbury

*A*fter Columbus's first landfall in the Caribbean in 1492, encounters between Indians and Europeans became gradually more frequent. By 1650, these encounters had given way to permanent relationships at many places on the eastern and southern peripheries of what is now the United States. The colonial era of American history had begun.

We know a great deal about the historical changes in Europe that coincided with and facilitated Spanish, Portuguese, French, Dutch, and English imperialism in America and other parts of the globe. The Renaissance, the Reformation, the rise of merchant banking and capitalism, and the advent of the nation-state in its modern form all contributed to the process whereby Europeans established colonies throughout the Western Hemisphere. Colonization entailed, directly or indirectly, the deaths of millions of Native Americans and the dispossession of many more. Yet colonization was never a one-way process. Native American history, too, was driven by dynamic processes that shaped Indians' attitudes and conduct toward Europeans and, thereby, the history of the colonists themselves.

This chapter seeks to illuminate some of those dynamics. It reviews developments in pre-Columbian North America in historical terms, including some of those discussed in the preceding chapter. But whereas Chapter One ends with the arrival of the first Europeans, this chapter encompasses the colonial period in order to show how certain indigenous patterns and processes continued to shape the continent's history after the beginnings of contact, for an understanding of the colonial period requires an understanding of its American background as well as of its European context.

Above: Detail from engraving. See page 41.

As Chapter One demonstrates, indigenous Americans living north of what is now Mexico exhibited a remarkable range of languages, economies, political systems, beliefs, and material cultures by the time Columbus made his first landfall. What is so striking, given this diversity, is the extent to which Native peoples' histories intersected one another.

At the heart of these intersections was exchange, meaning not only the trading of material goods but also the exchanges across community lines of marriage partners, resources, labor, ideas, techniques, and religious practices. Longer-distance exchanges frequently crossed cultural and linguistic boundaries as well and ranged from casual encounters to widespread alliances and networks that were economic, political, and religious. For both individuals and communities, exchanges sealed social and political relationships. Rather than accumulate material wealth endlessly, those who acquired it gave much of it away, thereby earning prestige and placing obligations on others to reciprocate with gifts of their own. Many goods were not given away to others in this world but were buried with individuals to accompany them to another.

Archaeologists have found evidence of ongoing exchange relations among even the earliest known Paleo-Indian inhabitants of North America. Ten thousand years before Columbus, in the wake of the last Ice Age, bands of two or three dozen persons regularly traveled hundreds of miles to hunt and trade with one another at favored campsites such as Lindenmeier in northern Colorado, dating to ca. 8800 B.C. At the Lindenmeier site, differences in the flaking and shaping of stone points distinguished regular occupants in two parts of the camp. The two groups' diverse geographic origins are evident from the fact that the obsidian each used came from about 350 miles north and south of Lindenmeier, respectively. Evidence from a wide range of settlement sites makes clear that, as the postglacial warming trend continued, so-called Archaic peoples (ca. 8000–1500 B.C.) in much of the continent developed wider ranges of food sources, more sedentary settlement patterns, and larger populations. They also expanded their exchanges with one another and conducted them over greater distances. Highly valued materials such as Great Lakes copper, Rocky Mountain obsidian, and marine shells from the Gulf and Atlantic coasts have been found in substantial quantities at sites hundreds and even thousands of miles from their points of origin. In many cases, goods fashioned from these materials were buried with human beings, indicating both their religious significance and, by their uneven distribution, their role as markers of social or political rank.

While the Archaic pattern of autonomous bands persisted in most of North America until the arrival of Europeans, complex exchange relationships in some parts of the continent produced the earliest evidence of concentrated political power. This was especially so for peoples who, after the first century A.D., developed food economies that permitted them to inhabit permanent, year-round villages. In California, for example, competition among communities for coveted acorn groves generated sharply defined political territories and elevated the role of chiefs who oversaw trade, diplomacy, and warfare for clusters of villages. Similar competition for prime fishing and trading locations strengthened the authority of certain village chiefs on the Northwest Coast. In the Ohio and Illinois valleys, where a greater abundance of food sources precluded such competition, long-distance exchange contributed to centralization. The Hopewell peoples there imported copper, shell, and other raw materials over vast distances to their village centers, where specialists fashioned them into intricately crafted ornaments, tools, and other objects. They deposited massive quantities of these goods with the dead in large mounds, differentiating even more sharply than had their Archaic forebears between commoners and elites by the quantity and quality of grave

An early-eighteenth-century engraving of Swedish settlers along the Delaware River emphasizes trade and political alliances between Europeans and Native Americans. Courtesy, The Newberry Library.

goods accompanying each. They also exported the finished objects to communities scattered throughout the Mississippi Valley. In the Southwest, meanwhile, a culture known as Hohokam emerged in the Gila and Salt river valleys among some of the first societies based primarily on agriculture. Hohokam peoples lived in permanent villages and maintained elaborate irrigation systems that enabled them to harvest two crops per year.

By the twelfth century, agricultural production had spread over much of the Eastern Woodlands as well as to more of the Southwest. In both regions, even more complex societies were emerging to dominate widespread exchange networks. In the Mississippi Valley and the Southeast, the sudden primacy of maize horticulture is marked archaeologically in a variety of ways—food remains, pollen profiles, studies of human bone (showing that maize accounted for 50 percent of people's diets), and in material culture by a proliferation of hoes made of chert (a type of quartz), shell-tempered pottery for storing and cooking, and pits for storing surplus crops. These developments were accompanied by the rise of Mississippian societies characterized by fortified political and ceremonial centers and outlying villages. The religious centers were built around open plazas featuring platform burial mounds, temples, and elaborate residences for elite families. Again, evidence from burials makes clear the wide social gulf that separated commoners from elites. Whereas the former were buried in simple graves with a few personal possessions, the latter were interred in the temples or plazas along with many more, and more elaborate, goods such as copper ornaments, massive sheets of shell, and ceremonial weapons. Skeletal evidence indicates that elites ate more meat, were taller, performed less strenuous physical activity, and were less prone to illness and accident than were commoners. Spanish and French observations of some of the last Mississippian societies confirm that political leaders, or chiefs, from elite families mobilized labor, collected tribute, redistributed agricultural surpluses, coordinated trade, diplomacy, and military activity, and were worshipped as deities.

The largest, most complex Mississippian center was Cahokia, located not far from the confluence of the Mississippi and Missouri rivers, near modern East St. Louis, Illinois, in the rich floodplain known as American Bottoms. By the twelfth century, Cahokia probably numbered 20,000 people and contained over 120 mounds within a five-square-mile area. One key to Cahokia's rise was the area's combination of rich soil and nearby wooded uplands, which enabled inhabitants to produce surplus crops while enjoying an abundance and diversity of wild food sources and ample supplies of wood for fuel and construction. A second key was the site's easy access to the great river systems of the North American interior.

Cahokia had the most elaborate social structure yet seen in North America. Laborers used stone and wooden spades to dig "borrow pits," from which they carried soil in wooden buckets to mounds and palisades often more than half a mile away. The volume and concentration of craft activity in shell, copper, clay, and other materials, both local and imported, suggests that specialized artisans provided the material foundation for Cahokia's exchange ties with other peoples. Although most Cahokians were buried in mass graves outside the palisades, their rulers were treated even more lavishly than their

"A Chief Lord of Roanoke," an engraving published by Theodor DeBry in 1590, executed from a drawing made by John White along the North Carolina coast in 1585. Courtesy, The Newberry Library.

earlier counterparts. At a prominent location in the largest of Cahokia's platform mounds, a man had been burned atop a platform of shell beads. Accompanying him were several group burials: fifty young women, aged 18 to 23, four men, and three men and three women, all encased in uncommonly large amounts of exotic materials. As with the Natchez Indians observed by the French in Louisiana, Cahokians appear to have sacrificed individuals to accompany their leaders in the afterlife. Cahokia was surrounded by nine smaller mound centers and several dozen villages from which it obtained much of its food and through which it conducted its waterborne commerce with other Mississippian centers in the Midwest and Southeast.

At the outset of the twelfth century, the center of production and exchange in the Southwest was in the basin of the San Juan River at Chaco Canyon in New Mexico, where Anasazi culture achieved its most elaborate expression. A twelve-mile stretch of the canyon and its rim held twelve large planned towns on the north side and 200 to 350 apparently unplanned villages on the south side. The canyon's total population was probably about 15,000. The towns consisted of 200 or more contiguous, multistoried rooms, along with numerous *kivas* (underground ceremonial areas), constructed of veneered masonry walls and log beams imported from upland areas nearly fifty miles distant. The rooms surrounded a central plaza with a great kiva. Villages typically had ten to twenty rooms that were decidedly smaller than those in the towns. Nearly all of Chaco Canyon's turquoise, shell, and other ornaments and virtually everything imported from Mesoamerica are found in the towns rather than the villages. Whether the goods were considered communal property or were the possessions of elites is uncertain, but either way the towns clearly had primacy. Villagers buried their dead near their residences, whereas town burial grounds were apparently located at greater distances, although only a very few of what must have been thousands of town burials have been located by archaeologists. Finally, and of particular importance in the arid environment of the region, the towns' locations at the mouths of side canyons enabled them to control the collection and distribution of water run-off.

The complex of communities in the canyon was the core of an extensive network of at least seventy towns or "outliers," as they are termed in the archaeological literature, and 5,300 smaller villages located as far as sixty miles from the canyon. Facilitating the movement of people and goods through this network was a system of roads radiating outward from the canyon in perfectly straight lines, turning into stairways or footholds rather than circumventing cliffs and other obstacles.

What archaeologists call the "Chaco phenomenon" was a multifaceted network. Within the canyon, the towns controlled the distribution of precious water. The abundance of rooms in each canyon town reinforces the supposition that many of them were used to store agricultural surpluses for redistribution, not only within the canyon but to the outliers. The architectural uniformity of towns throughout the system, the straight roads that linked them, and the proliferation of great kivas point to a complex of shared beliefs and rituals. Lithic (stone) remains indicate that the canyon imported most of the raw materials used for manufacturing utilitarian goods and ornamental objects from elsewhere in the Southwest. Particularly critical in this respect was turquoise, beads of which were traded to Mexico in return for copper bells and macaws and to the Gulf of California for marine shells. The Chaco phenomenon thus entailed the mobilization of labor for public works projects and food production, the control and distribution of water, the distribution of prestige goods of both local and exotic origin, and the control of exchange and redistribution both within and outside the network. In distinct contrast to Cahokia and other Mississippian societies, no evidence exists for the primacy of any single canyon town or for the primacy of certain individuals as paramount leaders.

Fundamental to the social and economic patterns of virtually all North American Indian communities were exchanges linking them directly or indirectly with other communities, often across geographic, cultural, and linguistic boundaries. The effects of these links are apparent in the spread of raw materials and finished goods, of beliefs and ceremonies, and of techniques for food production and for manufacturing. By the twelfth century, some exchange networks had become highly formalized and centralized. Exchange constitutes an important key to conceptualizing American history before Columbus.

Although it departs from our familiar image of North American Indians, the historical pattern sketched so far is recognizable in the way it portrays societies "progressing" from small, egalitarian, autonomous communities to larger, more hierarchical, and centralized political aggregations with more complex economies. Less recognizable are developments in some regions during the three centuries immediately preceding the arrival of Europeans. In both American Bottoms and the San Juan River basin, where twelfth-century populations were most concentrated, agriculture was most productive, exchange most varied and voluminous, and political systems most complex and extensive, there were scarcely any inhabitants by the end of the fifteenth century. What happened and why?

Cahokia and other Mississippian societies in the Upper Midwest peaked during the late twelfth and early thirteenth centuries. Data from soil traces indicate that even then laborers were fortifying Cahokia's major earthworks against attack. At the same time, archaeologists surmise, Cahokia was headed toward an ecological crisis: expanded settlement, accompanied by especially hot dry summers, exhausted the soil, depleted the supply of timber for building and fuel, and reduced the habitat of the game animals that supplemented the people's diet. By the end of the fourteenth century, Cahokia's inhabitants had dispersed over the surrounding countryside into small farming villages.

Cahokia's abandonment reverberated among other Mississippian societies in the Midwest. Fortified centers on the Mississippi River from the Arkansas River northward and on the Ohio River appear to have been strengthened by influxes of people from nearby villages but then abandoned, and signs from burials indicate a period of chronic, deadly warfare in the Upper Midwest. One archaeologist refers to the middle Mississippi Valley and environs during the fifteenth century as "the vacant quarter." A combination of ecological pressures and upheavals within the alliance that linked them appear to have doomed Cahokia and other midwestern Mississippian centers, leading the inhabitants to transform themselves into the village dwellers of the surrounding prairies and plains observed by French explorers three centuries later.

The upheavals may even have extended beyond the range of direct Mississippian influence to affect Iroquois and Hurons and other Iroquoian speakers of the lower Great Lakes region. These people had been moving from dispersed, riverside settlements to fortified, bluff-top villages over the course of several centuries; the process appears to have intensified in the fourteenth century, when it also led to the formation of the Iroquois and Huron confederacies. The Hurons developed fruitful relations with hunter-gatherers to the north, with whom they exchanged agricultural produce for meat and skins, and Iroquois ties with outsiders appear to have diminished except for small-scale interactions with coastal peoples to the south and east. Across the Northeast, political life was characterized by violence and other manifestations of intense competition. It is unclear whether the upheavals in exchange ties occasioned by the collapse of Cahokia were directly linked to the formation of the Iroquois and Huron confederacies or were simply part of a larger process generated by the advent of farming and its demographic and political effects. Whatever the cause, the repercussions were still evident when Europeans began to frequent the Northeast during the sixteenth century.

Violence and instability also were apparent across the Southeast. Unlike in the Midwest, where enormous power had been concentrated in a single center, southeastern Mississippian societies were characterized by more frequently shifting alliances and rivalries that prevented any one center from becoming as powerful as Cahokia was from the tenth to thirteenth centuries. A pattern of instability prevailed that archaeologist David Anderson terms "cycling," in which certain centers emerged for a century or two to dominate regional alliances consisting of several chiefdoms and their tributary communities and then declined. Whole communities periodically shifted their locations in response to ecological or political pressures. Thus, for example, the great mound center at Etowah, in northwestern Georgia, lost its preeminence after 1400 and, by the time of Hernando de Soto's arrival in 1540, had become a tributary of the nearby upstart chiefdom of Coosa.

From the mid-twelfth century through the fourteenth century, the demographic map of the Southwest was also transformed as Chaco Canyon and other Anasazi and Hohokam centers were abandoned. Although southwesterners had long made a practice of shifting their settlements when facing shortages of water and arable land and other consequences of climatic or demographic change, the severity and duration of drought conditions in this period undermined the great centers. Archeologists point to signs that the centralized systems lost their ability to mobilize labor, redistribute goods, and coordinate religious ceremonies and that such loss was followed by outmigration to surrounding and upland areas where people farmed less intensively while increasing their hunting and gathering. Trade between the Southwest and Mesoamerica was disrupted at the same time, though whether as a cause or an effect of the abandonments is unclear.

Most Anasazi peoples dispersed into small groups, presumably joining others to form new communities in locations with sufficient rainfall. These communities are what we know today as the southwestern pueblos, extending from Hopi villages in Arizona to those on the Rio Grande. These dispersals and convergences of peoples reinforced an emerging complex of beliefs, art, and ceremonies relating to *kachinas*—spirits believed to have influence in both bringing rain and fostering cooperation among villagers. Given their effort to forge new communities under conditions of severe drought, it is not surprising that southwestern farmers placed great emphasis on kachinas. The eastward shift of much of the southwestern population also led to new patterns of trade in which recently arrived Athapaskan speakers (later known as Apaches and Navajos) brought bison meat and hides and other products from the southern Great Plains to semiannual trade fairs at Taos, Pecos, and Picuris pueblos in exchange for maize, cotton blankets, obsidian, turquoise, and ceramics as well as shells from the Gulf of California. By the time of Francisco Vasquez de Coronado's *entrada* in 1540, new ties of exchange and interdependency bound eastern Pueblos, Athapaskan speakers, and Caddoan speakers on the Plains.

When Europeans reached North America, then, the continent's demographic and political map was in a state of profound flux. A major factor was the collapse of the great centers at Cahokia and Chaco Canyon and elsewhere in the Midwest and Southwest. Although there were significant differences between these highly centralized societies, each ran up against the capacity of the land or other resources to sustain it. This is not to argue for a simple ecological determinism, for, although environmental fluctuations played a role, the severe strains in each region resulted above all else from a series of human choices that had brought about unprecedented concentrations of people and power. Having repudiated those choices and dispersed, midwestern Mississippians and southwestern Anasazi formed new communities in which they retained kinship, ceremonial, and other traditions that antedated their former more complex societies. At the same time, these new communities and neighboring ones sought to flourish in their new political and environmental settings by establishing, and in some cases endeavoring to control, new exchange networks.

Such combinations of continuity and change, persistence, and adaptability arose from concrete historical experiences rather than timeless traditions. The remainder of this chapter indicates some of the ways that both the deeply rooted imperatives of reciprocity and exchange and the relatively recent legacies of competition and upheaval continued to inform North American history as Europeans began to make their presence felt.

The Southeast was the scene of the most formidable attempts at colonization during the sixteenth century, primarily by Spain. Yet in spite of several expeditions to the interior and the undertaking of an ambitious colonizing and missionary effort, extending from St. Augustine over much of the Florida Peninsula and north to Chesapeake Bay, the Spanish retained no permanent settlements beyond St. Augustine itself at the end of the century. Nevertheless, their explorers and missionaries introduced and began the spread of smallpox and other epidemic diseases to which Native Americans had little or no natural immunity over much of the area south of the Chesapeake and east of the Mississippi.

The town of Coosa, as previously noted, attained regional supremacy during the fifteenth century, a phase in the apparently typical process whereby paramount chiefdoms rose and fell in the Mississippian Southeast. But Coosa's decline was far more precipitate than others because Spanish diseases ravaged the province, forcing the survivors to abandon the town and move southward. By the end of the sixteenth century, several new provincial centers emerged in what are now Alabama and western Georgia, but these did not feature the mounds and paramount chiefs of their predecessors. As with earlier declines, a new formation emerged out of the resulting power vacuum. What was different in this case was the external source of the decline, its devastating effects, and the inability or unwillingness of the survivors to resume concentrating power in the hands of paramount chiefs. However, the absence of Spanish or other European colonizers in the Southeast from the late sixteenth century to late seventeenth century afforded the relocated Natives a sustained period of time in which to recover and regroup. When English traders encountered the descendants of refugees from Coosa and its neighbors late in the seventeenth century, they labeled them "Creek."

Just as Coosa's demise was eventually followed by the rise of the Creeks, the comparable decline of two Mississippian centers to the west fostered the emergence of the Choctaws. Unlike Coosa, Moundville in Alabama and a second center on the Pearl River in Mississippi were probably declining in power before the onset of disease in the 1540s hastened the process. Like the Creeks, the Choctaws were a multilingual, multiethnic society in which individual villages were largely autonomous.

As in the Southeast, Spanish colonizers in the sixteenth-century Southwest launched several ambitious military and missionary efforts, hoping to extend New Spain's domain northward and to discover additional sources of wealth. Even before arriving, the Spanish had acquired notoriety among the Pueblos as purveyors of dreadful diseases, offensive religious prosyletizers, and the enslavers of Indians to the south, in what is now northern Mexico. The best-documented encounters of Spanish with Pueblos—most notably those of Coronado's expedition (1540–1542)—ended in violence and failure for the Spanish who, despite vows to proceed peacefully, violated Pueblo norms of reciprocity by insisting on excessive tribute or outright submission.

The Spanish also affected patterns of exchange throughout the Southwest. Indians resisting the spread of Spanish rule to northern Mexico stole the Spaniards' horses and other livestock, some of which they traded to neighbors; by the end of the sixteenth century, a few Indians on the periphery of the Southwest were riding horses, foreshadowing the combination of theft and exchange that would later spread horses to Native peoples throughout the region and, still later, the Plains and the Southeast. In the meantime, some Navajos and Apaches moved near the Rio Grande Valley, strengthening ties with certain pueblos. These ties were reinforced when inhabitants of those pueblos sought refuge among their new neighbors in the face or wake of Spanish *entradas*.

Yet another variation on the theme of Indian-European contacts in the sixteenth century was played out in the Northeast, where Iroquoian-speaking villagers on the Mississippian periphery and Archaic hunter-gatherers still further removed from developments in the interior met Europeans of several

An early European illustration of a North American beaver (in French, castor). From Baron De Lahontan, Nouveaux Voyages Dans L'Amerique, *published in France in 1704. The pelts of beavers, highly desired in Europe for use in fur hats, was the principal commodity in Indian-European trade in the Northeast during the seventeenth and early eighteenth centuries. Courtesy, The Newberry Library.*

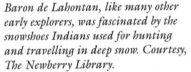

Baron de Lahontan, like many other early explorers, was fascinated by the snowshoes Indians used for hunting and travelling in deep snow. Courtesy, The Newberry Library.

nationalities. At the outset of the century, Spanish and Portuguese explorers enslaved several dozen Micmacs and other Indians from the Nova Scotia–Gulf of St. Lawrence area. Three French expeditions to the St. Lawrence itself in the 1530s and 1540s followed the Spanish pattern by alienating most Indians encountered and ending in futility. Even as these hostile contacts were taking place, fishermen, whalers, and other Europeans who visited the area regularly had begun trading with Natives. As early as the 1520s, Abenakis on the coast of Maine and Micmacs were trading the furs of beavers and other animals for European goods of metal and glass. By the 1540s, specialized fur traders, mostly French, frequented the coast as far south as the Chesapeake; by the 1550s or soon thereafter, French traders rendezvoused regularly with Indians along the shores of upper New England, the Maritimes, and Quebec and at Tadoussac on the St. Lawrence.

What induced Indians to go out of their way to trap beaver and trade the skins for glass beads, mirrors, copper kettles, and other goods? Throughout North America since Paleo-Indian times, exchange in the Northeast was the means by which people maintained and extended their social, cultural, and spiritual horizons as well as acquired items considered supernaturally powerful. Members of some coastal Indian groups later recalled how the first Europeans they saw, with their facial hair and strange clothes and traveling in strange boats, seemed like supernatural figures. Although soon disabused of such notions, these Indians and many more inland placed special value on the glass beads and other trinkets offered by the newcomers. Recent scholarship on Indians' motives in this earliest stage of the European-Indian trade indicates that they regarded such objects as the equivalents of quartz, mica, shell,

Locations of Native American groups mentioned in this essay and nearby European communities, ca. 1645. Adapted from a map by Blackmer which appeared in William and Mary Quarterly *(by permission).*

and other sacred substances that had formed the heart of long-distance exchange in North America for millennia. Such substances were regarded as
sources of physical and spiritual well-being, on earth and in the afterlife. Indians initially altered and wore many of the utilitarian goods they received from
their European trading partners, such as iron axe heads and copper pots, rather
than use them for their intended purposes. Moreover, even though the new
objects might pass through many hands, they more often than not ended up
in graves, presumably for their possessors to use in the afterlife. Finally, the
archaeological findings make clear that objects crafted of shell and native copper predominated over European-made articles in sixteenth-century exchanges,
indicating that the new goods did not suddenly alter indigenous patterns of
exchange. While northeastern Indians recognized Europeans as different from
themselves, they interacted with them and their materials in ways that were
consistent with their own customs and beliefs.

By the late sixteenth century, the effects of European trade began to
overlap with the effects of earlier upheavals in the northeastern interior. Sometime between Jacques Cartier's final departure in 1543 and Samuel de
Champlain's arrival in 1603, the Iroquoian-speaking inhabitants of Hochelaga
and Stadacona (modern Montreal and Quebec City), abandoned their communities. The communities were crushed militarily, and the survivors dispersed
among both the Iroquois and Huron confederations. Whether the perpetrators of these dispersals were Iroquois or Huron is a point of controversy, but
either way the St. Lawrence communities appear to have been casualties of
the rivalry, at least a century old, between the two confederations as each
sought to position itself vis-a-vis the French. The effect, if not the cause, of
the dispersals was the Iroquois practice of attacking antagonists who denied
them direct access to trade goods; this is consistent with Iroquois actions
during the preceding two centuries and the century that followed.

The sudden availability of many more European goods, the absorption
of many refugees from the St. Lawrence, and the heightening of tensions with
the Iroquois help to explain the movement of most outlying Huron communities to the Simcoe County area of what is now Ontario during the 1580s.
This geographic concentration strengthened the Huron confederacy and gave
it the form it had when allied with New France during the first half of the
seventeenth century. Having formerly existed at the outer margins of an arena
of exchange centered in Cahokia, the Hurons and Iroquois now faced a new
source of goods and power to the east.

The diverse Native societies encountered by Europeans as they began to
settle North America permanently during the seventeenth century were not
static isolates lying outside the ebb and flow of human history. Rather, they
were products of a complex set of historical forces, both local and wide-rang-
ing, both deeply rooted and of recent origin. Although their lives and
worldviews were shaped by long-standing traditions of reciprocity and spiri-

tual power, the people in these communities were also accustomed—contrary to popular myths about inflexible Indians—to economic and political flux and to absorbing new peoples (both allies and antagonists), objects, and ideas, including those originating in Europe. Such combinations of tradition and innovation continued to shape Indians' relations with Europeans, even as the latter's visits became permanent stays.

The establishment, by the mid-seventeenth century, of several lasting European colonies began a phase of American history that led eventually to the displacement of Indians to the economic, political, and cultural margins of a new order. But during the interim natives and colonizers entered into numerous relationships in which they exchanged material goods and often supported one another diplomatically or militarily against common enemies. These relations combined native and European modes of exchange. While much of the scholarly literature emphasizes the subordination and dependence of Indians in these circumstances, Indians as much as Europeans dictated the form and content of their early exchanges and alliances. Much of the protocol and ritual surrounding such intercultural contacts was rooted in indigenous kinship obligations and gift exchanges, and Indian consumers exhibited decided preferences for European commodities that satisfied social, spiritual, and aesthetic values. Similarly, Indians' long-range motives and strategies in their alliances with Europeans were frequently rooted in older patterns of alliance and rivalry with regional neighbors. Such continuities can be glimpsed through a brief consideration of the colonial-era histories of the Five Nations Iroquois in the Northeast and the Creeks in the Southeast

Post-Mississippian and sixteenth-century patterns of antagonism between the Iroquois and their neighbors to the north and west persisted, albeit under altered circumstances, during the seventeenth century when France established its colony on the St. Lawrence and allied itself with Hurons and other nearby Indians. France aimed to extract maximum profits from the fur trade, and it immediately recognized the Iroquois as the major threat to that goal. In response, the Iroquois turned to the Dutch in New Netherland for guns and other trade goods while raiding New France's Indian allies for the thicker northern pelts that brought higher prices than those in their own country (the supply of which they exhausted by midcentury) and for captives whom they could adopt to replace Iroquois people who had died from epidemics or in wars. During the 1640s, the Iroquois replaced raids with full-scale military assaults (the so-called Beaver Wars) on the Hurons' Iroquoian-speaking communities in the lower Great Lakes, routing their communities and absorbing most of the survivors as refugees or as captives. All the while, the Iroquois elaborated on a vision of their confederation, which had brought harmony within their own ranks, as one bringing peace to all peoples of the region. For the remainder of the century, the Five Nations fought a grueling and costly series of wars against the French and their Indian allies in order to gain access to the better pelts and French goods circulating in lands to the north and west.

Meanwhile, the Iroquois were also adapting to the growing presence of English colonists along the Atlantic seaboard. After the English supplanted the Dutch in New York in 1664, Iroquois diplomats established relations with the proprietary governor, Sir Edmund Andros, in a treaty known as the Covenant Chain. The Covenant Chain was an elaboration of the Iroquois' earlier treaty arrangements with the Dutch, but whereas the Iroquois had termed the Dutch relationship a chain of iron, they referred to the one with the English as a chain of silver. The shift in metaphors was appropriate, for what had been strictly an economic connection was now a political one in which the Iroquois acquired power over other New York Indians. After 1677, the Covenant Chain was expanded to include several English colonies, most notably Massachusetts and Maryland, along with those colonies' subject Indians. The upshot of these arrangements was that the Iroquois cooperated with their colonial partners in subduing and removing subject Indians who impeded settler expansion. The Mohawks in particular had already played a vital role in the New England colonies' suppression of the Indian uprising known as King Philip's War and in moving the Susquehannocks away from the expanding zone of English settlement in the Chesapeake after Bacon's Rebellion (1675–1676).

For the Iroquois, such a policy helped expand their "Tree of Peace" among neighboring Indians, who served as buffers against European encroachment around their homelands. The major drawback in the arrangement proved to be the weakness of English military assistance against the French. This inadequacy, and the consequent suffering experienced by the Iroquois during two decades of war after 1680, finally drove the Five Nations Iroquois to make peace with the French and their Indian allies in the Grand Settlement of 1701. Together, the Grand Settlement and Covenant Chain provided the Iroquois with the peace and security, the access to trade goods, and the dominant role among northeastern Indians they had long sought. That these arrangements in the long run served to reinforce rather than deter English encroachment on Iroquois lands and autonomy should not obscure their pre-European roots and their importance in shaping colonial history in the Northeast.

In the southeastern interior, descendants of refugees from Coosa and neighboring communities regrouped in clusters of Creek *talwas* (villages), each dominated by a large talwa and its "great chief." In the late seventeenth century, these latter-day chiefdom/provinces forged alliances with English traders, first from Virginia and then from Carolina, who sought to trade guns and other manufactured goods for deerskins and Indian slaves. In so doing, the Creeks were ensured that they would be regarded by the English as clients rather than as commodities. The deerskin trade proved to be a critical factor in South Carolina's early economic development, and the trade in Indian slaves, most of whom were from groups allied with the Spanish in Florida, significantly served England's imperial ambitions. But Anglo-Indian tensions flared in 1715 as a result of continued abusive treatment of natives by English traders and of Carolina colonists' seizing the lands of hitherto allied Yamassees. Siding with the Yamassees and other aggrieved Indians, the Creeks led an alliance that nearly crushed Carolina colony; only the timely assistance of settlers from Virginia and the anti-Creek Cherokees saved the colony. With France having established a colony in Louisiana in 1699, the Creeks moved after 1715 toward a policy of neutrality in which they maintained economic and diplomatic ties with the three imperial powers in the Southeast—Spain, France, and England. Thereafter the several Creek alliances often acted in concert as a confederacy—the Creek Nation. As a result, they achieved a measure of success in playing off the European powers and maintaining neutrality in their conflicts with one another. While much differentiates Creek political processes in the colonial period from those of the late Mississippian era, there are strong elements of continuity in the transformation of Mississippian chiefdoms into great Creek talwas.

Europeans and Indians often allied themselves for mutual protection. This scene of peacemaking was contained in Antoine Simon Le Page du Pratz, Histoire de la Louisiane, *published first in Paris in 1758. Courtesy, The Newberry Library.*

*A nineteenth-century image of the Ottawa
leader, Pontiac, which demonstrates how
the memory of his "rebellion" persisted
among European Americans. Courtesy,
The Newberry Library.*

In many ways, the four decades from 1715 to 1744 represented the high tide of Iroquois and Creek power in colonial America. Both confederacies avoided destructive wars, maintained lucrative exchange ties with Europeans, and reigned supreme among their Indian neighbors. Having made peace with the Great Lakes Indians, the Iroquois persuaded their new allies to trade with them for English goods rather than carrying their furs to Montreal for the more paltry returns offered there by the French. In 1722 the Iroquois incorporated into their confederacy a sixth nation, the Tuscaroras, fellow Iroquoian-speakers who had been driven from their North Carolina homelands by colonists. In the same year, the Iroquois reached agreements with Pennsylvania and Virginia in which those colonies recognized Iroquois hegemony over Delawares, Shawnees, and other Indians in the vicinity, none of whom were present at the conference. While the Creeks were obliged to cede some land for the establishment of Georgia in 1733, they were rewarded with a fourth source of trade goods that they could play off of in their dealings with Carolina, Louisiana, and Florida. The Creeks demonstrated their continued independence when England and Spain went to war in 1739 and most of them remained neutral.

Yet other forces at work during this period were beginning to undermine North American European empires and Indian confederacies alike. One such force was the collision course between England and France for preeminence in Europe, North America, and other parts of the world. Complicating this imperial rivalry was an even greater threat, the phenomenal growth of the

English North American colonial population and its economy. Finally, in response to the second factor, a proliferation of Indian refugees and other Natives who had been displaced or rendered vulnerable as a result of English expansion were determined to gain their own independence from all external powers. The explosive potential of these forces became apparent during the War of the Austrian Succession (known in America as King George's War, 1744–1748) and exploded during the Seven Years War (1756–1763, known in America, where it began in 1754, as the French and Indian war). In the upper Ohio Valley, Shawnees, Delawares, Seneca Iroquois refugees, and other Indians challenged French, English, and Iroquois claims to authority over them. After the arrival in 1755 of British troops under General James Braddock, these Indians sought the outcome that would leave them with maximum autonomy. Accordingly, they leaned toward France in the early stages of the war. Many Iroquois themselves, reacting to English expansion on to Mohawk lands in New York, likewise leaned toward the French. But after several French victories, the Indians sought to maintain a balance between the two by shifting their support to the English. But French fortunes quickly failed and the English emerged victorious in 1761. In the Southeast, meanwhile, South Carolina's continued catering to the Creeks led their rivals, the Cherokees, to ally with the French. With the French defeated, British troops devastated Cherokee villages and corn crops in 1761.

Thereafter the area between English settlements and Indians to the west was fraught with tensions and gradually escalating violence. Attempting to control the Ohio Valley Indians, British authorities alienated them by ceasing to issue them guns and ammunition, which they badly needed in order to procure meat for the coming winter. Inspired by a Delaware religious prophet, Neolin, who urged them to throw off their dependence on Europeans, the Indians rallied behind the Ottawa leader, Pontiac, and others to mount a coordinated siege of British forts in the Ohio Country and the Great Lakes. Known as Pontiac's Rebellion, the uprising did not dislodge the British but did motivate the Crown to issue a proclamation in 1763, which established a boundary along the crest of the Appalachians beyond which colonists could not trespass and colonial governments could not claim authority without approval from London. But the British proved unable to enforce the proclamation effectively, and in 1768 they signed the Treaty of Fort Stanwix with the Iroquois, in which the latter approved the cession of large tracts of Shawnee, Delaware, and Cherokee land on the Ohio. In the same year, British authorities returned control of Anglo-Indian trade to colonial governments. The repeal of major components of the Proclamation of 1763 emboldened squatters throughout the east to move on to Indian lands and begin building homes and communities. Shawnees, Delawares, Cherokees, and other Indians retaliated against the trespassers, many of whom had inflicted violence on Native Americans. The frontier had become a zone of anarchy where Natives and colonists alike resented those who claimed to rule them and fought for their survival as well as their independence. In 1775 the many regional conflicts would be absorbed into the larger war between Britain and its American colonies.

For varying periods of time after their arrival in North America, Europeans adapted to the social and political environments they found, including the fluctuating ties of reciprocity and interdependence as well as rivalry, that characterized those environments. They had little choice but to enter and participate in the existing conditions if they wished to sustain their presence on the continent. Eventually, one route to success proved to be their ability to assert themselves as regional powers in new networks of exchange and alliance that arose to supplant those of the Mississippians, Anasazis, and others.

To emphasize continuities between the older centers and those dominated by Europeans is not to minimize the radical transformations effected by Europeans' colonization of the continent. Arising in the wake of the great Mississippian powers, new centers at Montreal, Fort Orange/Albany, Charleston, and New Orleans permanently altered the primary patterns of exchange

Army Officer Seth Eastman's nineteenth-century drawing of Atotarho, the mythical Onondaga Chief who first opposed the "peacemaker" Hiawatha's proposal to form a "league" of Iroquoian tribes, and who late became the confederacy's first leader. Courtesy, The Newberry Library.

in eastern North America. The riverine system that channeled exchange toward the interior of the continent gave way to one in which growing quantities of goods arrived from, and were directed to, coastal peripheries and ultimately Europe. In the Southwest, the Spanish revived Anasazi links with Mesoamerica at some cost to newer ties between the Rio Grande Pueblos and recently arrived, nonfarming Navajos and Apaches. More generally, European colonizers arrived with a complex set of demographic and ecological advantages over the native peoples, most notably the epidemic diseases, to which they themselves were largely immune, that utterly devastated Indian communities. At the same time, they arrived with ideologies and beliefs proclaiming their cultural and spiritual superiority to Native peoples and their entitlement to Natives' lands. Finally, they organized economic, political, and military systems for the engrossment of Indian lands and the subordination or suppression of Indian peoples.

Europeans were anything but uniformly successful in realizing their goals, but the combination of demographic and ecological advantages and imperial intentions, along with the Anglo-Iroquois Covenant Chain, enabled land-hungry colonists from along the seaboard from New England to the Chesapeake to break entirely free of ties to dependence on Indians before the end of the seventeenth century. This success proved to be only the beginning of a new phase of Indian-European relations. By the mid-eighteenth century, the rapid expansion of land-based settlement in the English colonies had sundered older ties of exchange and alliance linking Natives and colonizers nearly everywhere east of the Appalachians, driving many Indians west and confining those who remained to small, politically powerless communities in which Indian identities persisted but in isolation. Meanwhile, the colonizers threatened to extend this new mode of Indian relations across the Appalachians. An old world, rooted in indigenous exchange, was giving way to one in which Native Americans had no certain place.

For Further Reading

A book that can serve as either an overall introduction or as a handy reference work on North American Indians before and after the first encounters with Europeans is *The Cambridge History of the Native Peoples of the Americas*, vol. 1: *North America*, eds. Bruce G. Trigger and Wilcomb E. Washburn (Cambridge, 1996). The volume of essays edited by Alvin M. Josephy, Jr., ed., *America in 1492: The World of the Indian Peoples Before the Arrival of Columbus* (New York, 1992), provides an excellent view of Native lives and cultures on the eve of European contact.

The long history of North America before the arrival of Europeans is known primarily through the work of archaeologists. The best surveys, based on the latest scholarship, are Brian Fagan, *Ancient North America: The Ar-*

chaeology of a Continent (1991); and Stuart J. Fiedel, *Prehistory of the Americas* (2d ed., Cambridge, 1992).

For interdisciplinary studies that link the pre-Columbian past with the subsequent history of European contact, see Charles Hudson and Carmen Chaves Tesser, eds., *Forgotten Centuries: Indians and Europeans in the American South, 1521–1704* (Athens, Ga., 1994); Patricia Galloway, *Choctaw Genesis, 1500–1700* (Lincoln, Neb., 1996); Bruce G. Trigger, *Natives and Newcomers: Canada's "Heroic Age" Reconsidered* (Kingston, Ont., 1985).

There are many excellent studies of Indian-European relations during the colonial era. The best general survey is Colin M. Calloway, *New Worlds for All: Indians, Europeans, and the Remaking of Early America* (Baltimore, 1997). James Axtell, *The Invasion Within: The Contest of Cultures in Colonial North America* (New York, 1985), compares English Protestant and French Jesuit missionary efforts in eastern North America. Discussions that link Indian history to environmental studies include Alfred W. Crosby, *Ecological Imperialism: The Biological Expansion of Europe, 900–1900* (Cambridge, 1986); William Cronon, *Changes in the Land: Indians, Colonists, and the Ecology of New England* (New York, 1983); and Timothy Silver, *Indians, Colonists, and Slaves in the South Atlantic Forests, 1500–1800* (Cambridge, 1990). Ian K. Steele, *Warpaths: Invasions of North America* (New York 1994), is a solid military history of Indian-European contact.

The history of the Iroquois and their relations with other Indians and with Europeans can be surveyed through Daniel Richter, *The People of the Longhouse: The Peoples of the Iroquois League in the Era of European Colonization* (Chapel Hill, 1992), and two volumes by Francis Jennings, *The Ambiguous Iroquois Empire: The Covenant Chain Confederation of Indian Tribes with English Colonies from Its Beginnings to the Lancaster Treaty of 1744* (New York, 1984), and *Empire of Fortune: Crown, Colonies, and Tribes in the Seven Years War* (New York, 1988). On New England, see Neal Salisbury, *Manitou and Providence: Indians, Europeans, and the Making of New England, 1500–1643* (New York, 1982); and Francis Jennings, *The Invasion of America: Indians, Colonists, and the Cant of Conquest* (New York, 1975). For studies of Indians in the Ohio and Great Lakes regions, see especially Richard White, *The Middle Ground: Indians, Empires, and Republics in the Great Lakes Region* (Cambridge, 1991); and Gregory Evans Dowd, *A Spirited Resistance: The North American Indian Struggle for Unity, 1745–1815* (Baltimore, 1992).

Studies of the Southeast in the colonial era also have proliferated in recent years. James Axtell, *The Indians' New South* (Baton Rouge, 1997), provides a comprehensive introduction. On particular Native groups and regions, see Kathryn E. Holland Braund, *Deerskins and Duffels: Creek Indian Trade with Anglo-America, 1685–1815* (Lincoln, Neb., 1993); Joel W. Martin, *Sacred Revolt: The Muskogees' Struggle for a New World* (Boston, 1991); Tom Hatley, *The Dividing Paths: Cherokees and South Carolinians through the Era of Revolution* (New York, 1993); Daniel H. Usner, Jr., *Indians, Settlers, and Slaves in a Frontier Exchange Economy: The Lower Mississippi Valley before 1783* (Chapel Hill, 1992); and James H. Merrell, *The Indians' New*

World: Catawbas and Their Neighbors from European Contact through the Era of Removal (Chapel Hill, 1989).

On the colonial Southwest, the most useful studies are Jack D. Forbes, *Apache, Navaho, and Spaniard* (Norman, Okla., 1960); Elizabeth A. H. John, *Storms Brewed in Other Men's Worlds: The Confrontations of Indians, Spanish, and French in the Southwest, 1540–1795* (Lincoln, Neb., 1981); Andrew L. Knaut, *The Pueblo Revolt: Conquest and Resistance in Seventeenth-Century New Mexico* (Norman, Okla., 1995).

Chapter Three

Indians in the Colonial Spanish Borderlands

Henry F. Dobyns

*I*n 1821, the United States annexed Spanish Florida, and Missouri merchants set out for Santa Fé, New Mexico, to initiate a highly profitable international commerce with newly independent Mexico. By 1854, the United States had added to its territory vast regions of northern Mexico from Texas to California. In these "Spanish Borderlands," U.S. citizens encountered Native Americans riding horses derived from Spanish stock, growing wheat (domesticated in the Old World), and speaking some dialect of Spanish as a second language. Many Natives wore Spanish-style clothing and were at least nominal Roman Catholics. Clearly, it seemed, Native American peoples south of a line through San Francisco and St. Louis had experienced post-Columbian events and processes different from those that shaped the cultural behavior of Native inhabitants in other sections of North America.

In 1492, the inhabitants of what became the western Spanish Borderlands already differed from Native Americans farther north. They intensively cultivated summer-season domesticated food crops. Those living in the arid Southwest irrigated their cultivated plants, building diversion dams of poles and brush, and excavating canals to carry spring, creek, or river flows to their fields.

The Southwestern frontier lay where horticulture ended. On the west, that frontier ran through the southern Nevada-California desert. Colorado River Valley Yuman-speakers grew crops, as did the Imperial Valley Cahuilla and the Southern Paiutes, Goshutes, and several of the Ute tribes in Nevada, Utah, and Colorado. In the upper Arkansas River basin, southern Athapaskan-

Above: Detail from engraving. See page 74.

speakers and/or Pueblo dwellers also cultivated crops. In the east, Pueblos gardened from the upper Pecos River south to the lower Rio Grande.

In addition to horticulture, many Southwesterners shared similar social patterns and architectural styles. Spaniards called compact defensive towns in the uplands *pueblos,* while the riverine settlements came to be known as *rancherías.* While there were a variety of belief systems in the region, they all exhibited some degree of Mesoamerican influence.

Southwesterners were also linked to southeastern communities through trade. Southern Athapaskan-speakers and Jumanos wintered along the eastern edge of the irrigated Southwest, trading Plains hides, dried meat, and bone tools for horticultural and high-value commodities. They crossed the southern Plains during warm weather to trade fairs conducted in frontier towns of riverine gardeners on the western edge of the Southeast.

In the Southeast, Native gardeners grew crops with direct precipitation and lived in a variety of settings. The Caddoan-speakers who lived between the Plains and Mississippi River inhabited rancherías with large thatched houses and fields spread along fertile river valleys. Members of densely populated Southeastern polities east of the Mississippi inhabited compact villages, typically palisaded for defense. Noble lineages closely resembling those that dominated Aztec and Mayan society ruled these vertically stratified groups. Priest-kings conducted ethnic ceremonials in temples built atop man-made mounds or platforms. Many if not all ruling families resided on mound summits.

Native Americans living in what became the borderlands played regional versions of the Mesoamerican ball game. Rancherían peoples moved earth to make simplified ball courts, copying carved stone masonry Mesoamerican prototypes. Southeasterners poured their enthusiasm into playing the game without building courts.

Beginning in the early sixteenth century, the Columbian Exchange of human populations, plants, animals, and their predatory parasites decimated Borderlands Natives. Depopulation brought dramatic contraction of settlements, followed and accompanied by migration into the region of peoples residing elsewhere prior to the demographic collapse. Immigrants included Native North Americans and Mesoamericans, Europeans, Africans, Mestizos, and Mulattoes. In 1492, the Borderlands population (within the present United States) probably numbered more than 5 million. Sixteenth-century epidemic diseases—smallpox, measles, bubonic plague, and influenza—reduced that total to perhaps 250, 000 by A.D. 1620. Thereafter, surviving Native ethnic groups struggled to endure. Between epidemic diseases, women bore enough children to increase small populations about 1 percent annually. Then Old World pathogens reinvaded, wiping out temporary gains. Some groups such as Florida and Georgia Timucuan-speakers and Texas Coahuiltecan-speakers did not survive after 1770.

A portrait of a Lipan Apache warrior from William H. Emory's Report on the United States and Mexican Boundary Survey, *published in 1857. Courtesy, The Newberry Library.*

During the sixteenth-century population collapse, sedentary peoples retreated from peripheral regions. As a result, the Natives who survived to, say, 1620 had amalgamated into far fewer settlements than their ancestors required in 1520.

Following on the heels of this demographic contraction, colonizing Spaniards sought out populated areas in order to subsist on horticultural products of Native American labor. Thus they created a series of hierarchical, multiethnic societies throughout the Hispanicized zone. In these communities, peninsular-born Spaniards nearly monopolized government positions and the power these endowed. *Creoles* (genetic Spaniards born in the New World) envied the Peninsulars but served as their assistants and stood with them against all lower castes and classes.

The Spanish conquest was also characterized by unions of European males and Native American women, a phenomenon that reduced the number of Native American births and produced a genetically mixed new American race. Called *Mestizos* in Spanish, the members of this new race played a significant role in the historical development of the region. Culturally, they ranged from persons who "passed" as Creoles to those who lived as traditional Native Americans, depending on which parent reared each child, and how effectively that parent imparted his or her heritage. The group was particularly prominent in North America because Spanish prejudice against the new American race often stimulated mestizo migration toward *El Norte* as Mestizos sought upward social mobility and economic opportunity.

From the beginning of the Spanish colonial enterprise in the Americas, soldiers captured Native Americans in "just wars" according to Christian-legalistic concepts. Turning captives into slaves, captors typically sold them into servitude at a profit. Missionaries, merchants, miners, farmers, and even housewives purchased native captives to toil for them. While mortality ran high among such captives, some survived. Those who did were inevitably detribalized. Genetically Native American, they became culturally Hispanic and socially lower class. Known in New Mexico as *genízaros,* such detribalized Natives founded several eighteenth-century frontier villages that by 1821 could hardly be distinguished from other rural frontier settlements.

The colonial market for slaves and Native demand for manufactured goods also stimulated Native American slave raiding. Some tribes selling agricultural produce—Wichitas for example—put purchased slaves to working their own fields. Seminoles, Creeks, Choctaws, and Cherokees emulated Spanish, French, and English plantation owners by keeping black slaves.

Lower in the sociopolitical hierarchy was the traditionalist Native American population. It furnished the bulk of colonial labor and food supplies during the early colonial period. That population was divided into tribal groups whose cosmological and cultural differences militated against their joining ranks to oppose European colonists. At the bottom of the social strata labored African slaves.

Christian priests and other social theorists in central New Spain defined at least 128 ranked categories to classify members of the new American race according to their relative proportions of European, African, and Native Ameri-

The Spanish Borderlands on the Eve of the Spanish Incursions

Illinois

Mosopelea

Monacan

Powhatan
Chiefdom
(post 1570)

Kaskaskia

Pamlico

Shawnee

Cherokee

Tuscarora

Chickasaw

Quapaw

Numerous groups
amalgamating into
late colonial "Catawba"

Caddoans

Yuchi

River

Creek

Cusabo

Timucuan
Chiefdoms

Tunica

Choctaw

"Guale"

A   Yustega
B   Utina
C   Saturiwa
D   Potano
E   Tocobaga
F   Ocali
G   Acuera
H   Mocozo
J   Agua Dulce

Natchez

Alabama

Hitchiti

nkawa   Atakapa

Huma

Mobile

Apalachee

Biloxi

Acolapissa

Karankawa

Chitimacha

Ais

Calusa   Tekesta

Mississippi River Chiefdoms

A   Taposa   E   Koroa   K   Tioux
B   Chakchiuma F   Yazoo   L   Koroa
C   Ibitoupa   G   Tunica M   Bayopgoula
D   Ofo   H   Taensa N   Tangipahoa
             J   Grigra

can ancestry. Even though frontier conditions discouraged such complicated discriminations, inhabitants of Spanish regions annexed by the United States constituted a settled and complex society.

Spaniards colonized St. Augustine on the Atlantic coast of Florida in 1565. Thereafter, they resettled Timucuan speakers native to northern Florida at Christian missions. There the latter labored to raise wheat and other foods to supply the large garrison that defended Spain's vital sea route home from the wealthy viceroyalties of Perú and New Spain. From that time forward, the *presidio* (military post) and the Indian mission characterized New Spain's northern frontier.

In 1598, Spaniards, Mestizos and Mesoamerican Tlaxcalans colonized the upper Rio Grande valley. The Spaniards established themselves as a socioeconomic elite exploiting Pueblo labor. They based their domination on military force—the superiority of armored horsemen and war-horses, lances, and steel swords over bows, arrows, and wooden war clubs. The elite exacted tribute in the form of textiles, piñon nuts, and other commodities as well as forced labor.

The Spaniards introduced sociological structures new to the Natives. St. Augustine functioned not only as a military stronghold but also as the administrative headquarters for missionaries and civil officials governing Timucuan, Apalachee, and other Native Americans. In 1610, Spaniards created the administrative town of Santa Fé, a similar outpost in the Southwest: Roman Catholic priests had accompanied colonists there in 1598 and initiated Indian missions in existing pueblos. The New Mexico elite collected tribute and forced labor through a feudalistic system called the *encomienda*. Under this system the governor put various pueblos "in charge" of elite *encomenderos* legally responsible for the communities' conversion to Christianity and defense. This "responsibility" in turn gave encomenderos the right to exact payments and labor from their native charges. Pueblo people resented the missionaries' "extirpation of idolatry" as much as Spanish and Creole domination.

The Pueblo and Timucuan areas lacked silver and gold deposits, although Timucuans obtained through trade with south Florida Calusa some of the bullion salvaged from ships wrecked after 1545. The Piman area in Arizona did contain some silver lodes. The colonial mining frontier reached rich deposits within a few miles of the present international boundary only after Spaniards, Mestizos, and their Native American allies defeated a Northern Piman army in 1649. Mine owners soon forced Pimans living well within the present-day United States to mine the ores, and the mining camp became a primary frontier institution that changed Piman lifeways.

Aedes egyptii mosquitoes and the deadly yellow fever they transmit spread to Florida in 1649. Peninsular Natives there suffered the same decimation as had those around the Gulf of Mexico and Caribbean seashores. As Florida's Native population declined, blacks became an increasingly large component of the area's population. Its Natives perished faster than the inland peoples whom yellow and dengue fevers did not reach.

While invisible pathogens decimated Native Americans everywhere, survivors benefited from an expanded food supply as a result of the Columbian Exchange. Spaniards introduced domesticated horses, cattle, donkeys, sheep, goats, swine, and poultry, and several crops. During the seventeenth century, Southwestern Natives traded slaves for horses—or stole them—until ethnic group after ethnic group became equestrian. Apaches on horseback using Spanish-type lances gained military domination on the southern Great Plains. They hastened Pueblo horticulturists' westward retreat, and the eastward retreat of Native gardeners living along western tributaries of the Mississippi River.

Early in the seventeenth century, Apache bands began creating the purely historic "Plains Indian" cultural pattern. That way of life in its ultimate 1870s form became fixed in the United States popular consciousness as the primary stereotype of "Indians"—mounted, feather-bonneted, bison-hunting, warlike. That lifestyle actually did not develop until the eighteenth century, when French traders furnished guns to Native American groups migrating onto the Plains to exploit bison from horseback. Plains Native Americans exported human captives, processed furs, and horses to pay for firearms, powder, lead, metal tools and utensils, glass beads, blankets, and many other imports. The "Plains Indian" of popular perception, was actually thoroughly integrated into the world fur and horse market, and depended upon European trade goods.

Like horses, many Old World domesticated plants spread to innovative Native horticulturists beyond the frontier. Economically and biologically, wheat became the most important new crop. Wheat grows through the winter, while all New World food crops cannot survive freezing temperatures and must be grown during the summer. Thus, wheat practically doubled the cereal-growing capacity of surviving Native American gardeners. In addition, the introduction of a variety of Old World summer-season crops increased the variety of foods and condiments that Natives in the Hispanicized zone consumed. These crops included watermelons, cantaloupes, broad beans, coriander, and other spices. New World tomatoes and piquant peppers also spread through the region during colonial times.

Old World sheep raised by Pueblo families enabled men to supplement or replace pre-Columbian cotton fabrics with woolen textiles. In a remarkable cultural transformation, a small group of Athapaskan-speakers on the northern Pueblo frontier combined sheep flocks with horses and gardening to create a distinctive pastoral lifeway and a new ethnic group. They became the group known as Navajos early in the seventeenth century. A steady mutton diet also enabled the new entity to increase in numbers from its creation to the present day. Periodic accretions of Pueblo refugees plus captives whom raiders brought back from New Mexican villages also added to the Navajo population.

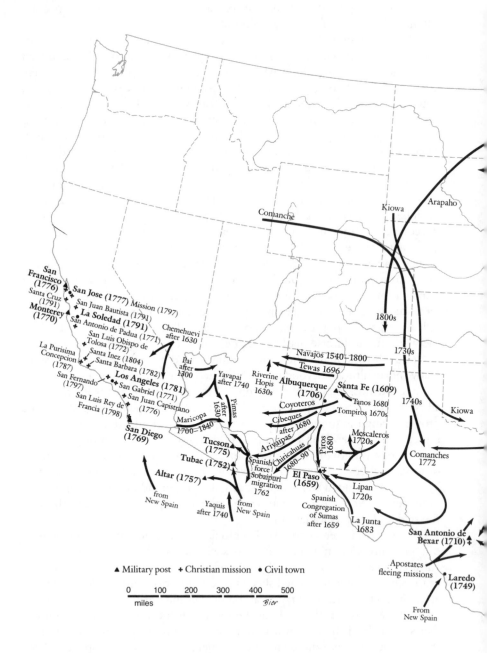

Spanish and Native American Migrations, 1565–1800

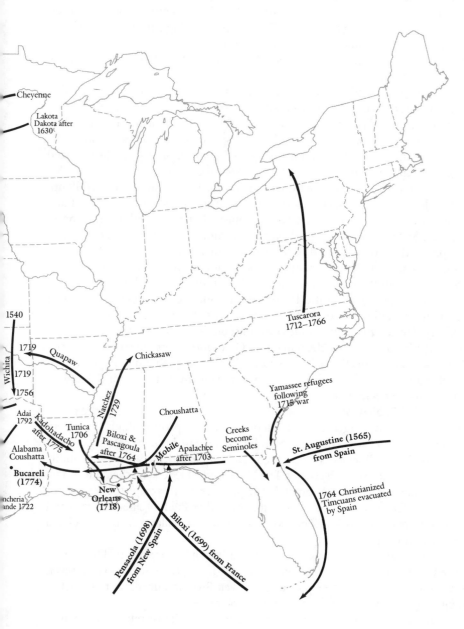

Cheyenne

Lakota
Dakota after
1630

1540

1719

1719

1756

Wichita

Quapaw

Chickasaw

Tuscarora
1712–1766

Adai
1792

Kadohadacho
after 1775

Tunica
1706

Natchez
1729

Biloxi &
Pascagoula
after 1764

Choushatta

Mobile

Apalachee
after 1703

Creeks
become
Seminoles

Yamassee refugees
following
1715 war

St. Augustine (1565)
from Spain

Alabama
Coushatta

Bucareli
(1774)

ancheria
ande 1722

New
Orleans
(1718)

Pensacola (1698)
from New Spain

Biloxi (1699) from France

1764 Christianized
Timcuans evacuated
by Spain

The most significant Pueblo increment to Navajo population came between 1692 and 1700 in the guise of Jemez Pueblo refugees from Spanish
colonialism. A serious environmental crisis began in New Mexico during the
late 1660s. Its effects prompted eastern Pueblo residents to migrate to Rio
Grande pueblos during the 1670s. Their Apache trading partners, whose horse
herds were also being decimated by new diseases in the 1670s, turned to
raiding to replace their lost animals. This accelerated Pueblo abandonment of
eastern outposts.

This prolonged environmental and cultural crisis culminated in 1680.
Traditionalist Pueblo leaders successfully united for a militant effort to regain
their autonomy. They resorted to arms on 10 August, killing more than twenty
missionaries and four hundred colonists. Spaniards and other colonists retreated south to El Paso, accompanied by inhabitants of several Christianized
pueblos, especially the southernmost Piro-speakers.

Widespread Native American population change followed the 1680 uprising. Jócomes, Sumas, and Janos peoples united to eject colonists west and
south of El Paso in 1684 (or nervous colonists thought they did). As a consequence, Spanish officials forced Northern Pimans to treat as enemies these
peoples with whom they had previously intermarried, traded, and shared irrigated fields. In addition, Spanish colonists forced the Pimans to break off
their trade with the rebellious "apostate" western Hopi Pueblos.

In the aftermath of the Pueblo revolt, Spain devised new methods of
extending its influence. In 1687, it sent the first Jesuit into Northern Piman
country. During the next decade, Rev. Eusebio F. Kino explored Piman territory north and west to the Gila and Colorado rivers, meeting ancestral
Maricopas and Quechans. Kino laid an institutional foundation for a new
northward thrust of colonial expansion, a movement that began in 1732 with
a missionary at *Bac* (Reeds) near modern Tucson.

In 1692, New Mexican Governor Diego de Vargas explored the possibility of reconquering the rebel Pueblos. First he probed Pueblo territory
from his El Paso base. Then, in 1694, he led an expedition of reconquest and
reoccupation of Pueblo New Mexico. De Vargas did not, however, simply
recreate the older Spanish colony. The Hopi were able to keep their autonomy
both because of their isolation and their willingness to accept the temporary
residence of many eastern Pueblo refugees. Other Pueblos amalgamated and
survived in new forms, the Zuñi consolidation of six villages into one being a
representative case.

The Spaniards were also more wary of possible opposition. They established presidios at Santa Fé, El Paso, and La Junta, the last protecting seven
missions founded in 1683 along the lower Rio Grande near its Conchos
confluence. These stood guard against "enemy" tribes.

In addition to providing protection against Native rebellion, Spanish
posts guarded their province against other European powers. Thus, when

An early Spanish illustration of the "Heathen Seris" who came to the Jesuit missions near the modern Arizona-Mexico border in the early eighteenth century. Courtesy, The Newberry Library.

French fur trader Louis Juchereau de St. Denis crossed Texas from Caddoland in 1714, viceregal officials rushed colonists to the Tejas. A month after their arrival in 1715, Catholic chapels stood among Caddoan-speaking tribes, the Neches and Nabedaches, Hainais, Nacogdoches and Naconos, and Nasoni and Nadacos. Within a year, two more missions influenced Adaes and Ais—Caddoan-speakers who would amalgamate as Spanish-transmitted diseases diminished their numbers. This Spanish thrust confronted the French Natchitoches outpost in theory; in fact, the Spanish colonists actually depended on the good will of St. Denis and related French traders for survival.

Native American and Spanish dependence upon French trade goods demonstrated that Southeastern Native Americans were integrated into the world market and that the Spanish presidio and mission would not be successful against people with access to plentiful quantities of manufactured items.

A missionary who had found San Pedro Springs at the head of the San Antonio River capitalized on official concerns to obtain approval for founding a mission there among three Coahuiltecan bands. In 1718, the provincial governor founded San Antonio de Béxar presidio nearby.

As a consequence of internal and external pressures during the early eighteenth century, the Spanish military post became the dominant Borderlands institution. The cavalry garrison at Santa Fé, aided by Pueblo auxiliaries, proved able to defend even the outlying trading pueblos of Taos and Pecos, plus the genízaro trading center at Abiquiú. The frontier stabilized at those trading centers where equestrian peoples came to fairs at which they exchanged slaves, horses, hides, and meat for textiles, agricultural produce, metal tools, and weapons.

Florida's equivalent to the environmental crisis in New Mexico was man-made. In 1672 Spanish officials began to replace St. Augustine's series of rotting wooden fortifications with stone walls. The 1672 project is still visible: a stone, Vauban-style fortress. Its construction placed additional life-threatening stress on Timucuans forced to labor in the Anastasia Island coquina quarries, as masons or their helpers, and as oarsmen on barges and canoes carrying food supplies from the missions.

The new Castillo de San Marcos was a strong eastern anchor for the Spanish empire. Because it withstood later enemy assaults, it enabled the Spanish

An early nineteenth-century engraving of the pueblo of Santa Ana. Note the chapel and the burros, two products of Spanish rule. Courtesy, The Newberry Library.

to expand their domination of the Timucuans. The consequences were devastating for the Indians' villages, economies, and lives.

In 1703–1704, a South Carolina militia with Native allies attacked and destroyed Florida's mission communities. The Carolinians captured thousands of Timucuans and Apalachees, marching them into English slavery. Thereafter, small Native remnant groups congregated close to St. Augustine and St. Marks, leaving northern Florida open to colonization during the eighteenth century by equestrian, cattle-raising, more or less dissident groups from the Creek Confederacy. Known to Spaniards as *cimarrón* (wild folk), these immigrants became known to English speakers as Seminoles. Spanish Florida and the Seminoles themselves offered refuge to Africans who escaped slavery on plantations in English colonies.

Similar patterns of demographic adjustment were apparent in the Southwest, where Plains Apache bands crossed the Río Grande and migrated southwestward during the demographic turmoil following 1680. By the late 1690s, an Apache vanguard allied with Jócomes, Sumas, and Janos, native to the territory on the Piman frontier, raided Piman riverside rancherías. By about 1725, the Apaches had absorbed the remnant Natives, as eastern Apaches absorbed the remnant Jumanos south Plains Natives by 1718. Thereafter, Apaches constituted the primary ethnic enemy of colonists and Native Americans within or near the frontier from central Arizona to central Texas. Aggressive mounted Comanches migrated south to become the second major ethnic enemy of northern New Mexicans early in the eighteenth century, and of Texans soon after.

In 1719, Comanches, Utes, Pawnees, Wichitas, and other Caddoans armed with French muskets decisively defeated the Apaches who had dominated the southern Plains for a century. Plains Apaches retreated to the Spanish frontier near San Antonio or the Rio Grande; Jicarillas fell back on Taos and Pecos Pueblos. Retreating eastern Apaches drove remnant Coahuiltecans into the south Plains *Ranchería Grande* amalgam of decimated groups.

Priests from three suppressed Caddoan missions moved to San Antonio in 1731, recruiting nearly one thousand Coahuiltecan neophytes. The 1731 arrival in San Antonio of fifty-six Canary Islanders insured the settlement's Hispanic heritage and urbanization.

Apaches, whom Spaniards perceived as perfidious aggressors, faced a dilemma. They were no match for mounted Natives armed with guns. Spanish policy prohibited trading firearms to Natives. As a result, Jicarillas, Lipans, Mescaleros, Warm Springs, and Chiricahuas (and older tribes that amalgamated into these) had no choice but to raid colonists to acquire needed weapons, metal tools, and horses to ride and eat. By 1735, the Apaches' search for these materials carried them as far south as Saltillo and Monclova in Coahuila.

During the eighteenth century, Spanish colonial border warfare took its toll in lives lost in battle and through forced migration of captives. Yet, contagious diseases continued to be the main determinant of Native population trends throughout the period. If known Pueblo population reports are reliable, the number of people under colonial control fell to their lowest numbers during the 1740s and then began a slow, jerky recovery. No later than 1760, however, immigrant Spaniards and Mestizos outnumbered New Mexican Pueblos. During the 1750s, in fact, colonists began expanding their ranching and farming west from the Rio Grande valley to the Rio Puerco and Mount Taylor. By this time that well-watered area was the core of the Navajo sheep range, so attempts at colonization precipitated conflict. The colonists fell back after several frustrating years, but their children returned with reinforcements beginning in the 1770s.

Northern Piman tribes united to throw back the colonial frontier in late November 1751. The Pimans killed more than one hundred Spaniards, Mestizos, and Christianized Native Americans from other groups. Then Spain established presidios at Tubac in southern Arizona in 1752, and at Altar on the far northwestern frontier in 1757. Soon after taking command of Tubac, Creole Juan Bautista de Anza in 1760 killed the son of the leader of the 1751 action, ending the small-scale continuation of the Piman movement.

While the western portion of the Borderlands continued to be preoccupied with regional interethnic relations, the worldwide Seven Years' War between European powers greatly affected the eastern portion. Having defeated France and Spain, England dictated the terms of the 1763 Treaty of Paris. England annexed Spanish East Florida as well as French Canada and Louisiana east of the Mississippi River. France ceded Louisiana west of that great stream to Spain. This cession greatly increased the number of Euro-American settlements in northern New Spain, such as at St. Louis, as well as the number of Native groups under nominal Spanish jurisdiction.

When Spanish officials left Florida, they evacuated the entire population, including all of the Christian Natives they could persuade or coerce aboard ship. That number was but a few thousand individuals, who soon perished in fever-ridden coastal, Cuban and Mexican settlements.

France had maintained alliances with Native Americans by giving them annual presents and trading with them on a large scale. Spain perforce had to continue the pattern in Louisiana or risk losing Native allegiances to British traders. Spanish adherence to New Spain's no-trade policy in Texas cost Spain Caddoan allies and colonial lives, leaving surviving Caddoans more influenced by French and English traders than by Spaniards. Similarly, English officials at St. Augustine conveyed many presents to Seminole chiefs in an effort to win the immigrants as allies and trading partners. Seminoles occupied most of the peninsula, which Englishmen failed to colonize effectively.

Spain's King Charles III appointed able ministers who galvanized Spain's cumbersome imperial apparatus into action after the Seven Years' War and several years' investigations. Resulting changes profoundly affected thousands of Hispanicized Native Americans. In just seven years, 1769–1776, Spanish missionaries and officers advanced the frontier more than five hundred miles from Lower California to San Francisco Bay. Priests founded San Diego Mission in 1769. Tubac's Captain Juan Bautista de Anza led colonists to San Francisco in 1776. Missionaries continued to found intervening missions until nearly the end of the century. Infectious diseases, malnutrition, and overwork reduced a 1770 Native population of not less than 64,500 in the missionized coastal zone to 21,100 by 1821.

Having sent a trusted nobleman to inspect frontier presidios in 1766–1767, Charles III in 1772 issued a *New Regulation* governing them. The new rules empowered governors to grant only truces to hostile Natives; only the viceroy in distant Mexico City could approve a peace agreement. The regulations created a new Frontier Provinces administrative unit. Its Commandant Inspector, Colonel Hugo O'Conor, carried out provisions for repositioning presidios to form a defensive line.

In 1775, O'Conor ordered the Tubac garrison to move north to Tucson. Gila River Pimas ninety miles farther north gained military strength by providing refuge for Pimans escaping colonial domination and Yumans fleeing more powerful Colorado River Yuman tribes. Thereafter the Pima-Maricopa Confederation sold Quechan, Yavapai, and Apache captives and wheat in Tucson for guns, munitions, clothing, liquor, oxen, and carts. Like numerous other amalgamated groups just north of the colonial zone, these Native Americans picked and chose the European cultural traits that they adopted. Even so, wheatfields, oxen, and Spanish-style wooden plows gave an Hispanic cast to confederation economics, and it became so militarized that by 1821 it maintained a standing equestrian army.

The royal regulations of 1772 further urbanized San Antonio by moving there the residents of East Texas presidios and missions. In 1774 former Adaes presidio inhabitants won viceregal approval for returning eastward, and thereafter they energetically traded with Caddoan and Plains Natives from the new town of Bucareli on the Trinity River. These Spanish individualists adopted the French trading pattern to profit from Native American dependence on world-market commodity exchange.

Another world war began in 1776 when English-speaking colonists on North America's Atlantic coast declared their independence from Britain's authority. That same year Spain's King Charles III implemented his 1772 provision creating the Frontier Provinces. Charles sent the Cavalier Teodoro de Croix from Spain as Commandant General with authority independent of the viceroy of New Spain. Traveling from Sonora to New Mexico as its new governor, Colonel Juan B. de Anza conferred with Croix in Chihuahua City. With other frontier military commanders participating in a key council of war, in July of 1778 they forged an energetic Indian policy.

Once in Santa Fé, Anza began mobilizing resources for war against hostile Native Americans. In 1779, he rode north with 600 soldiers, militiamen, and Native American auxiliaries. Anza kept west of the Rocky Mountain front

A nineteenth-century photograph of Alejandro Padilla of Isleta Pueblo, wearing an outfit of combined Indian and Spanish origin. Courtesy, The Newberry Library.

range through the San Luis Valley. Crossing to the Arkansas River headwaters, Anza posted sentinels. They soon descried dust raised by a major Comanche community on the move. Anza spurred to attack, cutting off the Comanche chief. Chief Green Horn's horseback heroics availed him nothing against the colonial troopers, who killed this principal Comanche leader, his son, and a shaman after they had forted up behind their horses' carcasses.

Meeting the Comanches on their own ground in the core of their own territory, Anza inflicted a crushing defeat. Other Comanche chiefs sued for peace and permission to trade. Governor Anza then demonstrated a diplomatic skill equal if not superior to his skill in battle. He refused to agree to treat any Comanches peacefully until the entire ethnic group selected a single head chief with authority sufficient to enforce the terms of a treaty of peace and commerce.

By 1786, the Comanches had apparently transformed their political structure to meet Anza's terms, even though eastern Comanche tribes had long been able to obtain French guns from Wichita trading partners. Anza granted Comanches the privilege of trading at Pecos Pueblo. He and the new Comanche head chief thus established a mutually (very) profitable and pacific exchange relationship. It insured the transfer of manufactured goods as well as livestock and New Mexican (Pueblo and Euro-American) farm products to Comanches and their Plains trading partners. Moreover, the agreement was permanent. That is, Anglo-Americans entering Texas and the southern Plains encountered Comanche opposition while New Mexican traders always traveled and traded safely among Comanches.

During Anza's long negotiations with Comanche leaders, another Treaty of Paris, this one signed in 1783, recognized the political independence of England's thirteen North Atlantic coastal colonies. England ceded East Florida back to Spain and evacuated its nationals, but it left Minorcan colonists who had drifted to St. Augustine. Florida welcomed Spanish officials. Florida and the Gulf coast continued to be plagued by tropical fevers that sharply limited European colonization so that Seminoles and escaping African slaves continued to be the most successful immigrants into Florida. Now Charles III appointed Bernardo de Galvez, a Spanish hero of the late war against England, as New Spain's viceroy. Bernardo de Galvez was the nephew of former Visitor General Jose de Galvez. Young Galvez had commanded troops of provincial Nueva Vizcaya and Sonora and gained a broad knowledge of the kingdom. In 1786, he promulgated instructions for governing the Frontier Provinces.

From his wartime experience on the Gulf coast, Galvez knew that Spain must make allies of Native Americans on the Plains and in the Mississippi River valley if it was to compete successfully with the new United States. Yet, Apache tribes comprised the main military and economic problem of the Frontier Provinces, forcing Spain to divert men and material from the Florida and Mississippi River frontier.

Appropriately, Galvez's instructions made the negotiation of peace treaties with the Apaches a principal goal. He ordered governors and presidial commanders to conduct search-and-destroy missions into the Apacheria, the Apache homeland, with the objective of forcing Apaches to sue for peace. Once they did, Galvez called for them to migrate to and settle at presidios. "Peaceful Apaches" were to receive rations, tobacco, and distilled alcoholic

Spanish Borderlands in 1819, on the Eve of Mexican Independence

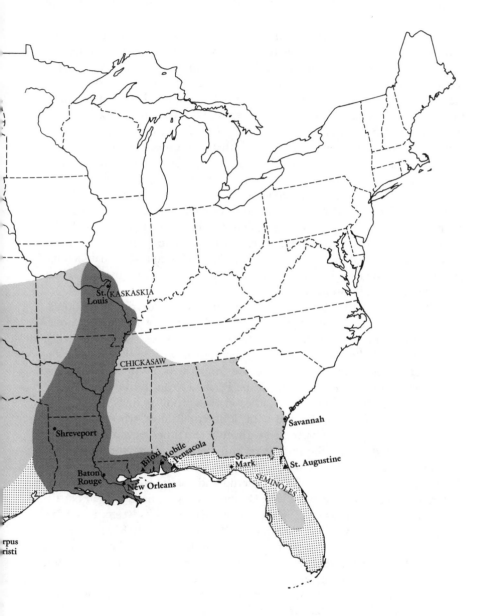

beverages. Galvez stated the goal of this Spanish version of what Englishmen called an "Indian reservation": rations, tobacco, and especially liquor were to be given Apaches to make them economically and psychologically dependent upon Spaniards.

Spurred by Galvez's instructions and a succession of energetic Frontier Provinces commandants, presidial troops coordinated campaigns through the Apacheria. Troops that included Pueblo, Opata, and Northern Piman companies and auxiliaries killed scores of Apaches and captured scores more. In the search-and-destroy sweeps, troops burned rancherías and food stores, captured horse herds, and harried Apaches throughout their territory.

Apache band after band sued for peace. Most Mescaleros moved to Janos. Arivaipas went to Tucson. In little more than half a decade Spanish troops achieved what had seemed impossible for a century—they pacified the Apaches.

By the end of the eighteenth century, Native peoples in the Frontier Provinces had entered an unprecedented era of peace and prosperity. In 1800, Creole, Mestizo, and Mulatto populations were rapidly increasing in the Rio Grande valley and adjacent provinces, and non-Indian families were colonizing irrigated farmlands and grazing areas. Mestizo entrepreneurs began exporting thousands of sheep every year from New Mexico to Chihuahua mine towns. Their activity—and the press of rising wealth—posed a growing threat to Pueblo land and water control.

By the 1820s, the Hispanic, Mestizo, Mulatto, and detribalized population of New Mexico outnumbered the Pueblo peoples by about five to one. Mexican Governor Antonio Narbona's 1827 census reported 43,433 residents, while Friar José Pedro Rubin de Celis had reported only 8,716 Pueblos in 1821.

Small as their numbers were, Native Americans continued exchanging commodities over ancient trails from the Pacific Ocean to the Great Plains. Mission Indians traded shells and other marine products to Serranos, who traded with Mojaves, who traded with Southern Paiutes, who traded with Hopis of Oraibi Pueblo, who traded with Zuñi and other New Mexico Pueblos, who traded with Abiquiu, Taos, and Pecos traders who dealt with Comanches, Jicarillas, Cheyennes, and Arapahos. Also, Gabrielinos dealt with desert Cahuilla, who traded with Northern Band Panya (*Hal Chedom*) on the Colorado River, who exchanged with Oraibis directly or through their Northeastern Pai relatives, thus tapping the Pueblo market via its western gateway.

United States explorers did not cross Pai country until 1851. Yet, Spanish loan words in the language attest to how fundamentally the Columbian Exchange had long before altered Native life. Pai used Spanish terms for horses, cattle, wheat, bread, sugar, and honey—a few indices of basic Old World cultural traits spread by Native American merchants. Standard strings of marine shells functioned as the standard of value among these Southwestern native merchants, an astonishing continuity from pre-Columbian times. Abalone shell employed in traditional Pueblo rituals carried as high an intrinsic value as any item traded along the traditional trails.

Native Americans on the southern Plains, in the Mississippi River valley, and the Florida peninsula were firmly integrated into the world market by the beginning of the nineteenth century. In other words, they were dependent peoples, militarily and politically. Their military success depended on imported guns and powder and colonial powers' policies. The Creek Confederation experienced the bitter reality of dependency in 1798–1802. A European adventurer announced a Muskogee State; several hundred Creek warriors mobilized and seized a major trading post and Spanish presidio. Spanish gunboats promptly ousted the invaders and put an end to the Muskogee State.

The French Revolution affected Native Americans quite unaware of it. France's Napoleon Bonaparte forced Spain's weak king to cede Louisiana back to France in 1800. Yellow-fever mortality soon demonstrated to Bonaparte that French troops could not hold sugar-exporting Haiti against rebelling blacks resistant to the disease. So Bonaparte changed his view of Louisiana and in 1803 sold it to the United States. The transfer of Louisiana greatly diminished the number of Native Americans under Spanish jurisdiction and equally increased the number in the United States. Native Americans living near the vague international boundary were embroiled in the Spanish-American turmoil until 1821.

When Napoleon invaded Spain, Spanish patriots resisted and were later reinforced by the British at the same time (1810) that a populist revolt broke out in New Spain. The professionalism of Frontier Provinces officers preserved New Spain for Spain by suppressing rebels. In that conflict, Native American soldiers fought with both rebels and loyalists.

In 1813, claiming that West Florida was part of Louisiana, the United States occupied Mobile. Dominated by France, Spain could do nothing about it. The Americans pressed their advantage during the 1812–1815 war with the English. Cynically pitting Creek collaborationists against so-called "Red Stick" Creek patriots, Andrew Jackson broke the military might of the French and Spanish–influenced Creeks at the Battle of Horseshoe Bend. The split Creek confederacy lost 2,000 warriors, and the United States seized half of the Creek lands. The surviving Red Sticks fled to Florida. In 1818, Jackson invaded Spanish Florida, without presidential approval, and seized St. Marks and Fort Barrancas at Pensacola.

Beset by Creole rebellions throughout its overseas empire, Spain jettisoned Florida. The 1819 Adams-Onís Treaty (not ratified by Spain until 1821) ceded Florida to the United States, creating conflict between the U.S. Army and the Seminoles that persisted for decades at varying levels of intensity. Three Seminole wars showed that regular U.S. troops could not win a guerrilla war in a subtropical area.

The Arkansas River became the western boundary between the United States and New Spain in 1803. That kept Comanches, Kiowas, Lipans, Tonkawas, Karankawas, Caddos, and trans-Mississippi Cherokees, Choctaws, Creeks, Acolapissas, and many others in Hispanicized Borderlands territory. New Mexican traders flocked to the south bank to continue trading with "Plains" Native Americans ranging on what had recently become U.S. territory.

Creole officers in New Spain reassessed their situation in the light of Spain's cession of Florida and the cumulative success of South American independence movements. In 1821, these New Spain officials themselves led the viceroyalty to political independence from Spain. They terminated Spain's policy of excluding foreign merchants, allowing Missouri entrepreneurs to open the Santa Fé trade. That became the opening wedge for U.S. conquest of complex, multiethnic societies in the Southwest. Borderlands Native Americans who had survived centuries of deadly infectious diseases and adapted culturally to revolutionary technical and social change would now face yet another century of biological, military, and social challenge.

For Further Reading

Alfred W. Crosby, Jr., *The Columbian Exchange: Biological and Cultural Consequences of 1492* (Westport, Conn., 1972) remains the best single-volume summary of fundamental processes of both biological and cultural changes unleashed by the Columbian voyages. J. Leitch Wright, Jr., *Anglo-Spanish Rivalry in North America* (Athens, Ga., 1971) describes the broad sweep of Timucuan, Apalachee, and Seminole experience in 1821, as well as that of many other Natives. Frank Raymond Secoy, *Changing Military Patterns on the Great Plains (Seventeenth Century Through Early Nineteenth Century)*, American Ethnological Society, Monograph 21 (Locust Valley, N.Y., 1953) is a comprehensive reconstruction of North American behavioral changes on the Plains stemming from adoption of Spanish horses and French-British trade muskets. Elizabeth A. H. John, *Storms Brewed in Other Men's Worlds: The Confrontation of Indians, Spanish, and French in the Southwest, 1540–1795* (College Station, 1975) relates events on the southern Plains to those in New Spain's Old Northwest and those on the southeastern theater of colonial confrontation. Abraham P. Nasatir, *Borderland in Retreat: From Spanish Louisiana to the Far Southwest* (Albuquerque, 1976) fills in the period that John does not treat, focusing on Spain's confrontation with the United States through Native Americans, trading partners, and "peace medal" chiefs between Santa Fe and St. Louis. Edward H. Spicer's pioneering ethnohistorical synthesis, *Cycles of Conquest: The Impact of Spain, Mexico, and the United States on the Indians of the Southwest 1533–1960* (Tucson, 1962) transcends international borders, comparing not only policies pursued by three colonial powers but also the responses thereto by two score and more Native American groups. D. H. Thomas, ed., *Columbian Consequences*, 3 vols. (Washington, D.C., 1989–1991) presents useful archaeological and historical perspectives on the Spanish

Borderlands. Thomas D. Hall, *Social Change in the Southwest, 1350–1880* (Lawrence, 1989) offers an engaging overview.

Bartolmé Barrientos' laudatory biography, *Pedro Menendez de Aviles: Founder of Florida,* translated by Anthony Kerrigan (Gainesville, 1965) focuses on Spain's contest with France but also includes useful information about Native Americans. Sherburne F. Cook perceptively analyzes *The Conflict between the California Indian and White Civilization* (Berkeley, 1976). Michael V. Gannon, *The Cross in the Sand: The Early Catholic Church in Florida, 1513–1870* (Gainesville, 1965) falls in the priestly tradition of mission interpretation, influenced by historian Herbert E. Bolton's Spanish Borderlands school. Max L. Moorhead, *The Presidio: Bastion of the Spanish Borderlands* (Norman, 1975) deals with the Indian-fighting Spanish garrisons on New Spain's frontier, while Marc Simmons, *The Last Conquistador: Juan de Oñate and the Settling of the Southwest* (Norman, 1991) offers a portrait of this significant figure. Henry F. Dobyns, *Spanish Colonial Tucson: A Demographic History* (Tucson, 1976) focuses on native Northern Pimans and examines one riverine settlement continuously occupied since pre-Columbian times. Paul H. Ezell, *Hispanic Acculturation of the Gila River Pimas* (Menasha, Wis., 1961) reconstructs colonial period militarization and parallel cultural changes. John L. Kessell, *Kiva, Cross, and Crown: The Pecos Indians and New Mexico, 1540–1840* (Washington, D.C., 1979) is a multifaceted study of the major eastern frontier trading center of the Pueblo market. Anthropologist Charles H. Lange's *Cochiti: A New Mexico Pueblo, Past and Present* (Austin, 1959) is much fuller for postcolonial periods than for the Spanish-Mexican years, but is useful in examining the historic experience of a Rio Grande Valley, Keresan-speaking pueblo representative of others that survive today. Jane Quinn, *Minorcans in Florida: Their History and Heritage* (St. Augustine, 1975) narrates how surviving Minorcan laborers from the New Smyrna plantation fled to St. Augustine, insuring its Hispanic culture. Alfred Barnaby Thomas, trans., *The Plains Indians and New Mexico, 1751–1778* (Albuquerque, 1940) provides documents concerning trade and raid at and near the Taos and Pecos Pueblo trading centers from mid-eighteenth century to the eve of Anza's defeat of and negotiation with Comanches. (Kavanagh) Robert H. Jackson, *Indian Population Decline: The Missions of Northwestern New Spain, 1687–1840* (Albuquerque, 1993) and Robert H. Jackson and Edward Castillo, *Indians, Franciscans, and Spanish Colonization: The Impact of the Mission System on California Indians* (Albuquerque, 1995) offer scathing portraits of the missions and their devastating effects upon Native peoples.

George P. Hammond and Agapito Rey, eds. and trans., *Don Juan de Oñate, Colonizer of New Mexico, 1595–1628,* 2 vols. (Albuquerque, 1953) is a brief synthesis of Spanish colonization of Pueblo country, with copious translated documentation. A Franciscan administrator's description of New Mexico's Native Americans as affected by a Roman Catholic mission is given in *Fray Alonso de Benavides' Revised Memorial of 1634,* translated and edited by Frederick Webb Hodge, George P. Hammond, and Agapito Rey (Albuquerque, 1945). Charles Wilson Hackett, ed., *Revolt of the Pueblo Indians of New Mexico and Otermin's Attempted Reconquest, 1680–1682,* 2 vols., translated by Charmion

Clair Shelby (Albuquerque, 1942) summarizes the successful Pueblo use of force to oust colonists from their territory and translates Spanish records of events.

Herbert Eugene Bolton synthesizes much archival research in his biography of the first Jesuit priest sent into Northern Piman territory, *Rim of Christendom: A Biography of Eusebio Francisco Kino, Pacific Coast Pioneer* (New York, 1936). Bolton also translated Kino's *Historical Memoir of Pimería Alta*, 2 vols. (Cleveland, 1919). J. Manuel Espinosa, *Crusaders of the Rio Grande* (Chicago, 1942) is a narrative of New Mexico Governor Diego de Vargas's reconquest of eastern Pueblos.

Nicolàs de La Fora accompanied King Charles III's special inspector of New Spain's frontier Indian-fighting presidios. *The Frontiers of New Spain: Nicolàs de La Fora's Description, 1766–1768*, translated by Lawrence Kinnaird (Berkeley, 1958; New York, 1967) contains significant details about Native Americans. Herbert Eugene Bolton, ed. and trans., *Athanase de Mézieres and the Louisiana-Texas Frontier, 1768–1780*, 2 vols. (Cleveland, 1914) translates many documents that clearly describe Native American dependence upon the world market. Coauthors Sidney B. Brinckerhoff and Odie B. Faulk provide useful translations of regulations in *Lancers for the King: A Study of the Frontier Military System of Northern New Spain, with a Translation of the Royal Regulations of 1772* (Phoenix, 1965), and Alfred Barnaby Thomas, ed. and trans., summarizes the career of the first Commanding General of the Frontier Provinces of New Spain in *Teodoro de Croix and the Northern Frontier of New Spain, 1776–1783* (Norman, 1941). Herbert Eugene Bolton, ed. and trans., *Anza's California Expeditions*, 5 vols. (Berkeley, 1930) synthesizes and translates documents that record Captain Juan Bautista de Anza's leading colonists to San Francisco, and his negotiations with numerous Native American peoples along the Sonora–San Francisco land route. Bolton also has edited and translated *Pageant in the Wilderness: The Story of the Escalante Expedition to the Interior Basin* (Salt Lake City, 1950). In *Bernardo de Galvez in Louisiana, 1776–1783* (Berkeley, 1934), John W. Caughey narrates the successes of one of Spain's ablest military leaders during the Revolutionary War on the Gulf of Mexico coast. Francisco Atanasio Domínguez provides an inspecting priest's description of Pueblo Catholic missions at the beginning of the American Revolution in *The Missions of New Mexico, 1776*, translated and edited by Eleanor B. Adams and Angélico Chavez (Albuquerque, 1956). Alfred Barnaby Thomas, ed. and trans., *Forgotten Frontiers: A Study of the Spanish Indian Policy of Don Juan Bautista de Anza, Governor of New Mexico, 1777–1787* (Norman, 1932) narrates the New Mexican career of the remarkable Creole Anza, treating extensively Spanish–Native American interactions from conquest and pacification of Comanches to standoff with Hopis. Bernardo de Galvez, *Instructions for Governing the Interior Provinces of New Spain, 1786*, translated and edited by Donald E. Worcester (Berkeley, 1951) contains the translated text of Viceroy Galvez's 1786 policies governing Spanish–Native American interaction in the Frontier Provinces.

Chapter Four

Native Americans and the American Revolution:
Historic Stories and Shifting Frontier Conflict

Kenneth M. Morrison

*F*or many Americans, the story of who they are winds back to the Revolution. It matters how we think of that event and how we see ourselves and others in the tableau. At the same time, history books tend to discount the power of that mythology and to turn the human meaning of the event into dull facts. Rather than appearing as some kind of collective creation, the Revolution is too often reduced to the product of disembodied forces, inevitable outcomes, and foreordained action. In response to that rather gray vision, impatient students have called for a new story, one that includes women and working people and that allows for human heroism. They want a story that conveys some of the passion of the age; they want history "from the bottom up!"

To write a history of the Revolution "from the bottom up" requires us to take seriously the experience and perspective of American Indians. The first aspect of the Indian side of the Revolution—their contributions—is easily managed. Most Indians sided with the British and fought alongside their allies in New England, New York, Pennsylvania, the Carolinas, and the Great Lakes. This is the story of the Indians in the Revolution.

The Indian perspective on the Revolution is a second—and far more important—aspect of the story. This perspective tells us about Indians *and* the Revolution. To tell that tale we should begin with a single question: What can the Indians—the outsiders—teach us about the character of the Revolution? An explanation does not come easily.

An overview of the American Indian *and* the Revolution should begin with a concern for story. For years historians have struggled to include Native Americans—people who were thought of as preliterate and therefore

Above: Detail from seal. See page 91.

ahistorical—in the great American history of progress. The struggle has been marked by anguish: without written documents Native American history remained mired in sentiment and myth, and Indian people themselves stood by chiding historians that they had gotten the story wrong. This should not surprise us, for Indians were not insiders to the Revolution. They were excluded by the principal actors and they rejected involvement themselves. Except for interaction in trade and conflict over land, Native and Euro-Americans had few common experiences. The war derived from and affected people who were usually far from the tribal world.

But the revolutionary era inspired acts of storytelling that addressed the cultural divisions of Indians and whites and set the course of relations between the races far into the future. Whether spoken by Native or Euro-Americans, the stories tried to explain why brutality was the order of the day. The world was coming apart and all the old stories had to be revised.

The era of the Revolution confronted both cultures with a new age. Behind an array of shifting economic, diplomatic, and military events lay a mythic urgency. Native and Euro-Americans alike plumbed events seeking answers to new, fundamental questions: Who are we? Why are we?

Imperial Story: 1760–1774

Native and Euro-Americans had once met as equals, but that equality ended in the 1750s. Since all the British colonies pressured the tribes to surrender their lands, Native Americans had had to favor the French during the Great War for Empire. The Iroquois Confederacy epitomized the situation Indians faced. The English pushed the Six Nations to abandon their fifty-year policy of neutrality in Euro-American conflicts—a policy that had been a very successful story of powerful aloofness by which the Iroquois played the French against the English. During the Seven Years' War, the confederacy was driven one way and then another. To placate English allies, the Iroquois declared war on New France. They also hedged their bets by failing to march against Canada. Their indecision proved costly. Colonial officials attributed the tribes' ambivalence to Indian untrustworthiness. Indian duplicity was always the story whenever the tribes followed their own interests.

With the defeat of the French, trust was even harder to come by. The Iroquois Covenant Chain—an alliance system linking the English colonies with the Indian tribes of the Old Northwest—began to come apart. More seriously, the Six Nations' Confederacy began to collapse from within. It took forty years for this external and internal disintegration to occur, a length of time which measures the complex challenge Indians faced in coming to grips with growing American power. To be successful, Native Americans faced two related tasks. First, they needed to achieve intertribal unity to counter that favorite Euro-American strategy: divide and rule. And second, each tribal group needed to revitalize the core kinship values that shaped their community life.

The conquest of Canada in 1763 made the achievement of these goals all the more urgent. Unfortunately, an old story that had been long in the making came immediately into play. The English colonies had fought the Catholic French and their Indian allies since the end of the seventeenth cen-

Joseph Brandt, or Thayendanega (1743–1807), the Mohawk leader who allied himself with the British during the American war for independence. Courtesy, The Newberry Library.

tury. By the 1760s, the English had little sympathy for Indian "savages" who had fought by the side of the equally "savage" French. Such sentiments reflected something more than bald racism: religious dogma, intellectual presupposition, and bitter experience had taught the English to stand on guard. Ideologically, then, the 1760s opened with little hope for cross-cultural communication.

Other stories had their impact, particularly the contrasting meanings Native and Euro-Americans placed on exchange. Gifts played a prominent role in Indian-white relations because, for Native Americans, symbolically charged acts of sharing structured positive social relations. In contrast, colonials limited the meaning of exchange to the merely economic: profit considerations prevailed. For example, they often thought of presents given to Indian allies as a form of bribery. That was one story that seemed to work. Gifts did win friends. So, gifts were given for as long as Euro-Americans needed Indian furs, land, and military assistance. Visiting Indian dignitaries were dined, and especially wined, and eventually sent on their way sporting new finery: shirts, jackets, and hats. Moreover, colonial or British officials paid the bills for food and entertainment at the public conferences that frequently drew hundreds of Indian people. As it turned out, Indian relations became more expensive in the 1760s, just as Euro-Americans felt more powerful, and official largesse turned into resentment.

Euro-Americans' frustration at the cost of Indian relations hid from them the Indian story about the significance of exchange. The gifts that sweetened discourse, opened and closed councils, and expressed enduring friendship had a religious value in Indian society. One's closest kin did not give presents; they shared with no thought of reward. Others, including distant relatives and strangers seeking to express good faith, gave gifts. Expectation of profit may well have been a part of such reciprocal exchange, but the achievement of something like kinship solidarity was the real goal of the forms Indians imposed on commercial give-and-take.

Still, colonial governors, imperial administrators, and American officials alike groaned under the cost of the conversation. There were always expenses that seemed more important. As a result, the major misunderstandings endured. In the 1760s, British officials contributed substantially toward alienating the tribes by slashing the Indian budget. Funding rose dramatically during the War for Independence, when much was at stake. After the war, American officials cut expenditures and so ensured the survival of tribal resentment. To the Indians, every refusal to honor Native American exchange values was an expression of disdain.

In 1763 budgetary retrenchment and the heritage of years of mutual animosity fused into violence. In the first place, the tribes were alarmed that France had ceded their lands to England. Second, the British had taken a hard line against what they saw as the "conquered" allies of the French. Major

*Seal of the Society for the Propa-
gation of the Gospel, founded in
London in 1704. Courtesy, The
Newberry Library.*

General Jeffrey Amherst, not one to truck with subordinates, made British policy clear. "It is not my intention," he declared, "ever to attempt to gain the friendship of Indians by presents." Moreover, he limited trade to a few posts to profit the English without regard for Indian cost, convenience, or sentiment.

English dominance was not to come easily. When the native peoples of the Old Northwest struck back in 1763, they effectively communicated, in the language of power that the English understood, the necessity for both economic and diplomatic reciprocity. The British government compared the cost of war to trading profits and, for a while, trade won. In the early 1760s, British officials had moved to control commerce from London to protect the tribes from abusive traders. But before long, control of the trade was returned to the individual colonies, and it fell into the hands of those who served private rather than public interests.

Imperial authorities in London claimed general powers over Indian-white relations, but in practice they abdicated their role to particular colonial merchants. Expediency became the main theme of British colonial Indian policy. For example, when faced with effective Indian opposition, the British shifted their story that the tribes had been conquered along with the French. To win peace (and also to streamline imperial direction of unruly colonial governments), the Proclamation of 1763 provided for the erection of a boundary between Indian and colonial lands.

The British even proceeded in good faith and for a time abated Indian resentments. In the South, the Cherokees led the way in surveying the border, hoping that it would at last control grasping frontiersmen. The Cherokees knew that the boundary was vital. In 1760 they had attacked squatters whom the southern colonies would not, and could not, control. The result had been a bitter war. Cherokee towns were devastated, and the tribe sued for peace even though the treaty confiscated lands under that classic story called reparations.

By the mid-1760s, then, several stories were shaping Indian-white relations in a way that would profoundly affect the tribes' reaction to the War for Independence. At every point on the frontier—at trading posts, forts, missions, and on borders breached by settlers—Indians rejected the grand story of Euro-American superiority. Native Americans countered with stories of their own, insisting on their own humanity, political independence, and territorial integrity. The Indian war of 1763 drove this message home.

The Indian defeat in the 1763 war communicated that the British might do as they wished because the tribes could not cooperate. Their disunity had its source in two related mythic orientations. The first was the story of tribalism itself, especially the religious conviction that solidarity was possible only between kinfolk. The second story derived from a major effort to deal with the divisive impact tribalism had on Native Americans' ability to achieve peace between and within the tribes. Not only had the Six Nations Confederacy abolished the law of revenge (and thereby extended the bonds of kinship beyond the clan), but it had also developed a new metaphor of solidarity—the Great Tree of Peace—a powerful symbol of diplomatic dominance over its Indian and Euro-American neighbors. By the mid-eighteenth century, the confederacy had come to claim that its tree (and its sovereignty) extended over the tribes and lands of the entire Old Northwest. In the 1760s it suited British interests to recognize and manipulate these Iroquois pretensions.

The devastating result of this story of an Iroquois empire can best be seen in the first Treaty of Fort Stanwix of 1768, an agreement that set the scene for the Revolution itself. The British used the treaty to establish the northern boundary between Indian and colonial lands. As in every treaty that negotiated a new border, the tribes were required to surrender more land. Even in the South, these land cessions fueled resentment but, as in the case of the Creeks and the Cherokees, the tribes had usually been able to see some value in compromise. In the North, the situation was different because Iroquois claims of territorial sovereignty effectively disenfranchised the Shawnees and the other tribes of the Old Northwest. When the Six Nations ceded all land south of the Ohio and the Susquehanna rivers (opening Kentucky, West Virginia, and western Pennsylvania to settlement), they lost face with their former Indian allies. A new confederacy arose beyond the Ohio determined to resist not only British manipulation but also the interference of the Six Nations.

Thus, the principle of divide and rule had again been used to further colonial interests.

The boundary line negotiated at Fort Stanwix was an illusion, the real effect of a story about centralized British and Iroquois authority that simply was not so. Settlers immediately swarmed beyond the Ohio with utter disregard for Indian rights. Worse, Delaware and Shawnee people who refused to abandon their homes found themselves facing racist frontiersmen who were now hostile neighbors. These rowdy settlers felt free to deal with Indians as they pleased. By 1774, government itself was breaking down throughout the American colonies. In Virginia such tensions produced a bloody frontier conflict, Lord Dunmore's War, as Indians moved to defend themselves against frontiersmen who were unwilling to discriminate between friendly and hostile Indians. The same situation prevailed all along the frontier; entirely apart from the growing American-British quarrel, Creeks, Cherokees, Delawares, Iroquois, Penobscots, and Passamaquoddies faced the prospect of war since neither the British nor colonial authorities seemed capable of protecting their lands. The 1770s were years of such dramatic confrontation between England and America that everyone overlooked these dangerous local disagreements. Americans and British expected Native Americans to remain neutral but did not examine the effect of what they asked.

Revolution: The Story of Conquest

Because the Patriots failed to comprehend the Indians' need to protect themselves from individual American citizens, they constructed an Indian policy on false premises. These erroneous principles were established in the official United States' story about Indian involvement in the Revolutionary War. As expressed in treaties, laws, and executive proclamations, the story was simple, having only two themes. First, Native Americans had proven themselves incapable of friendship. They had waged an unprovoked war against the United States. And second, since they had sided with the British, the tribes were conquered when Great Britain admitted defeat. It followed, therefore, that Indians had lost ownership of their lands. In other words, the United States contended that it had waged a "just war"; the new government could call upon international law and the doctrine of conquest to further buttress its claims. It is worth comparing this story with the facts of Indian participation in the War for Independence. The official story forgot that the war had many complex causes and that the outcome was not nearly as simple as conquest theory would have it.

In the Northeast, the Penobscots and Passamaquoddies suffered because they supported the American cause. Having survived a century of warfare with the English of Massachusetts, the two peoples aligned with their old enemies to ingratiate themselves. Both tribes, in fact, obtained written guarantees protecting their land from further encroachments in exchange for their support. During the war, the Indians' assistance was appreciated. Afterwards, Massachusetts returned to its old tactics.

Despite the fact that individuals were legally barred from settling on Indian land, Massachusetts looked the other way. Dispossession proceeded apace. Then, as the Penobscot and Passamaquoddy people found themselves in direct economic competition with English squatters, government commissioners offered them a new, protected reserve. In actual defiance of laws requiring federal participation in land transactions, Massachusetts pushed the two peoples into treaties that dispossessed them against their will. The conquest story did not fit the Penobscots and Passamaquoddies, but it was applied anyway.

In the South we find variations on these themes. Despite British promises and the enthusiastic endorsement of the Cherokees, the boundary established in the 1760s fell before settlers and traders. John Stuart, the British Indian superintendent, used the resulting Cherokee resentment to animate them against the American cause. Still, the Cherokees followed their own interests. They concluded in 1776 that further protests to either the British or colonial governments were futile. Speaking a new language, the tribe attacked the two newest white settlements. This action flouted the British request that the Cherokees remain neutral. Nevertheless, southern governments interpreted the attack as a British plot. Instead of discussing the real issue of territorial encroachment, colonial military forces set out to teach the Cherokees a lesson. Militiamen attacked and burned Cherokee villages across the tribe's vast lands. Witnessing these harrowing events, and richly benefiting from British trade, most Creeks remained quiet on the sidelines. Indeed, except for a few Cherokee warriors who continued to resist individual settlements, most southern Indians remained neutral. After the war, the Cherokees lost half of their remaining lands, and even the Creeks accepted a new boundary.

The conquest story was directly applied against the Six Nations and their supposed allies in the Old Northwest. Here, again, the story failed to mesh with the facts. Two of the Six Nations (the Oneidas and Tuscaroras) not only sided with the United States, they also paid a stiff price when the other members of the confederacy attacked them as traitors. Moreover, despite promises to the Oneidas and Tuscaroras that their lands would be protected, it was only a short time after the war before they too were dispossessed.

The struggle for land was so intense in the Old Northwest that it would have been self-destructive for Indians to side with the Patriots, an option Americans rarely considered. The Iroquois understood that it would be disastrous to side with Great Britain. The confederacy therefore resurrected the old play-off policy and told the new American government that the Six Nations would remain neutral. It also stipulated that its promise hinged on several conditions, all of which were soon violated. American forces engaged the British on Iroquois soil; Patriots attempted to arrest the Mohawk ally, Sir

John Johnson, and forced other Loyalist friends to flee. Worse, the government did not examine long-standing Mohawk complaints that settlers were encroaching on their lands. These American refusals to meet the Iroquois halfway demonstrate that the first theme of the conquest story, Indian perfidy, was not true. The confederacy did its part in trying to keep the peace, but no government succeeded in reining in the advancing settlers.

The conquest story also directed the confederacy's actual wartime activity. Although the British provided much needed goods and war materiel, everyday strategy remained in Iroquois hands. Waging traditional war, the confederacy succeeded in laying waste a vast area of New York, Pennsylvania, and Virginia. Since these were agricultural regions on which revolutionary forces depended, the Iroquois thus proved themselves a formidable force. Retaliating American armies inflicted comparable losses on confederacy towns but failed to dampen Iroquoian resistance. When Great Britain made peace, the Iroquois were ready to fight on. The confederacy considered itself undefeated.

The conquest story failed to account for either the causes or the course of the Indian side of the Revolutionary War. The story also made it necessary for the new United States to fight the tribes. The heritage of the Revolution produced such a clamor for land that the federal government found itself committed to the proposition that Native Americans were subjects who held their land only on sufferance. In the Old Northwest, at least, Native Americans acted to make clear their rejection of this idea. Armies under Generals Harmar and St. Clair met the assembled tribesmen and were soundly defeated in 1790 and 1791. The latter encounter cost the Americans 647 lives, more than any other Indian battle in the nation's history, including the celebrated Custer massacre of 1876. Shocked, the United States intensified its efforts and, in the process, learned an important lesson: war is more costly than diplomacy.

The conquest story had another result: Americans soon transformed their deep seated contempt for Indian people into a story of superiority and inferiority. Thomas Jefferson, for a single example, admitted that Native Americans were people. He added, however, that they were less developed and more backward than advanced Europeans. Thus, the president was equipped with a linguistic tool for dealing with headstrong Native Americans who needed restraint. Having found it too expensive to enforce its will, the federal government declared itself a father with ultimate disciplinary authority. Paternalism turned out to be the ultimate story for eroding Native American independence.

Religious Revitalization: An Indian Story

For people of the Revolutionary era, brutal realities demanded effective action. As we have seen, those actions were organized around new stories that not only justified policy but also shaped it. The new stories swept away earlier beliefs in the possibility of constructive relations between Native and Euro-Americans. The old stories were now thought to be false. Native Americans apparently were doomed to dispossession and destruction. Seen in the light of historical facts (facts that fit the "stories"), the era of the American Revolution epitomizes the passive victimhood of Indians in every age.

There is another side to this story. If, as many have held, the history of Indian-white relations has been shaped by federal paternalism, we should recognize that this was not a father who knew best. Rather, we must conclude that this was a father who killed—sometimes by neglect and sometimes with righteous fury. The image is uncomfortable, but it helps us to understand better the side of the Revolution that eludes our understanding of the apparent facts. The very image of the Great White Father often hides his habit of using power with little qualm of conscience.

In actuality, both the facts of the American Revolution and the paternal symbols in which they are often expressed hide another element of the story: from their own point of view, Native Americans never accepted the role of mere victim. Before, during, and after the American Revolution, Native Americans took responsibility for defining themselves in ways that made sense to them. And, in achieving both success and failure in that struggle for identity, Native peoples have a good deal to teach us about the social dynamics of the Revolution itself.

Native American failure stemmed from the inability of the tribes to effectively unite—a failing that rested partly on their economic dependence and partly on their tribal traditions. Such problems also affected the revolutionary effort: economic immaturity and states' rights troubled both the American confederation and the new republic. As it turned out, republicanism was achieved at the cost of some personal and political freedoms, a price that Native Americans largely refused to pay. Thus Native and Euro-Americans shared a similar vision of unity, but they sought to achieve it in entirely different ways.

For Indians, the era of the Revolution was sandwiched between two acts of prophecy. In the early 1760s, Neolin, a Delaware prophet, called the nations of the Old Northwest to revitalize themselves. The 1790s witnessed a number of such passionate individuals, the most prominent of which, Handsome Lake, led the way in reshaping Iroquois tradition and culture. In both the short and the long term, these religious movements were more important to tribal survival than were the military events of the war.

Grounded in tradition as they were, prophetic stories became historic forces. They called the people themselves to renewal, reminding them that responsible action effectively countered victimhood. The Iroquois say that whenever the people find themselves up against the wall, a prophet will come forth to help them. Oral tradition trained Indian people to listen attentively to the stories such prophets related. They did not always heed the prophet, but when they did revolutionary results were possible.

The Delaware prophet was neither the first nor the last religious leader who attempted to save disintegrating tribes with a new vision. But Neolin stands out for three reasons. First, Neolin's message was a syncretism of Indian and Christian teachings mixed to speak to the crisis of the 1760s. Second, unlike the old, traditional prophets, Neolin attempted to unite religiously several independent Indian nations. Third, Neolin's teachings ideologically fueled the Indian war of 1763. When the Creator spoke to Neolin, it became clear that the Christ of the missionaries and the Indian spirit were one and the same. Like Christ, the Creator communicated directly with human beings; this came as a radical change in Indian religious experience. The Creator's message was radical. Unlike Christ, the Creator recognized that Indians and Euro-Americans were culturally different peoples. In this way, the Creator, working through Neolin, validated Indian culture and began to undermine Christian beliefs among the tribes.

Sometime in 1760, Neolin had a vision in which the Creator warned that the Indian peoples were in grave danger. They had rejected the Creator's teachings and would, therefore, lose everything in this world and be damned in the next. The catastrophe could be averted. Euro-Americans could be driven from Indian lands and Native peoples themselves could return to their original, reciprocal relationship with nature. In effect, the Creator called Native Americans to recognize their own responsibility for their situation. He condemned their addiction to alcohol, quarrelsomeness, and sexual licentiousness.

Most of all, the Creator declared to Neolin that Indians tolerated the settlement of their lands only because they wanted trade goods. This desire led to two kinds of moral failings. First, Indians who hunted with guns violated the reciprocity that was supposed to exist between themselves and animals. The Creator observed that he had placed animals on earth to provide the people with food. He had not intended that they be sold to Euro-American traders. Second, the Creator warned that such commercial relationships had created severe social strife even within the individual tribes. This vicious conflict was so grave a violation of kinship values that the Creator had removed the animals as a punishment. Neolin's message was clear. Either the people would repent and return to proper ways of living, or they would starve and lose their lands to the Americans.

Religious stories like Neolin's put forward a special kind of truth. In becoming the voice of truth itself, Neolin attempted to bridge the gap between absolute and relative truth. He attempted to speak from tradition to the unprecedented troubles of the 1760s. Neolin's tale shows the extreme difficulty of bridging past and present, of conserving the best of the old while changing to ensure survival.

Given the problems facing the Old Northwest tribes, Neolin's message had to have been heard with some uncertainty. It is not known whether Indians perceived themselves as dependent on trade; at least that is not the thrust of Neolin's story. Rather, the Creator demanded that Indian people act positively and take responsibility. Neolin told the people that they could return to traditional values, if they so chose.

The initially successful war of 1763 was partly based on Neolin's vision of moral and cultural liberation. The failure of that war has obscured much that is valuable in Neolin's story. Behind the failure stand the harsh facts of economic need. The tribes could not drive the British away without ammunition, but that was only one part of the situation. At the intertribal level, Neolin's story became a call to arms. But at home, where kinship mattered, the story had another meaning: Neolin urged Indians to renew themselves as family members whose first commitment had to be to each other.

Little is known about the impact of Neolin's teachings, but something of their importance can be seen in the career of the Seneca prophet, Handsome Lake. As one of the forty-nine sachems of the Iroquois Confederacy, Handsome Lake had considerable prominence. But he was also a dispirited drunk, a state of being all too common for end-of-the-century Senecas. The American Revolution had terminated an ancient way of life, bringing an end to hunting, warfare, and diplomacy and to a social life in which men and women contributed equally. The Revolution also accelerated a beginning made long before the War of Independence, when the Iroquois first selected aspects of Euramerican culture. George Washington's troops had destroyed frame houses and barns, blacksmith shops, and sawmills. The Seneca continued to draw profitably from Euro-American culture in the 1790s, but the changes sparked little optimism. And, therein lies the importance of Handsome Lake.

As a prophet, Handsome Lake focused on the Senecas' most pressing issue, the survival of the people themselves. For the Senecas, prophets exist only to call the people to moral and social renewal. It did not seem remarkable to them that Handsome Lake had been a drunk. The Senecas knew that prophetic authority derived from no merely human act and certainly not from individual choice, ability, or ambition. Rather, the prophet is called because he is representative. Handsome Lake the man had internalized both the social and psychological difficulties afflicting his people. Like other Senecas, he felt ashamed, but not even Quaker missionaries could help him, or them, to change.

Instead, Handsome Lake fell "dead." He returned transformed by power, now a vehicle and a voice of the basic reality of things. The Senecas recognized Handsome Lake's transformation in a traditional way: the prophet spoke an archaic form of their language, a style of speaking that could not have been learned in everyday speech. Handsome Lake returned with mythic truth about the sad story of Seneca life. The Senecas listened and in time they themselves were transformed.

Red Jacket (1756–1830), a Seneca orator and chief who fought with the British during the revolution, and who forcefully defended traditional ways afterwards. When asked at one point why he refused to welcome missionaries among his people, he replied, "Because they do us no good." Courtesy, The Newberry Library.

Handsome Lake's visions spoke to the Senecas' total condition. The visions located the source of the Senecas' problems in their religious lapses. They directed the prophet to aid his people in bringing their social lives back into line with the old values. The visions thus made it possible for the Senecas to choose wisely from Euro-American culture. Because he spoke of these concerns using the concepts and language of Seneca myth, Handsome Lake's words galvanized the people in ways that Quaker missionaries had not been able to achieve. One of them reported that after hearing Handsome Lake recite his first vision the Senecas were "solid and weighty in spirit," and that he "felt the love of God flowing powerfully amongst us."

Handsome Lake's story resembled Neolin's. Its overall message—that the Senecas must accept responsibility for their sorry condition—was the same. Like Neolin, Handsome Lake pointed to antisocial behavior as the major cause of declension, and he summed up Seneca failings in four sins: whiskey, witch-craft, love-magic, and abortion medicines. In his second vision, Handsome Lake not only saw the resulting damnation of the Senecas but he also met Jesus. "Now tell your people that they will become lost when they follow the ways of the white man," was Jesus' frightening message.

Unlike Neolin, Handsome Lake devised a program of cultural change that worked within preexisting forms of cultural organization, made sense of

Boston's Columbian Centinel *for December 3, 1791, carried on its front page the text of the recently negotiated treaty with the Cherokees. Courtesy, The Newberry Library.*

adaptations to Euro-American culture, and led to genuine and long-range reform. Handsome Lake stressed that traditional values had to shape Seneca adjustments. In particular, the prophet's grasp of the socioreligious implications of economic change reveal the main characteristics of an effective story.

Handsome Lake squarely faced the facts. The Senecas' ancient hunting economy had been swept away. Hence, the demoralization of the men. The Senecas were also moving toward a life-style based on the nuclear, patrilineal family farm instead of the matrilineal clan. Again, the result was social strife as women repulsed male authority. Moreover, acceptance of a money economy threatened the exchange values that had always stressed putting group welfare before private profit.

The prophet identified and responded to each of these concerns. He understood that the authority of the clan mothers had to be wielded with more discretion, and he advised them to avoid interfering in their daughter's marriages. In effect, Handsome Lake validated a shift toward men and women sharing work and power. Similarly, Handsome Lake advised maternal uncles that they ought to defer to fathers in disciplining their nephews, a new rule appropriate to the new social arrangement.

More remarkably, Handsome Lake shaped the Senecas' transition to a Euro-American economy, and he did so in a way that countered the social divisiveness of capitalism. He warned the Senecas against pride in material worth, stipulated that they were not to sell agricultural produce among themselves, and required that they maintain collective ownership of tools and resources. In these ways the prophet showed the Senecas that close contact with the American people threatened communal life because it undercut the traditional value of sharing and an economy of reciprocal exchange.

Handsome Lake's story spoke to the Indians' situation with a remarkable sensitivity. The story recognized the excruciating emotional pain individuals experienced during the recent war. In doing so, it helped people to act responsibly. Specifically, the story urged Indians to take collective action: that people should work together was the main theme of Handsome Lake's tale. Moreover, the story accounted for both the psychological and the social impact of Euro-American culture. Finally, Handsome Lake's story taught an attitude of tolerance. Unlike Neolin, whose teachings urged a violent solution, Handsome Lake recommended cooperation between Indian and Euro-American people. In all these ways, the prophet not only reinvigorated Indian identity but he also realistically confronted the fact of cultural pluralism.

Conclusion: Story and Conflict

Handsome Lake illustrates the ways in which even the most revolutionary story can actually have a conservative character. Like the Seneca revival, the American Revolution was built on old mythic foundations, particularly the precepts of Christian faith and the certainty of civilized progress. Religious and secular truths bolstered each other, thereby obscuring many of the class divisions within the Euro-Americans' social order. Revolutionaries achieved political independence, and they promulgated far-reaching republican and democratic principles. But those principles and real life were something else again. Initially, the Revolution excluded not only Native Americans but also blacks, women, and many rural and urban workers from decision making. The rights of man made for fine-sounding political rhetoric, but in the early national period those rights were limited.

Like Native American prophets, revolutionaries spoke hopeful stories— stories of freedom, stories of possibility. But Euro-Americans did not share Handsome Lake's insight that the new American order had to embrace cultural pluralism. As they were applied to Native Americans, both official and unofficial Euro-American stories camouflaged colonialism in the cover of friendly help. The Northwest Ordinance expressed the story in 1787: "The utmost good faith shall always be observed towards the Indians; their land and property shall never be taken from them without their consent. . . ." The ordinance also contained an escape clause, declaring that Indians' property and liberty would never be compromised except "in just and lawful wars authorized by Congress."

Changing the tale to suit the case, Euro-Americans sooner or later won the land, thereby alienating Indian peoples from tried and true ways of life. The result was an enduring crisis as Native Americans sought a workable synthesis of traditional values and new culture, and Euro-Americans insisted on the veracity of their revolutionary stories. Thus federal agents and missionaries hastened to reform Indians in the name of progress and Christian love even though their program ran afoul of three additional American myths.

First, even though Euro-Americans claimed to offer Indians membership in the American nation, they built a segregated society. Federal policy envisioned Native American cultural transformation but did not take into consideration either Native American culture or Euro-American reactions to having Indians as neighbors. Much of the brutality of American history can be attributed to the fact that EuroAmericans did not have Handsome Lake's appreciation of the delicate balance of Indian values, culture, and social well-being.

Moreover, the offer of civilization failed to account for the conventional reaction to Indians as the ultimate outsiders—the wilderness personified. Fear of the stranger had always fueled Indian-white distrust, and it continued to do so after the war. Since the governing American symbol was now the vigorous pioneer transforming the land, government promises of peaceful cooperation contradicted new facts. Even Christianity failed to make sense of cultural pluralism. The idea of one God contradicted the multifaceted nature of tribal solidarity. That solidarity rested on kinship, custom, and obligation, not on ideological unanimity.

The second undercutting constructive association was based on cultural ethnocentrism. Euro-Americans were convinced of the superiority of their way of life. From first contact centuries before, Native Americans had been defined in negative terms. They were not religious and had neither laws nor property. The same continued to shape federal-Indian relations. Forgetting the economic upheaval caused by massive dispossession, federal officials claimed that Indians knew nothing of agriculture and so began a program to civilize them. This story not only failed to recognize Indians' sophisticated agricultural knowledge, it also attacked tribal values directly. Unlike Handsome Lake, who strengthened the social reciprocity at the heart of Indian life, federal officials sought to detribalize Indian people. Individually held property, they argued, would transform the Indian into a citizen.

The final story line had ominous implications for Indian-white relations. Americans contended that theirs was a government of laws. They therefore failed to see that laws surrounding Indian relations often did not govern. Treaties with Indian nations were ostensibly the highest law of the land, but they were respected only in the breech. In frontier areas, lawlessness became a way of life. Individuals and states purchased Indian lands in violation of the federal government's constitutional authority. Traders used credit, shoddy goods, sweet talk, and rum to defraud Indians everywhere. Indian agents and missionaries embezzled annuity funds and skimmed the money sent out to uplift Indians morally and culturally. In these ways, the story of law became a cover for continuing oppression.

In the end, each of these stories has had a history extending from the Revolution to the present, and all three share an important characteristic. Like Neolin's tale, and unlike Handsome Lake's, the Euro-American stories that shaped Indian-white relations enshrined a fatal mistake. Neither Neolin nor the Euro-Americans were inclined to test their stories against possible contradiction. They didn't realize that their stories failed to fit the facts. Many Native Americans have understood the essential flaw: they have come to know that stories often have a hidden agenda. The Revolution, and its continuing aftermath, have refreshed for them a traditional truth: all stories have a history and, when amnesia strikes the teller, history can repeat itself. But that's another story.

For Further Reading

For general discussions of the Revolution, see Robert S. Allen, *His Majesty's Indian Allies: British Indian Policy in the Defense of Canada, 1774–1815* (Toronto, 1992); Colin G. Calloway, *The American Revolution in Indian Country: Crisis and Diversity in Native American Communities* (Cambridge, 1995); Edward Countryman, *The American Revolution* (New York, 1985); Ronald Hoffman, Thad W. Tate, and Peter J. Albert, eds., *An Uncivil War: The Southern Backcountry during the American Revolution* (Charlottesville, 1985); Francis Jennings, "The Indians' Revolution," in Alfred E. Young, ed., *The American Revolution: Explorations in the History of American Radicalism* (DeKalb, 1976); and Dorothy V. Jones, *License for Empire: Colonialism by Treaty in Early America* (Chicago, 1982).

For discussions of the Revolution in the South, see David H. Corkran, *The Carolina Indian Frontier* (Columbia, 1970); Michael D. Green, "Alexander McGillivray," in R. David Edmunds, ed., *American Indian Leaders: Studies in Diversity* (Lincoln, 1980); James Howlette O'Donnell, III, *Southern Indians in the American Revolution* (Knoxville, 1973); Thomas M. Hatley, *The Dividing Paths: Cherokees and South Carolinians Through the Era of the Revolution* (New York, 1992); and James H. Merrell, *The Indians' New World: Catawbas and Their Neighbors from European Contact through the Era of Removal* (Chapel Hill, 1989).

For similar treatments of the North, see Barbara Graymont, *The Iroquois in the American Revolution* (Syracuse, 1972); William T. Hagan, *Longhouse Diplomacy and Frontier Warfare: The Iroquois Confederation in the American Revolution* (Albany, 1976); Isabel Thomas Kelsay, *Joseph Brant 1743–1807: Man of Two Worlds* (Syracuse, 1984); Daniel K. Richter and James H. Merrell, eds., *Beyond the Covenant Chain: The Iroquois and Their Neighbors in Indian North America* (Syracuse, 1987); Anthony F. C. Wallace, *The Death and Rebirth of the Seneca* (New York, 1969); and Richard White, *The Middle Ground: Indians, Empires, and Republics in the Great Lakes Region, 1690–1815* (Cambridge, 1991).

The immediate postwar conflicts are the subject of Colin G. Calloway, *Crown and Calumet: British-Indian Relations, 1783–1815* (Norman,1987); Gregory Evans Dowd, *A Spirited Resistance: The North American Indian Struggle for Unity, 1745–1815* (Baltimore, 1992); Joel W. Martin, *Sacred Revolt: The Muskogee Struggle for a New World* (Boston, 1991); and Wiley Sword, *President Washington's Indian War: The Struggle for the Old Northwest, 1790–1795* (Norman, 1986). For a discussion of the role of myth in shaping relations with Native Americans, see Helen Carr, *Inventing the American Primitive: Politics, Gender and the Representation of Native American Literary Traditions, 1789–1936* (New York, 1996); and Richard Slotkin, *Regeneration Through Violence: The Mythology of the American Frontier, 1600–1860* (Middletown, Conn., 1973).

Chapter Five

Indian Tribes and the American Constitution

Charles F. Wilkinson

Texts on constitutional law and history uniformly give short shrift to American Indians and to Indian tribal governments. This failure to recognize the proper place of Indian issues in constitutional law traces largely to an implicit presentist bias in the teaching of law: the thrust of legal education is to teach modern, real-world law in order to train professionals who can serve real-world clients. In response to this, constitutional texts for undergraduate and graduate nonlaw students tend to offer a perspective that is more balanced in historical terms. One leading book for undergraduate students explains by way of introduction that "as the amount of current doctrine has increased, historical materials [in law texts] have been curtailed. The normal solution [in books for law students] has been to describe the John Marshall period rather well and then move briskly to at least 1937 before beginning thorough analysis. In undergraduate instruction . . . we have more time to spend on developing the historical continuities, believing that such an investment of time comports well with the general goals of liberal arts as opposed to professional education."

Yet the undergraduate constitutional texts have done little better than the law books in integrating American Indian law into the larger body of constitutional law and history. We should not overstate the point: Indian issues are *not* decisive in constitutional law. At the same time, there are several concepts and events from Indian law and policy that simply cannot legitimately be extricated from the essence of constitutional law; others afford valuable enrichment and depth. What has happened, however, is that the constitutional law and history texts have unconsciously bought into the "Vanishing

Above: Detail from engraving. See page 106.

B.West inv.   Grignion sculp.

The Indians giving a Talk to Colonel Bouquet in a Conference at a Council Fire, near his Camp on the Banks of Muskingum in North America, in Octr. 1764.

"Indians Giving a Talk to Col. Bouquet." Formal proceedings of this kind were a staple of Indian-white relations under both the British and the Americans. Courtesy, The Newberry Library.

American" idea, and it has tainted the presentation of our most fundamental body of law. All of the books that exclude or minimize Indian issues on this basis are doubly wrong because the premise is wrong: since World War II, Native American issues have come to be of considerable social, political, legal, and economic importance, especially in the American West.

To highlight these conclusions, let us ask a few preliminary questions. *Worcester* v. *Georgia* was the legal centerpiece in the Cherokee-Georgia conflict of the 1820s and 1830s in which the Supreme Court held firm, on federalist grounds, against assertions of state power. The *Worcester* opinion has been cited more frequently by modern courts than all pre–Civil War Supreme Court opinions save three. In 1959 the Supreme Court described *Worcester* v. *Georgia* as one of Chief Justice John Marshall's "most courageous and eloquent opinions." Charles Warren, a leading historian of the Supreme Court, called the Cherokee-Georgia question "the most serious crisis in the history of the Court." How, as is the case, can *Worcester* v. *Georgia* be excluded from virtually all of the constitutional texts?

In *Worcester* v. *Georgia,* and in modern times, the Court has squarely held that Indian tribes possess inherent sovereignty and that the only other sources of sovereignty in this country are the states and the United States itself, which leads me to my second question. How can it be that our constitutional law texts resolutely instruct us that there are just two sources of governmental authority, state and federal, and wholly ignore Indian tribal sovereignty—a governmental authority that extends over 52 million acres, or 2.5 percent of all land in the country?

My third question involves the dramatic and historic dispute concerning Indian treaty fishing rights in the Pacific Northwest. This has been one of the great racial conflicts of our time, involving, among many other things, the allocation of 50 percent of the yield of the Northwest's famous and exquisite salmon and steelhead trout runs (so valuable to both commercial and sports fishers) to less than 0.5 percent of the population. In addition to that profound equal-protection question, the litigation proceeded against a backdrop of two decades of civil disobedience and refusals to obey federal court orders. In an assessment reminiscent of Charles Warren's description of the importance of the Cherokee-Georgia conflict in nineteenth-century jurisprudence, the Supreme Court in 1979 said no less than this: "The State of Washington's extraordinary machinations in resisting the [1974] decree have forced the district court to take over a large share of the management of the state's fishery in order to enforce its decree. Except for some desegregation cases, the district court has faced the most concerted official and private efforts to frustrate a decree of a federal court witnessed in this century." How is it that some of our most essential books—ones that instruct us on our society's most essential document—are devoid of any mention of this signally important conflict?

The study of constitutional law properly should include a treatment of Indian issues. Before turning to specific areas of constitutional doctrine, it will be useful to develop a foundation by briefly examining the constitutional provisions relating to Indians, the structure of Indian law, and three leading decisions by John Marshall that continue to influence constitutional law.

The Constitution, Indian Law, and the Marshall Trilogy

Indian tribes are mentioned three times in the Constitution. The phrase "Indians not taxed" is used twice, in Article I (allocation of seats in the House of Representatives and levying of direct federal taxes) and in the Fourteenth Amendment (revision of the apportionment formula for the House of Representatives to eliminate the slave fraction). The "Indians not taxed" provisions are of historical importance only; they were intended as a reference to noncitizen Indians, a distinction that was obviated in 1924, when all Indians were made citizens. The third express reference has been the most important to the group. The commerce clause authorizes Congress "to regulate Commerce with foreign Nations, and the several States, and with the Indian Tribes." This specific constitutional recognition of Indian tribal governments is complemented by two sections of Article VI: the reaffirmation of previously negotiated treaties, most of which were with Indian tribes; and the supremacy clause, which makes federal treaties and statutes superior to state laws.

Federal relations with Indian tribes have been carried out through some four hundred federal treaties and literally thousands of statutes, executive orders, and administrative rules. The most important Indian laws are the treaties, statutes, agreements, and executive orders establishing Indian reservations. Most of Indian law and policy is geographically based, and these are the basic organic laws defining the nature of law and policy within Indian reservations. These documents are exceedingly general so that it has been necessary for the courts to bring specific meaning to these laws by placing them in a larger context of constitutionalism, history, national policy, and morality.

The broad shape of the field of Indian law has been set by a relatively small number of opinions. Even today, perhaps the leading cases are three early opinions by Chief Justice John Marshall. This Marshall Trilogy has been refined by decisions in the century and a half since but, remarkably, the essential principles announced there remain good law today in spite of the societal changes that have occurred throughout the country.

The first decision in the Marshall Trilogy is *Johnson* v. *McIntosh*, handed down in 1823. Chiefs of the Illinois and Piankeshaw tribes had deeded away parcels of their aboriginal land to settlers—Johnson and others. Later, the tribes treatied with the United States, retaining some land as a reservation but transferring most tribal land, including the Johnson parcels, to the United States. Federal officials then issued homestead patents to McIntosh and others for the same land that the tribes had already transferred to the Johnson settlers. The owners of the Johnson parcels sued to establish title based on their prior, tribal deeds.

Chief Justice Marshall's decision is the beginning point for real property law in the United States and is essential to an understanding of the westward expansion. He ruled that the tribes, due to their possession that predated European settlement by so many centuries, held an ownership interest in their aboriginal lands. Their right to occupy, hunt, and fish on that domain was superior to all except the United States, which held a shared title with the tribes and which could obtain tribal title voluntarily by purchase or by military conquest. Marshall's federalist philosophy was then applied to the central issue in *Johnson* v. *McIntosh:* although the tribes held an ownership interest in

Miss Mary Eyre 2044 Vine
st Philadelphia

CONSTITUTION

OF THE

CHEROKEE NATION,

FORMED BY A CONVENTION OF DELEGATES FROM THE
SEVERAL DISTRICTS, AT

NEW ECHOTA, JULY 1827.

ᎠᎣᎦᎵᎾᎢ ᏩᏯ ᎤᎿᏍᎦ,

ᎫᎠᏫ ᎢᏍᏚ ᏫᎮᎵᎿᏩᎾ ᎤᎬᏃᎤᎾ, ᎫᏪᎾᏂ ᎤᎠᏇ 1827 ᎤᎲᏓᎢᏍᏆ.

We, THE REPRESENTATIVES of the people of the CHEROKEE NATION in Convention assembled, in order to establish justice, ensure tranquility, promote our common welfare, and secure to ourselves and our posterity the blessings of liberty; acknowledging with humility and gratitude the goodness of the sovereign Ruler of the Universe, in offering us an opportunity so favorable to the design, and imploring his aid and direction in its accomplishment, do ordain and establish this

The 1827 Cherokee constitution established a "civilized" government for the tribe; a government the Supreme Court refused to recognize in Cherokee Nation v. Georgia. *Courtesy, The Newberry Library.*

real property, they could not transfer it to anyone but the United States. Thus the tribes' attempted sale to Johnson was void, and the McIntosh homestead patent was valid because only the later transaction had a federal imprimatur. The ruling stabilized and federalized frontier property law. It also carried strong suggestions about the place of tribalism within the constitutional framework, notions that were sharpened less than a decade later by the other two cases in the Marshall Trilogy.

The Cherokee-Georgia dispute centered on Georgia state laws that, if valid, would have obliterated the Cherokee Nation by outlawing the tribal legislature and courts and by dividing up Cherokee lands among five counties. In 1831, the Cherokee Nation took the unusual step of bringing an action directly in the Supreme Court, claiming that the Court had original jurisdiction because the Cherokee Nation was a "foreign nation" and that the Court was empowered to hear filings in cases between foreign nations and states. The Court ruled against the tribe in *Cherokee Nation v. Georgia* and dismissed the case, holding that it lacked power to accept the case because the Cherokee Nation was not a "foreign nation."

But, having explained what the Cherokee Nation was not, the Chief Justice went on to explain what the tribe was. The Cherokee Nation did possess governmental powers—it was, Marshall declared, a "domestic, dependent nation." Further, the Cherokees and other aboriginal peoples had a special relationship with the United States: "The condition of the Indians in relation to the United States is perhaps unlike that of any two people in existence. . . . [T]he relation of the Indians to the United States is marked by peculiar and cardinal distinctions which exist no where else. . . . Their relation to the United States resembles that of a ward to his guardian." This special obligation has come to be called the trust relationship, and it is the essential concept that has provided Congress with vast power, for good and for ill, to deal in Indian affairs with a latitude found in few other corners of Congress's store of powers.

The final opinion in the Marshall Trilogy, the 1832 decision in *Worcester v. Georgia,* is the most expansive of the set. The controversy involved a Georgia statute requiring permission from the governor for anyone to enter Cherokee territory. The state law was enacted in spite of the federal Trade and Intercourse Acts, which reserved to exclusive federal authority the power to regulate travel in Indian country.

The case arose because two missionaries, Samuel Worcester and Elizur Butler, had refused to comply with the permit requirement and had been sentenced by the Georgia courts to four years of hard labor. Worcester and Butler appealed their convictions to the Supreme Court. Georgia was so contemptuous of the federal treaty and statute, and of asserted federal judicial power, that it refused to file a brief in the Supreme Court or to appear at oral argument. Needless to say, this constitutional, regional, and federal conflict—which coincided with South Carolina's Nullification Ordinance and with Andrew Jackson's second presidential campaign—fell under the eye of the nation.

In the first *Cherokee* case, Chief Justice Marshall had been able both to protect the Court's institutional integrity by avoiding a direct conflict with Georgia and, at the same time, to announce legal principles favorable to Indians by the procedural device of dismissing the Cherokee Nation's case and announcing the special trust relationship in a judicial aside. In *Worcester*, the Court ruled directly on the legal effects of Georgia's legislative assault and sided with tribal and federal authority.

Chief Justice Marshall's opinion explained that, like Georgia, the Cherokee Nation was a sovereign entity. Indeed, tribal sovereignty long antedated state or federal sovereignty: Indians always had been "a distinct people . . . having institutions of their own, and governing themselves by their own laws." To the Court, it was "an extravagant and absurd idea, that the feeble settlements made on the sea coast" somehow gave the Europeans "legitimate power" over the tribal governments. The Europeans treated the tribes with "great solicitude." Similarly, federal treaties did not obliterate tribal governments. As Marshall pointed out, the United States "treat[ed] them as nations." After the treaties, Indian tribes remained "distinct political communities, having territorial boundaries, within which their authority is exclusive, and having a right to all the lands within those boundaries, which is not only acknowledged, but guaranteed by the United States." With this matrix of overriding tribal and federal authority, Georgia law could have no place, and it was declared unconstitutional.

This mighty opinion, written in the deep heat of one of history's most charged situations, is by any standard one of the great constitutional, moral, and political statements ever produced by our jurisprudence. Historians still argue over whether President Jackson actually said the words attributed to him in response to the *Worcester* decision, but surely he thought them; and surely it can be said, even today, that the words "John Marshall has made his law, now let him enforce it" continue to epitomize the fragile, multifaceted relationship between the Supreme Court and the presidency.

And even today, although ultimately the force of *Worcester* must be kept in place by one of our smallest minorities and although the Indian and non-Indian societies at the time of the opinions are all but unrecognizable across the gulf of 150 years, John Marshall's words are still the law, and it is still enforced. To be sure, edges have been carved from the absolute tribal immunity from state law announced in *Worcester*, but most aspects of the immunity remain in force. How is it that the words of one human being can carry so much power across so much time? What are the things that make such a thing possible?

Taken together, the concepts embodied in the Marshall Trilogy continue to define the place of Indian tribes in the larger federal constitutional regime. Indian tribes possess aboriginal title to their ancestral lands, a property interest embedded at the base of American real property law. Indian tribes are sovereigns, governments with substantial legal and political power over their territory and their people and, in many cases, over people from outside the tribes who enter tribal territory. The United States has broad, almost unlimited, power over Indian affairs. Conversely, the United States has a high trust obligation to Indians. Indian law is federalized.

These special principles tracing to the Marshall Trilogy, with variations, help explain the preoccupation with Indian affairs in the First Congress in 1789 and 1790, when the national legislature enacted a comprehensive battery of laws dealing with Indian land transfers, crimes in Indian country, trade with Indians, Indian treaties, and a range of other subjects. The Marshall decisions are the premise for the emotional conflicts over authority, finances, and resources that have raged across Indian country in the twentieth century. They also provide the foundation for analyzing the several constitutional issues to which we now turn. In each instance, Marshall's words have both historical and contemporary ramifications.

The Place of Indian Tribes in the Constitutional Framework

As already noted, the existence of Indian tribes is acknowledged by the Constitution in the Indian commerce clause and in the treaty clause, which affirmed preconstitutional treaties, most of which were with Indian tribes. Relations with Indian tribes were established by means of treaties or treaty substitutes (such as agreements, statutes, and executive orders). An examination of the nature of treaties and treaty substitutes assists in determining the place of tribalism within the constitutional allocation of governmental authority.

Indian treaty negotiations were similar in concept to negotiations with representatives of prospective states over statehood. Both kinds of transactions sought to resolve territorial boundaries, land ownership, and governmental authority. The Tenth Amendment reserves to states the sovereign powers not delegated to the United States. The treaties and treaty substitutes reserve to tribes sovereign powers not expressly or impliedly relinquished to the United States.

In theory, state police powers are more permanent than tribal powers because they are constitutionally established, while tribal powers are lodged in treaties and treaty substitutes, which can be altered without recourse to the constitutional amendment process. In practice, however, congressional power to encroach on state prerogatives under the commerce clause is largely unfet-

MEMORIAL OF THE CHEROKEES.

One of the many Cherokee efforts to win support from whites, this bilingual memorial protested Georgia's efforts to abolish the Cherokee government. In 1832, the U.S. Supreme Court upheld the tribe's position in Worcester v. Georgia. Courtesy, The Newberry Library.

tered, just as there are few constitutional restraints on congressional authority over Indian affairs. Tribal and state police powers, in other words, were preserved in the same manner, by reservation and a bilateral contract; were manifested in different ways—the one by treaty or treaty substitute, the other by constitutional provision; and are both subject to the commands of Congress, although the political restraints on Congress are much greater in the case of states.

The two sets of transactions have produced different results in many respects. States are directly represented in Congress and possess much larger and wealthier citizenries. Accordingly, a greater quantum of reserved state powers remains undisturbed than is the case with reserved tribal powers. Nevertheless, in spite of these differences, treaties and treaty substitutes creating Indian reservations are best understood as organic government documents with legal characteristics similar in many respects to the Tenth Amendment for the states.

Perhaps Congress can unilaterally withdraw all federal recognition of all Indian governments, thereby effectively eliminating most actual exercises of tribal power. Even if such an event were to occur, no federal termination of tribes is final because Congress can and has restored recognition of tribes with which federal ties have previously been severed. Thus, whether under the current system of federal-tribal relationships that has existed for two centuries or under a hypothetical regime of termination, the rule of law requires that tribes continue to be reconciled into our constitutional system.

Indian tribes are part of the constitutional structure of government. Tribal authority was not created by the Constitution—tribal sovereignty predated the formation of the United States—but the Constitution acknowledged the existence of tribes. Although many assumed that Indian tribal governments would simply wither away, the tribes have not died out and the modern presidency, Congress, and the Supreme Court continue squarely to acknowledge this third source of sovereignty in the United States.

Accordingly, while the Supreme Court has recognized that inherent tribal sovereignty is both preconstitutional and extraconstitutional, it has found that direct analogies can properly be made to those governmental entities whose ultimate source of power is the Constitution. The Court made that point in 1982 in *Merrion* v. *Jicarilla Apache Tribe:*

> To state that Indian sovereignty is different than that of Federal, State, or local governments does not justify ignoring the principles announced by this Court for determining whether a sovereign has waived its taxing authority in cases involving city, state, and federal taxes imposed under similar circumstances. Each of these governments had different attributes of sovereignty, which also may derive from different sources. These differences, however, do not alter the principles for determining whether any of these governments has waived a sovereign power through contract, and we perceive no principled reason for holding that the different attributes of Indian sovereignty require different treatment in this regard.

The concept of Indian tribes as constitutionally recognized entities with reserved governmental rights on reservations free of most state authority is a fundamental constitutional principle that ought to be included in every course on constitutional law, history, and policy.

Due Process and Equal Protection

Civil liberties issues arising under the equal protection and due process clauses have long been among the most emotional and troublesome questions in Indian country. The Supreme Court has held that the restrictions on governments contained in the Bill of Rights and in the Fourteenth Amendment do not limit Indian tribes. That is, those amendments, taken together, apply to state governments and the United States government; they do not restrict tribal power. Thus, in 1896, the Supreme Court held in *Talton* v. *Mayes* that an Indian tribe was not bound by the Fifth Amendment and was not required to provide a grand jury to a criminal defendant in tribal court. More recently, courts have found that the First Amendment's establishment and free exercise provisions do not apply to Indian tribal governments.

In 1968 Congress passed the Indian Civil Rights Act (ICRA) which applied many of the provisions of the Bill of Rights and Fourteenth Amendment to Indian tribes. But rights under the Indian Civil Rights Act differ in several respects from constitutional rights of citizens outside of Indian country. The 1968 act, for example, does not prohibit the establishment of religion. Indian tribes, therefore, are the only governments in the United States that can legally operate as theocracies. Several Pueblos in the Southwest are just that, while other tribes across the country combine republican and theocratic forms of government by having some tribal council members chosen by election and some seats on their councils filled by hereditary chiefs.

Constitutional-type rights under the Indian Civil Rights Act differ in another important aspect. Under the reasoning in the 1978 decision, *Santa Clara Pueblo* v. *Martinez*, ICRA rights generally can be enforced only in tribal forums, not in federal courts. Thus if Indians have a grievance against their tribal government, they often lack recourse outside of the tribe. For example, a tribal council is prohibited by the free speech clause of the Indian Civil Rights Act from shutting down an opposition newspaper, but tribal forums— a tribal judge or the council itself—will interpret and implement that free speech guarantee and will decide if the newspaper continues.

These issues become magnified when non-Indians are involved, as has occurred at an accelerated pace since the 1960s when tribes began to reassert their sovereign powers. The Supreme Court ruled in 1978, in *Oliphant* v. *Suquamish Indian Tribe*, that Indian tribes lack criminal jurisdiction over non-Indians. Tribes do, however, possess civil authority over non-Indians when necessary to implement an important tribal interest. This means that in many circumstances tribal governments can, and do, try non-Indians in tribal courts in civil matters such as automobile accidents and contract disputes; regulate non-Indian reservation businesses; and zone non-Indian land located within tribal boundaries. In most situations, these decisions will be made by members of one race—Indians—against persons of other races. Under the Indian Civil Rights Act of 1968, federal judicial review is limited, and decision-making by tribal forums is emphasized.

These principles seem to clash with commonly held constitutional theory and can spark spirited debate. For example, John Hart Ely's influential book, *Democracy and Distrust*, argues that the essence of the Constitution is not substance but rather an open process that keeps all of the channels of representation open to diverse groups in order to produce truly democratic results. Yet these Indian governments, whose leaders are elected by a racially defined electorate, are outside of the system of constitutional restraints.

This race-based governmental system has been upheld by the Supreme Court, which has gone to considerable lengths to find that tribal governments are not in fact race based. The Court has concluded that political ties were established, by treaty or treaty substitutes, between the United States and tribal governments. This government-to-government relationship means that Indian tribes are recognized under federal law as political and governmental, not racial, entities and that there is no equal protection violation.

There is another context in which Indian law and policy energizes analysis of civil liberties issues. In 1954, *Brown v. Board of Education* rejected the "separate but equal" doctrine and struck down racial segregation in public schools. But Indian reservations are plainly racial enclaves where separatism prevails. On many reservations even the schools are effectively segregated.

This gives us a deeper insight into the antidiscrimination principle of the Constitution. Separatism for blacks was outlawed because it was forced upon them and because it demonstrably operated to their disadvantage. Indian separatism is allowable because Indians are separatists by choice, because most Indian leaders have voluntarily selected a measured separatism as the single best hope for the future of Indian people. Without the Indian experience, we are led to believe that our Constitution outlaws separatism; with it, we learn that the essential prohibition is against a forced policy that wounds minorities. Numerous aspects of federal policy have wounded Indians, but separatism is not one of them; thus it does not offend the Constitution.

Federal Preemption of State Law

We now accept, based on the body of law that has developed since 1937, the idea that Congress has expansive authority to preempt (i.e., oust or override) state laws. The supremacy clause makes valid federal law superior to a conflicting state law. Several constitutional provisions, most notably the commerce clause, provide ample basis for a far-ranging congressional authority to preempt state laws in most subject matter areas.

Of course, it was not always this way. And, of course, modern concepts of congressional authority do not trace just to 1937. The origins of federal plenary power in the Supreme Court decisions are found in the Marshall era. The Marshall Trilogy is central to this. Indian policy, along with shipping and banking, are the areas in which plenary federal power was first asserted, and first upheld by the Court, in derogation of state authority. Further, when the Federalist view waned after Roger B. Taney replaced Marshall as chief justice, the Court continued to recognize an expansive federal power over Indian affairs, one of the few fields in which federal preeminence was acknowledged. So there is a legitimate place for Indian law in the study of the historical development of federalism and preemption.

The Indian cases continue to be important in Supreme Court preemption law. Even though it is accepted that Congress can override state law, it is often difficult to tell from the face of a particular federal statute whether Congress has actually intended to exercise its broad power to preempt state law. Normally, the Supreme Court presumes that Congress has not intended to override state law unless it does so in a reasonably explicit manner. In the case of Indian law, however, the special traditions in the field are such that the Court has developed an opposite rule: state laws presumptively do not operate in Indian country unless Congress expressly has allowed state law to apply. This rule sharply limits the powers of state courts and legislatures within Indian country in key areas such as taxation, land-use controls, business regulation, and environmental protection.

The special rule for preemption in Indian law is relevant for two reasons. First, Indian law is a surprisingly large segment of the Supreme Court's work. Between 1960 and 1985, the Court handed down over seventy Indian law cases. The pace was especially swift during the 1970s and early 1980s, when the Court handed down more decisions about Indian law than it did decisions in established fields such as antitrust, securities, environmental, or international law. Thus the special Indian law rule on state power is significant in

Following their refusal to remove to the West, John Ross and other Cherokee leaders were arrested and confined in this house in Spring Place, Georgia. The house had been built in 1795 by Joseph Vann, a "civilized" Cherokee leader. Courtesy, The Newberry Library.

its own right. Further, the Indian preemption cases are a fit reminder that constitutional adjudication is not monolithic and that special rules sometimes must be developed to fit the particular history and circumstances of a discrete body of policy.

The Impact of Indian Law
on Constitutional Law in the American West

Regionalism is a major force in both American history and literature. Even though we think of law as existing mainly at the federal and state levels, we also have instances of regionalism in the law. One notable instance is the desegregation struggle, which focused on the South. An even better example is what can be called the Law of the American West, an amalgam of water, mining, public land, Indian, and national resources issues that arise most often in the arid western states with large concentrations of federal and Indian lands.

Indian law is central to the Law of the American West. A major political and constitutional development—the carving of new western states from the public domain to implement the westward expansion—cannot be fully understood without an appreciation of the role of Indian policy and law. The Marshall Trilogy established that Indian tribes, as governments, possessed a right of occupancy in their aboriginal lands; the westward expansion could not be consummated under the property law of the United States until questions of Indian title were resolved. Thus in most instances it was necessary to negotiate Indian treaties before statehood. When that was not done, as when Alaska became a state in 1959, development was thrown into question until the 1971 settlement with the Natives, a massive transaction involving the transfer of 44 million acres and $1 billion to Alaska natives pursuant to the Alaska Native Claims Settlement Act.

Political and constitutional power in the western states, then, must be placed in the context of the three landed sovereigns, the United States, the states, and the tribes. The tribes had prior rights. Then the United States acquired some, but by no means all, tribal political and property rights. In the treaties the tribes retained some lands—homelands—as reservations. The subsequent creation of new states by the statehood transactions, then, logically would deal only with the lands that had not previously been set aside for Indians. At that point, representatives of these future states bargained for the transfer of as much federal land as they could manage.

These arrangements, which provided for Indian reservations and the retention of most lands in federal ownership, explain the division of land in the West among the United States, the states, and the tribes, who own about 5 percent of all land in the eleven western states in addition to the extensive Native land holdings in Alaska. This progression of events also helps explain the continuing separatism, in a constitutionally egalitarian nation, of Indian tribes today.

The special status of Indian tribes raises particularly acute questions in regard to western natural resources. The Court has upheld extraordinarily favorable distributions of these resources to Indian tribes. *Winters* v. *United States,* in 1908, and *Arizona* v. *California,* in 1963, both recognized extensive Indian reserved water rights, outside of state water law, under dint of federal and tribal authority. Water, because of its scarcity in the American West and its importance to most forms of economic development, is especially controversial, and the question of Indian water is one of the foremost policy issues in the region. Somewhat similarly, in 1979 the Supreme Court upheld the right of the tribes in the Pacific Northwest to harvest up to 50 percent of the valuable salmon and steelhead trout runs. Tribes also possess important deposits of oil, gas, and coal.

All of these decisions, and others involving western resources, had to be made in the face of impassioned opposition based on states' rights and equal protection. Indians, it has been widely claimed, are "supercitizens" who have been allowed to operate outside of the state laws applicable to other citizens and to benefit from reverse discrimination based on race.

The Supreme Court's response has been the doctrine discussed above in another context, that the treaties are based on the governmental status of tribes, not on race. But debate still swirls over whether the distinction between Indian governments and Indian individuals is arbitrary and superficial, and whether this special, separate treatment is wise national and regional policy.

Conclusion

Indian issues ought to be accorded their rightful place in constitutional law and history. It is unthinkable to build a principled argument for the notion that the *Cherokee* cases—and the epochal controversy that surrounded them—should be excluded as principal cases from the study of constitutional law. The Cherokee-Georgia episode raises classic historical, institutional, and constitutional issues with all the drama and intellectual dynamism that our society can infuse into a set of confrontations and resolutions. These cases belong in the company of the *Dartmouth College Case, Gibbons* v. *Ogden,* and *Marbury* v. *Madison* itself, a conclusion proved in part by the fact that modern courts have cited the *Cherokee* cases nearly as often as the great cases just mentioned. In addition, constitutional scholarship should squarely acknowledge the existence of Indian tribes as one of the three sources of sovereignty within the constitutional structure.

Indian law bears on the other constitutional issues I have raised in a somewhat different way. Indian cases are not essential to a balanced treatment of freedom of religion, equal protection, or modern preemption law. But Indian law enriches our understanding of those areas demonstrably, and attention to it will breed stimulating debates.

The significance of Indians in the study of the Constitution does not rest on a patronizing or romantic view of Native issues. Indeed, the bottom reason that Indian issues are at least as relevant in the United States today as they were one hundred years ago is that Indian people themselves have demanded it. Rather than riding off into the sunset, Native Americans have dug in, insisted on choosing a measured separatism over assimilation, and have continued to press for their very existence as a discrete race. They, not white society, have dictated their place in constitutional law and history.

From the beginning of the Republic, then, our law has acknowledged the historical fact that Indian tribal sovereignty reaches back into the mists farther than most of us can conceive. Remarkably, that aboriginal authority, and the property rights that complement it, continue to have ramifications in our modern constitutional democracy. Indian law is a blend without peer of constitutional law, history, anthropology, international law, and political science. We lose far too rich an opportunity when we overlook it.

For Further Reading

Many of the ideas raised in this chapter are explored in Charles Wilkinson, *American Indians, Time, and the Law: Historical Rights at the Bar of the Supreme Court* (New Haven, 1987). The standard treatise on Indian law is Felix S. Cohen's *Handbook of Federal Indian Law* (Charlottesville, 1982), a revision of the original 1942 publication. These sources contain specific citations to the various court cases discussed in the essay. John R. Wunder, *"Retained by the People": A History of American Indians and the Bill of Rights* (New York, 1994) is a recent analysis by a legal historian. The matter of treaties is explored in detail by Francis Paul Prucha in *American Indian Treaties: The History of a Political Anomaly* (Berkeley, 1994).

For other examinations of Indians in American political and constitutional history, see Sidney Harring, *Crow Dog's Case: American Indian Sovereignty, Tribal Law, and United States Law in the Nineteenth Century* (New York, 1994); Russell L. Barsh and James Y. Henderson, *The Road: Indian Tribes and Political Liberty* (Berkeley, 1980); Vine Deloria, Jr., *Behind the Trail of Broken Treaties: An Indian Declaration of Independence* (New York, 1974); Francis Paul Prucha, *American Indian Policy in the Formative Years* (Cambridge, Mass., 1962); and Roy Harvey Pearce, *Savagism and Civilization* (Baltimore, 1966).

Chapter Six

Indians in Southern History

Theda Perdue

*H*istorians of the American South have pointed to a number of themes in southern history including agrarianism, patriarchy, and poverty; but overshadowing those is the South's long experience with racial slavery. Yet most textbook treatments of southern history divorce Indians from this major theme. Removal of the five large Indian nations from the Southeast is the only episode of the Native American past that receives substantial attention, and that event is placed primarily in the context of Jacksonian democracy or the United States' westward expansion. Removal was, of course, a part of the westward movement of whites and a feature of national policy that also included Native people outside the South. Nevertheless, the history of southern Indians is also intrinsically linked to the history of black and white southerners. Native Americans in the South cannot be understood apart from the plantation regime and its aftermath. Southern Indians had to contend with a society fueled by an economy based on the exploitation of nonwhite labor to cultivate crops that could produce enormous profits. They also had to contend with a people obsessed with issues of race.

As historian Daniel H. Usner, Jr. has pointed out, another South existed earlier, a South that was "swept into the vortex of antebellum racism and sectionalism," a South that had been characterized by fluid social and economic relations between races. This South lasted only until colonials realized the region's potential for growing valuable products, determined to profit from them, and developed the institutions necessary to realize this promise. Commercially profitable agriculture and racial slavery early became features of white southern society in the English colonies. Tobacco proved to be the

Above: Detail from photo. See page 129.

121

salvation of the Virginia colony and, by the end of the seventeenth century, the labor of nonwhite slaves had become the salvation of tobacco planters. Rice and indigo were followed by cotton and sugar; all became major products of slave labor that brought profits to the white South. For agriculture to be lucrative in the South, however, there had to be land and labor. Native peoples provided both.

From the British perspective, Indians had a right to the land, but that right was limited and circumscribed by European rights stemming from "discovery." The British based their claims to North America on the discoveries of Cabot and others who explored the New World under the auspices of the British crown. People, of course, lived in this "new found" land, but the British insisted that the Natives had only the right to occupy it temporarily. Limitations on the Indians' right to the land stemmed from the perception of native peoples as wandering hunters and gatherers who did not cultivate the soil or permanently inhabit a particular piece of real estate. Discovery entailed the right of preemption, that is, the right to possess the land when the Indians moved on, died out, or conveyed their limited claim to the "discoverer." When Indians relinquished their right of occupancy, the "civilized" nation that had discovered the land could then settle it, put it to proper use, and establish legitimate ownership. The British, therefore, viewed Indian titles as transitory and European titles as permanent.

Self-interest no doubt shaped British definition of land titles and clouded the British view of Indian culture. Observers overlooked or distorted important cultural characteristics; as a result, the claims of Native inferiority or inadequacy that whites used to dispossess indigenous peoples frequently had not been valid in the first place. In particular, southern Indians were not nomadic hunters as Europeans often portrayed them but farmers living in permanent villages. The former, masculinized, version of Native culture denied the economic role of women, who did most of the farming. For centuries before European contact, southeastern Indians depended on agriculture. Native peoples began to cultivate squash and gourds about 1000 B.C.; in approximately 200 B.C. they added corn and beans. Its broad fertile valleys, a long growing season, and an annual rainfall ranging from forty to sixty-four inches made the Southeast admirably suited for an agricultural economy. Agriculture permitted a stationary existence, and people built permanent houses, villages, and large earthen mounds which were the focus of an elaborate ceremonial life.

The agricultural base of southern Indian societies allowed a fairly high population density. Recent studies have suggested that some areas such as the Gulf Coast may have supported as many as 4.6 persons per kilometer for a total population of 1.1 million. Diseases took a heavy toll, particularly in the early years of exploration before Native peoples had acquired some immunity to new European diseases. Even after epidemics, however, a substantial Native population remained. To obtain the land belonging to these people for the expansion of their booming agricultural enterprises, southern whites had to eliminate southern Indians, or at least terminate their right of occupancy.

War provided one solution for land-hungry white southerners. In 1622 the Powhatan Confederacy rose up against the Virginia colonists, who had been abusing and exploiting Native people for a decade and a half. Those colonists who survived the assault welcomed the opportunity to abandon their facade of friendliness and their professed concern for the Indians' conversion to Christianity in favor of simply seizing the Indians' land under the guise of retribution. One rejoiced that the colonists were "set at liberty by the treacherous violence of the Savages. . . . Now their cleared grounds in all their villages (which are situated in the fruitfullest places of the land) shall be inhabited by us." This same scenario was repeated countless times in southern history: Native peoples went to war in defense of their homelands only to meet defeat, which Anglo-Americans then used to justify seizure of Indian lands.

War not only helped satisfy the southern planter's need for land, it also helped meet his demand for labor. Native prisoners of war often found themselves on the slave trader's auction block. In the seventeenth and early eighteenth centuries, many Indian slaves worked alongside Africans on southern plantations while others were exported to the West Indies. In 1708, for example, a South Carolina population of 9,850 included 2,900 African slaves and 1,400 Indian slaves. Also, many of the slaves listed as African on such censuses probably were in fact Indian; the total number of Indian slaves ultimately reached tens of thousands.

Indian slavery declined dramatically in the last half of the eighteenth century for several reasons. For one, the enslavement of Indians involved an escalation of Native warfare. By the end of the century, U.S. policy had come to focus on the temporary pacification of Native peoples and the appropriation of land by methods other than waging war. By this time the Indian population had been so depleted that slave raiding was no longer worth the trouble. Planters also feared collusion between free Indians and slaves, both Indian and black, and a joint resistance to white oppression seemed at times to be a real possibility. Furthermore, an emerging racial ideology among southerners, perhaps prompted partly by this fear of collusion, increasingly separated Indians and Africans. Thomas Jefferson's comments on the two races in *Notes on the State of Virginia* provide a good example of the new racial philosophy. While Jefferson recommended assimilation of Indians into U.S. society, he wrote that African Americans were "inferior to the whites in the endowments both of body and mind" and that their color was a "powerful obstacle to the emancipation of these people." Jefferson and others regarded the Indian as culturally inferior to whites but capable of change. The African, however, was incapable of change. The Indian was a "noble savage" whom "civilization" might save, but the African was an inferior being suitable only for service to his superiors.

Many Native peoples accepted this ideology. Southern society was becoming strictly biracial, and if they were given a choice between classification as black or white, Native peoples chose white. The Catawbas of South Carolina, for example, developed an antipathy toward blacks gradually. One scholar contends that by 1800, "Catawbas had become an anomaly. Neither useful nor dangerous, neither black nor white, they did not fit into the South's expanding biracial society. . . . No official policy arose that forced the Catawbas to become blacks; but in a culture that recognized only two colors, the danger was always present, and the Catawbas became acutely sensitive to it. . . . Natives cast their lot with the dominant culture and strengthened the barrier separating them from blacks by adopting white racial attitudes."

The fear of being classified as black may have been a factor that led to the cultural transformation of many southern Indians in the early nineteenth century. This transformation, most pronounced among the Cherokees, Chickasaws, Choctaws, and Creeks, took place under the U.S. government's program of "civilization." Proclaiming that the Indian was doomed unless he abandoned his "savage" ways, government agents and missionaries descended on these nations to promote among them commercial agriculture, republican government, English education, and Christianity. While genuine altruism probably motivated some whites to promote the program, the spectre of hunting grounds opened to white settlers after the Indians had been successfully "civilized" no doubt accounts for much of the enthusiasm for Indian "civilization."

Many southern Indians readily accepted the government's "civilization" program. The descendants of white traders and native women already were accustomed to Euro-American ways and capitalized on the material aspects of the program. Also many men who formerly had engaged in hunting and war, no longer viable occupations, found an avenue for self-fulfillment and an outlet for aggression in the individualistic economic system and acquisitive values that agents introduced. These men whose ancestry was Indian, plus others of mixed ancestry became "civilized," or at least they acquired that "love for exclusive property" on which Washington's Secretary of War Henry Knox believed "civilization" rested. They began to cultivate many acres of commonly owned land, to build and furnish elegant homes, to invest in toll roads, taverns, ferries, mills, and steamboats, and to emulate those who, as the Cherokee Charles Hicks phrased it, "kept their women & children at home & in comfortable circumstances."

These Indian planters also bought black slaves. Since they no longer considered farming to be appropriate for women and had little desire to perform what had been considered women's work themselves, Indian planters had to find a new source of labor. A brief experiment with white sharecroppers failed, and so Indian planters turned to the same labor source as their white counterparts—Africans. The exclusive enslavement of blacks reinforced the racial antipathy that southern Indians may already have felt toward them. Adoption of the white South's racial ideology combined with the economic advantage that accrued to those owning slaves to produce a Native society in which racial slavery became a significant feature.

In the late eighteenth and early nineteenth centuries, leadership of the southern tribes fell increasingly to a slaveholding, highly acculturated male elite. These were the people with whom the United States agents and treaty commissioners interacted most easily. In some cases, more traditional Indians deferred to these "progressives" and looked to them as interpreters of U.S. policies and as mediators of culture. In other cases, however, government officials grossly overestimated the power of people who supported federal policies and failed to realize that they had little support within Indian communities.

Most federal officials viewed the "civilization" program that helped produce this elite as a means to an end: the real objective of U.S. Indian policy

This portrait of a group of Creek leaders in Indian Territory, taken in the 1870s, indicates the tribe's racial diversity as well as its willingness to adopt the costumes and poses of "civilization." Left to right: Lochar Harjo, unidentified man, John McGilvry, Ho-tul-ko-mi-ko (Chief of the Whirlwind). The latter was also called Silas Jefferson. Courtesy, National Anthropological Archives.

was the acquisition of Indian land. At first, the prospects for acquiring Indian land seemed bright. Hunting (and therefore the need for hunting grounds) declined in the late eighteenth century. The demise of the deerskin trade resulted in part from land cessions and the depletion of game through overhunting or encroachments on Indian hunting grounds by white squatters. Many private trading houses, in particular the large British firm of John Forbes, began to shift their emphasis from deerskin to cotton. The invention of the cotton gin in the 1790s and the growth of the British textile industry made cotton a far more lucrative commodity than deerskins. Cotton production by whites grew dramatically after the War of 1812; and the demand increased for new cotton land, land which Indians claimed as hunting grounds but which whites regarded as unnecessary to support a Native population well on its way to "civilized" life.

The United States pressured southern Indians to relinquish their "surplus" land in a variety of ways. The War Department authorized the construction of government-owned trading posts, or factories, and instructed traders to permit Indians to run up sizable accounts. When the Indians were unable to settle their accounts, then authorities demanded payments in land. In 1802, for example, the federal government built a trading post among the Chickasaws who within three years owed $12,000. They paid their debts by ceding their territory north of the Tennessee River.

Treaty commissioners sent to negotiate land cessions also bribed chiefs and exploited internal factionalism. In the Cherokee removal crisis of 1806–1809, for example, the federal government took advantage of discord between the Cherokee upper towns of eastern Tennessee and western North Carolina and the lower towns of Alabama and Georgia. Lower towns were more committed to "civilization" and ultimate assimilation into white society. Espousing the political fiction of tribal unity, federal officials negotiated land cessions and exchanges of land claimed by the entire Nation with only lower-town chiefs and included secret treaty provisions appropriating funds to particularly cooperative chiefs. Treaty commissioners employed the same tactic in 1825 when they bribed William McIntosh and other lower Creeks to cede tribal lands in Georgia. In both cases, the Indian nations executed the miscreants, but considerable damage was done. The Senate ratified the Cherokee treaty, and although the president of the United States set aside the fraudulent treaty McIntosh signed, a subsequent treaty achieved the same cession from the Creeks, who succumbed to less overt pressure. The federal government's willingness to use bribery and factionalism to obtain land cessions demoralized southern Indians and encouraged self-serving individuals to cede tribal territory.

In response to these tactics, southern Indian nations began to devise ways of coping with incessant demands for their land. With the hearty approval of the "civilizers"—agents and missionaries—southern Indians adopted

Son of a Scottish trader and a Creek woman, William McIntosh rose to prominence among those in the tribe who urged friendship with the United States. McIntosh fought with Andrew Jackson against his fellow Creeks during the War of 1812 and cooperated in efforts to have the tribe cede its Georgia and Alabama lands and depart for the West. Following his approval of an 1825 agreement which would have extinguished the tribe's remaining claims in the East, McIntosh was executed on the orders of the Creek tribal council. Courtesy, The Newberry Library.

Anglo-American political institutions. The Cherokees, Creeks, Choctaws, and Chickasaws began to centralize their tribal governments, to formalize political processes and structures, to delegate authority to clearly designated chiefs, and to hold those chiefs accountable for their actions. Ceding land became a capital offense.

The national governments organized by these Indians also attempted to protect private property. National police forces and court systems dealt with theft and other property matters. Borrowing from their white neighbors, Native legislators also enacted slave codes that restricted the activities of slaves, prohibited marriages between Indians and blacks, and denied citizenship rights to African-Indian children. At the same time that they were trying to protect themselves from the onslaught of southern whites, southern Indians increasingly adopted white racial attitudes and practices.

The slow pace of land acquisition and the obstacles erected by native people angered many white southerners. As cotton prices rose, the white population in the South grew, the Cotton Kingdom expanded, and the desire for additional land suitable for cultivating cash crops increased. Consequently, southern states began to demand that the federal government, which controlled Indian relations, liquidate native title to land within their borders. Georgia, in particular, insisted on federal compliance with the Compact of 1802. In this agreement the state relinquished claims to its western land, which became Alabama and Mississippi, and the federal government promised to extinguish Indian land titles within what remained of the state at some unspecified future time. By the 1820s, Georgians thought that the federal government had delayed long enough. Indian land promptly became a political issue. Constitutional changes in 1825 providing for the direct election of governors (whom the State Senate previously elected) contributed to the uproar. Politicians seized upon Indian land as an issue with broad popular appeal. In 1826, Georgians rejoiced when the Creeks gave up their remaining land in the state and withdrew to Alabama. White Georgians then turned their attention to the Cherokees.

In 1827, the Cherokees established a republican government with a written constitution patterned after that of neighboring states. Georgia interpreted this act to be a violation of state sovereignty and renewed demands for the extinction of Indian land titles. The state legislature, hoping to make life so miserable for the Indians that they would leave on their own accord, extended Georgia law over the Cherokees and created a special militia, the Georgia Guard, to enforce state law in the Cherokee country. Laws prevented Indians from testifying against whites in court and required all whites, including missionaries, to take an oath of allegiance to the state. The Georgia legislature enjoined the Cherokee council from meeting and leaders from speaking publicly against Indian removal. Finally, legislators formulated plans for a survey and division of Cherokee lands in preparation for their distribution to whites by lottery. Other southern states soon followed Georgia's lead and extended oppressive state laws over their Indian populations.

In his 1829 message to Congress, President Andrew Jackson offered southern Indians two alternatives—they could become subject to the discriminatory laws of the states or move west and continue their own governments. The president and most southerners believed that they should move. In 1830, Congress passed the Indian Removal Act, which authorized the president to negotiate exchanges of territory and appropriated $500,000 for that purpose. Under the proposed removal treaties, the federal government would compensate emigrants for improvements (houses, cleared and fenced fields, barns, orchards, ferries, etc.) and assist them in their journey west.

Jackson, therefore, championed the rights of states to deal with Indian nations within their chartered borders. Ironically, this controversy coincided with the nullification crisis in which Jackson adamantly refused to permit an expansion of states' rights. This crisis pitted the state of South Carolina against the federal government over the immediate issue of the tariff and the broader issue of states' rights. In this context, Jackson's behavior seems inconsistent— bowing to states' rights in Georgia where Indian rights was the issue while defending federal authority to collect tariffs in South Carolina. Many in his administration may have feared that driving Georgia into the South Carolina camp would result in dissolution of the Union. Support of Georgia served to reassure southerners that the federal government would not interfere in their

By the early twentieth century, many Indians such as these eastern Cherokees survived in isolated cabins on marginal lands. Courtesy, National Anthropological Archives.

internal racial affairs, which ranged from laws regulating Native populations to those establishing and protecting the institution of slavery.

The Choctaws were the first tribe to go west under the provisions of the Indian Removal Act. In the fall of 1830, a group of Choctaw chiefs agreed to the Treaty of Dancing Rabbit Creek. In this treaty, the tribe ceded its land in the Southeast, but those who wished to remain in Mississippi (or could not pay their debts to citizens of the state) would receive fee simple (absolute) title to individual allotments of land and become citizens of the state. The federal government promised those who removed to the West reimbursement for improvements, transportation, subsistence for one year after removal, and an annuity for the support of education and other tribal services. There was much dissatisfaction with the treaty, particularly among Choctaw traditionalists who did not want to go west under any condition. Opponents had little opportunity to protest formally because the U.S. government refused to recognize any chief as long as the Choctaws remained in Mississippi. Consequently, the Choctaws began preparations for their westward migration.

Confusion surrounded the preparations for the journey west. After a dispute about routes, the Choctaws and the government agreed on a combination of water and land routes. Finally in late fall 1831, the first detachment of Choctaws left Mississippi. The War Department had divided the supervision of removal between an Indian trader who conducted the Indians to the Mississippi River and a Jacksonian Democrat who then assumed control. These men delegated their authority to supply the Indians to agents in the field. Many agents viewed removal only as an opportunity to increase their own fortunes, and so the Choctaws often failed to receive rations promised. The Indians who removed under government supervision suffered greatly as a result of winter weather, corruption, greed, and bureaucratic bungling, but so did those who received an insufficient $10 commutation fee from the United States and paid fellow Choctaws to conduct them west in an operation that proved a logistical nightmare. The later Choctaw removals of 1832 and 1833 were not as plagued by corruption and confusion, in part because military officials replaced civilian speculators as field agents. By the spring of 1834, between 13,000 and 15,000 Choctaws had been removed.

About 7,000 Choctaws remained in Mississippi under provisions of the Treaty of Dancing Rabbit Creek. Either they were heads of household who registered to receive an individual allotment of land or they could not leave the state because of indebtedness. Some who remained in Mississippi were highly acculturated such as Greenwood LeFlore, who subsequently embarked on a successful career in Mississippi politics. Others, however, were traditionalists accustomed to communal ownership of land who did not understand titles, deeds, and individual ownership. Frequently, traditionalists understood only their native language and, as a result, became the unwitting victims of unscrupulous speculators. Often tricked into running up debts or signing their deeds directly over to these landmongers, the traditionalists appealed to the federal government for help. U.S. officials, however, turned a deaf ear to their pleas and insisted that fraudulent contracts be honored. No longer entitled after 1834 to emigrate at government expense, these landless Mississippi Choctaws either struggled to Indian territory on their own or remained in the state as an impoverished and landless minority.

The federal government made allotment a major feature of the treaties signed with the Creeks and Chickasaws in 1832. The Creek chiefs agreed to cede much of their land in Alabama and to permit some Creeks to receive the remainder in allotments. After this, land speculators descended on the Indians and once again defrauded many of their individual allotments. Evicted from their homes and farms, most Creeks still refused to go west. Tension between white intruders and foraging Indians escalated and finally erupted into violence. In 1836, the War Department responded by forcibly removing thousands of Creeks as a military measure. Although many Creeks died during their westward trek as a result of the sinking of a steamboat, disease, hunger, and exposure, about 14,500 finally assembled in their new nation in the West.

The Chickasaws avoided some of the suffering of the Creeks, but once again corruption and fraud characterized their removal. Under the terms of the Treaty of Pontotoc, they ceded their eastern homeland, but the federal government delayed removal of the tribe until officials could locate a suitable tract of land in the West. In the interim, the Chickasaws received individual plots, and the federal government opened the remaining two-thirds of the Chickasaw territory to white settlement. Speculators promptly poured into the Chickasaw country defrauding hapless Indians of their property. Finally, in desperation, the Chickasaws agreed to purchase a tract of land from the Choctaws, and in 1837–1838 about four thousand Chickasaws migrated beyond the Mississippi.

The scandals affecting other tribes strengthened the Cherokees' resolve to resist removal. The Cherokee Nation challenged Georgia's claim of jurisdiction over Cherokee territory and won a decisive victory before the Supreme Court in *Worcester* v. *Georgia* (1832), but Georgia defied the Court order. Legal technicalities, along with President Jackson's disinclination to interfere, precluded federal enforcement of the decision. Instead of coming to the Cherokees' defense, the federal government turned to the old tactic of exploiting internal divisions and sent treaty commissioners to the Cherokee Nation. In 1835 a small unauthorized group of Cherokees signed a document providing not for allotment but for a total exchange of territory in the East for land west of the Mississippi. The legitimate leadership of the Cherokee Nation repudiated the treaty, but despite appeals to the U.S. Senate and popular outcry in the United States, the document was ratified and the Cherokees were forced west in 1838.

Cherokees had fought violation of their rights in the courts; the Seminoles resisted removal militarily. Most Seminoles were Creek refugees from the War of 1812 who had fought against the United States and its Creek allies. They fled to Spanish Florida where they joined with other Native peoples to resist the United States. With the Seminoles were many black slaves who had been seized during the war from white and Indian masters. In Florida these bondsmen acquired considerable autonomy. Runaway slaves augmented their number, and the Indian-black alliance so feared by colonial planters at last materialized. In 1835 the United States—now in possession of Florida—attempted to enforce a removal treaty that a Seminole delegation had signed under duress two years earlier. The treaty provided not only for Seminole removal but for merger with the Creeks, their old enemy. Desperate Seminole warriors attacked a company of soldiers sent to round them up, and the battle sparked the Second Seminole War. Skillfully employing guerrilla tactics in the swamps of southern Florida and led by superb warriors such as Osceola, the Seminoles and their black allies forced the United States to wage a costly military campaign; over the next seven years it committed a total of forty thousand men, spent $40 million, and suffered substantial casualties. In this attempt to defeat and remove Indians, the government resorted to even more duplicitous means than bribing chiefs and exploiting tribal factionalism: commanders in the field, with approval from Washington, repeatedly captured Seminole warriors under flags of truce. Even after the official end of the war in 1842, soldiers continued to capture and deport bands of Indians until three

A group of Seminoles photographed in southern Florida in the early twentieth century. Courtesy, The Field Museum #A 110449, Chicago.

thousand Seminoles resided in the West and only several hundred remained in the Florida Everglades.

When the federal government finally managed to remove the majority of the Seminoles from Florida, a major problem developed. The government reasoned that since the Seminoles and Creeks had been one people before the War of 1812, they now could share territory in the West. But U.S. officials were blind to a controversy between the two native groups. The Creeks had paid whites for the loss of slave property during the war, but the Seminoles had taken many of these slaves with them to Florida. Because they had paid for the slaves, the Creeks believed they were entitled to them. The Seminoles disagreed, and they feared that the Creeks would seize their blacks as soon as they entered the Creek Nation, their ultimate destination. Consequently, many refused to leave Fort Gibson in the western Cherokee Nation where they had disembarked from the boats bringing them from Florida. The Cherokees complained that the freedom enjoyed by the Seminole blacks had an adverse effect on their own bondsmen and attributed a slave revolt they had suffered in the early 1840s in part to Seminole influence. Finally, the United States arranged for a separate Seminole Nation.

The southern Indians who went west took with them not only enmities but institutions, lifestyles, and attitudes developed in the South that they had shared with a white slaveholding society for over two hundred years. In the West they reestablished the institution of slavery. Slaves proved to be an important asset. Their labor enabled Indian slaveholders to recover quickly from economic losses caused by removal. In addition to farming, slaves operated salines, herded cattle, worked on steamboats and docks, and performed other kinds of jobs. In 1860, over eight thousand slaves lived in the five southern nations west of the Mississippi. Slaves accounted for 14 percent of the total population, even though only 2.3 percent of the citizens of these nations owned slaves. As in the South, the wealth that slaves produced helped their masters dominate the political and economic life of their respective Nations.

Among the Seminoles, Creeks, and Cherokees, however, many people had serious misgivings about slavery. This attitude rose less from a belief in racial equality than from resentment of the power commanded by the slaveholding elite and a desire to preserve traditional culture. Furthermore, northern missionaries, particularly in the Cherokee Nation, actively encouraged abolitionism. When the Civil War broke out in the United States, the southern Indians faced a serious dilemma. As John Ross, the Cherokee chief, described the situation to the National Council: "Our locality and situation ally us to the South, while to the North we are indebted for a defense of our rights in the past and that enlarged benevolence to which we owe our progress in civilization." Nonslaveholding traditionalists, and even some slaveholders such as Ross, preferred neutrality, which meant that existing treaties with the United States remained in effect. Most slaveholders, however, favored a Confederate alliance. The Chickasaws and Choctaws, whose territory adjoined Texas, negotiated Confederate treaties in July 1861. Factions of the Creeks and Seminoles followed their example and, in August, Chief Ross of the Cherokees succumbed to pressure and signed a Confederate alliance.

The Confederacy quickly organized companies of Indian soldiers whose initial assignment was to capture Opothleyohola, a Creek traditionalist. Opothleyohola opposed the Confederate alliance and decided to conduct a group of loyal Creeks to Kansas where they intended to take refuge behind Union lines. Many Cherokee traditionalists in service to the Confederacy refused to attack the Creek chief and instead joined his flight to Kansas, where they enlisted in the Union Indian Brigade. The American Civil War produced among the Cherokees and Creeks their own civil wars.

Following the Civil War, the United States negotiated with the five southern Indian nations treaties that provided for the abolition of slavery and the extension of citizenship to freedmen. This latter provision was particularly important to those newly emancipated because Indians held their land in common, and any citizen was permitted to use unoccupied land. Problems arose, however, because former Indian slaveholders were as reluctant as white slaveholders to accept their former bondsmen as equals. During the war, many slaves had been taken to Texas by their Indian masters, who simply left them there following emancipation. Unable to return to their nations in time to assert their (land) rights, these people suffered greatly. In addition, the Choctaws delayed the grant of citizenship to freedmen for twenty years, and Chickasaw freedmen never managed to become citizens because of the legal maneuvering of their former masters. Nevertheless, many Indian freedmen did manage to acquire land, which gave them the economic base denied most former slaves in the white South.

Indian slaveholders turned to a variety of economic enterprises following the Civil War. These former Confederates supported the provision in Reconstruction treaties that provided for building railroads through Indian territory, a move opposed by traditionalists. Many former slaveholders such as Elias Cornelius Boudinot, Cherokee delegate to the Confederate Congress, actively lobbied for railroads and other forms of economic development on Indian land such as mining, ranching, logging, and oil exploration. Although traditionalists who had supported the Union in the Civil War objected strenuously to these activities that brought increasing numbers of whites into their nations, the federal government preferred "progress" and profits to loyalty. The outcome of this preference was the dissolution of Indian governments and the incorporation in 1907 of southern Indians into the new state of Oklahoma.

The Native peoples who remained in the Southeast after the removal of the large Indian nations were a tiny minority in their states. They fall into two groups—those tribes who did not negotiate removal treaties and remnants of removed nations. The latter included large numbers of Choctaws, Seminoles, and Cherokees. After the 1840s, the government occasionally expressed interest in removing these remnants, but little was done largely because they lived on land whites considered worthless. The Cherokees managed to purchase the land they occupied in the Smoky Mountains of western North Carolina, but neither Seminoles nor Choctaws had a formally recognized landbase until after 1890. The Seminoles adapted to life in the inhospitable Florida Everglades while the Choctaws eked out a bare subsistence in the sand hills and swamps of central Mississippi. A handful of Creeks in southern Alabama also managed to remain in the East, and although most of them ultimately lost their land, a community coalesced around a Creek allotment at Poarch.

The Indians who did not negotiate removal treaties often lived in small isolated enclaves and had an even more precarious existence. Their obscure histories and small numbers meant little attention from the government, benevolent associations, or anyone other than scheming whites. Few owned land; that is, few held deeds to the land they believed they owned. The absence of legal titles meant that unscrupulous people could force them from their homes. In 1841, for example, the captain of an "Indian patrol" established by local whites to supervise the activities of the Tunicas living in central Louisiana fenced in a section of Tunica Indian land and claimed it for himself.

When the Tunica chief pulled up the fence posts, the captain shot him in the head in front of most of the tribe. The white murderer never stood trial, and a Louisiana court subsequently awarded him a large portion of Tunica territory.

Some Indians managed to hold onto their land into the twentieth century; but individual whites, business corporations, and even local governments constantly sought opportunities to seize Native property. The loss of land by the Waccamaws of North Carolina provides a good example. In the 1920s, a surveyor employed by the state traveled through the eastern counties locating "vacant" land, that is, land to which no recorded deed existed. The Indians, of course, had been living on the land long before deeds existed but, according to white officials, they did not have legal title to it. The surveyor, who was also an agent for a group of timber companies, claimed thousands of acres of "vacant" land for the state and promptly sold it off for logging. North Carolina received the money from the land sales, the surveyor got a commission, and many Indians were forced off land they had occupied for years. (Finally, descendants of a Waccamaw whose land was sold in this transaction sued. In 1963, the North Carolina Supreme Court awarded these people title to 126 acres.) For most Indians with no land, there was no alternative to sharecropping, the fate of many black and white southerners as well, and many sank into debt and peonage.

In addition to economic exploitation, southern Indians often suffered racial discrimination. In the Civil War, both the Mississippi Choctaws and the North Carolina Cherokees provided troops for the Confederacy. In the ab-

Pushmataha (1764–1824), one of the most prominent Choctaw leaders of the preremoval era. Popularly known as "the Indian General," Pushmataha distinguished himself in both intertribal warfare and as a military ally of the United States. He fought with Andrew Jackson in Florida, but later opposed the American leader during the negotiation of the treaty of Doak's Stand, one of the first agreements requiring Indian removal to the West. When he died during a visit to Washington, D.C., in 1824, General Jackson attended his funeral. Courtesy, The Newberry Library.

surd racial lines drawn by southerners, however, the Lumbees of North Carolina were not permitted to serve as soldiers because of their designation as "free people of color." The Confederacy did conscript Lumbees to build fortifications, and this precipitated a Lumbee guerrilla war that lasted through Reconstruction. In the 1880s North Carolina recognized the Lumbees as Indians and set up a separate school system for them. Some have suggested, however, that this reclassification came about because the state's whites preferred to view the Lumbee guerrilla war as an Indian uprising rather than a black insurrection.

On the other hand, Virginia's Racial Integrity Act, passed in 1924, attempted to redefine the state's Native people as "colored." The Registrar of Vital Statistics regarded Indians as a threat to the racial purity of white Virginians and vigorously enforced the measure. Designation as "colored" not only denied Indians their ethnicity, but it relegated Native people, along with African Americans, to second-class status and inferior jobs, schools, and housing. In World War II, four Rappahannock men refused induction into the armed services, which were segregated, as "colored." Arrested, tried, and convicted, three of them received two-year sentences to a federal prison. Their refusal reflects the resistance of Virginia's Native people to the Racial Integrity Act and suggests that two decades of enforcement had only strengthened their identity as Indians.

In the nineteenth and early twentieth centuries, small Indian groups throughout the South confronted similar problems. White school boards frequently denied Indians admission to white schools and insisted that they attend schools established for blacks. Many Indians refused to enroll in black schools, in part because of their own racial prejudice but primarily because they feared that official designation as black would destroy their own ethnic identity and result in further discrimination. In addition, whites allocated far less funding for black schools than for white schools and, consequently, children who attended black schools normally received an inferior education.

Even when school boards established separate schools for Indians, the facilities were usually unsatisfactory. In 1950, an article in *The American Indian* gave the following description of a school provided for Native children:

> The present school is inadequate. It is poorly constructed, drafty, overcrowded, lacking in books and desks, and portions of it have never been ceiled on the inside. Bare studs in the room add to the general dismal appearance. There are no cloak rooms; no entry halls. Access to certain rooms are only through another. No playgrounds or playground equipment. Three of the rooms have an ordinary tin, wood heater. The fourth is provided with no heat at all. Its construction, as well as the lack of exits, create an extremely dangerous fire hazard. There is no fighting equipment or extinguisher. The only source of water is a hand pumped well which requires priming.

Segregation extended beyond the classroom, and so did Indian resistance to being classified as black. In 1981, a Coharie man in North Carolina recounted incidents of discrimination for a reporter from the *Winston-Salem Sentinel:*

> There [w]as a period of time here when the Indians were just classified as blacks. . . . I'd go down the courthouse, for example, and the white man would come in and chase me out. . . . And you'd pee upside the wall before you'd go to the black bathrooms. I remember one Indian veteran came home from Vietnam and he and his wife went to get a hot dog at one of these [white] restaurants and the owner tried to run him out and called a cop. The Indian fellow gathered up a crowd to stop it, but the cop shoved him out. . . . These things have become part of the past now. But it's only changed during the '70s.

In the 1960s civil rights legislation ended overt discrimination and committed the federal government to improving the lives of Native Americans. Greater recognition of Native sovereignty was an important component of the nation's new Indian policy. Native people replaced non-Indian bureaucrats at the Bureau of Indian Affairs (BIA), and tribes began to take firm control of their own affairs. The significant gains of the 1970s and 1980s, however, brought new problems, many of them grounded in racism. For example, when the Choctaws created the Chata Development Corporation in 1969 and awarded most reservation construction contracts to it, local white developers, who had rarely hired Choctaws and had kept profits rather than reinvesting them in the community as Chata did, regarded the arrangement as unfair, but Chata went on to become the county's largest employer. The Seminoles pioneered "smoke shops," which sold cigarettes free from state tax, and high-stakes bingo games, but once again, non-Indians complained that exempting Indians from certain state laws was unjust, even though federal courts sided with the Indians. While they voiced concerns ranging from increased traffic to compulsive gambling, opponents to a casino in Cherokee, North Carolina, ultimately focused on a report from the state commerce department that concluded: "Gambling may divert some dollars from existing businesses." Many Native southerners fear that a backlash to their new prosperity is just around the corner.

This recent perception of Indians as uniquely advantaged has spawned an even more bizarre phenomenon—a dramatic increase in individuals proclaiming Native ancestry. While many have legitimate claims to Indian ancestry, few have any cultural or historical identities as Indians. Although these "wannabees" did not share the oppression of the past, they eagerly seek to embrace a more rewarding future.

Today southern Indians continue to struggle against racism. This is why it is imperative that we study southern Indians in the context of southern

138 • THEDA PERDUE

history. Westward expansion and Jacksonian democracy have ended, but southern Indians still exist. The problems they encounter today are legacies of racial slavery and economic exploitation that began in the colonial South and continued in the antebellum period. The first Reconstruction gave slavery and exploitation new forms—sharecropping and economic peonage. Although the second Reconstruction has brought significant change for Indians as well as for other minorities in the South, its promises seem empty to those Native peoples who still must contend with poverty, racism, and ethnic anonymity. Divorcing southern Indians from southern history has obscured both their past and their present. By denying Indians a place in southern history, we run the risk of denying Native southerners a place in modern America.

For Further Reading

The best study of Native culture in the South is Charles Hudson, *The Southeastern Indians* (Knoxville, 1976). Henry F. Dobyns, *Their Numbers Become Thinned: Native American Population Dynamics in Eastern North America* (Knoxville, 1983) offers a provocative look at precontact populations and the impact of European disease on them. For an overview of preremoval Indian history in the region, see J. Leitch Wright, *The Only Land They Knew: The Tragic Story of American Indians in the Old South* (New York, 1981). Recent, more specialized studies of the early South include James H. Merrell, *The Indians' New World: Catawbas and Their Neighbors from European Contact through the Era of Removal* (Chapel Hill, 1989); Joel W. Martin, *Sacred Revolt: The Muskogee Struggle for a New World* (Boston, 1991); Daniel H. Usner, Jr., *Indians, Settlers, and Slaves in a Frontier Exchange Economy: The Lower Mississippi Valley Before 1783* (Chapel Hill, 1992); Tom Hatley, *The Dividing Paths: Cherokees and South Carolinians Through the Era of Revolution* (New York, 1993); Kathryn E. Holland Braund, *Deerskins and Duffels: Creek Indian Trade with Anglo-America, 1685–1815* (Lincoln, 1993); and Patricia Galloway, *Choctaw Genesis, 1500–1700* (Lincoln, 1995).

Annie H. Abel published the earliest study of Native southerners and African-American slavery. See her three-volume *The Slaveholding Indians* (Cleveland, 1915–1925). More recent works include Theda Perdue, *Slavery and the Evolution of Cherokee Society, 1540–1865* (Knoxville, 1979); Daniel F. Littlefield, *Africans and Seminoles: From Removal to Emancipation* (Westport, Conn., 1976) and *Africans and Creeks: From the Colonial Period to the Civil War* (Westport, Conn., 1979); Katja May, *Collusion and Collision: African-Americans and Native Americans in the Creek and Cherokee Nations* (New York, 1996); and a number of articles in William G. McLoughlin, Jr., *The Cherokee Ghost Dance: Essays on the Southeastern Indians, 1789–1861* (Macon, Ga., 1984). For one group's experiences in the racially polarized South, see James Merrell, "The Racial Education of the Catawba Indians," *Journal of Southern of History*, 50 (1984): 363–384.

The "civilization" program and the centralization of Native governments are covered in William G. McLoughlin, *Cherokee Renascence in the New Re-*

public (Princeton, 1986); Michael D. Green, *The Politics of Indian Removal: Creek Government and Society in Crisis* (Lincoln, 1982), and Clara Sue Kidwell, *Choctaws and Missionaries in Mississippi, 1818–1918* (Norman, 1995). A comparative overview can be found in Duane Champagne, *Social Order and Political Change: Constitutional Governments among the Cherokee, the Choctaw, the Chickasaw, and the Creek* (Stanford, 1992). For removal, Grant Foreman's classic study, *Indian Removal: The Emigration of the Five Civilized Tribes* (Norman, 1932) remains useful. More recent studies include Mary Elizabeth Young, *Redskins, Ruffleshirts, and Rednecks: Indian Allotments in Alabama and Mississippi, 1830–1860* (Norman, 1961); Arthur H. DeRosier, Jr., *The Removal of the Choctaw Indians* (Knoxville, 1970); William L. Anderson, ed., *Cherokee Removal: Before and After* (Athens, 1991); and Theda Perdue and Michael D. Green, eds., *The Cherokee Removal: A Brief History with Documents* (Boston, 1995).

For discussions of Indian territory in the period between removal and Oklahoma statehood, see William G. McLoughlin, *After the Trail of Tears: The Cherokees' Struggle for Sovereignty, 1839–1880* (Chapel Hill, 1993); M. Thomas Bailey, *Reconstruction in Indian Territory: A Story of Avarice, Discrimination, and Opportunism* (Port Washington, N.Y., 1972); H. Craig Miner, *The Corporation and the Indian: Tribal Sovereignty and Industrial Civilization in Indian Territory, 1867–1907* (Columbia, Mo., 1976); Angie Debo, *And Still the Waters Run: The Betrayal of the Five Civilized Tribes* (Princeton, 1940); and Theda Perdue, *Nations Remembered: An Oral History of the Five Civilized Tribes* (Westport, Conn., 1980).

Native people who remained in the East are the subject of John R. Finger, *The Eastern Band of Cherokees, 1819–1900* (Knoxville, 1984) and *Cherokee Americans: The Eastern Band of Cherokees in the Twentieth Century* (Lincoln, 1991); Harry A. Kersey, Jr., *The Florida Seminoles and the New Deal, 1933–1942* (Gainesville, 1989) and *An Assumption of Sovereignty: Social and Political Transformation among the Florida Seminoles, 1953–1979* (Lincoln, 1996); Samuel J. Wells and Roseanna Tubby, eds., *After Removal: The Choctaw in Mississippi* (Jackson, 1985); Helen C. Rountree, *Pocahontas's People: The Powhatan Indians of Virginia Through Four Centuries* (Norman, 1990); Gerald M. Sider, *Lumbee Indian Histories: Race, Ethnicity, and Indian Identity in the Southern United States* (Cambridge, 1993); Walter L. Williams, ed., *Southeastern Indians Since the Removal Era* (Athens, 1979); and J. Anthony Paredes, ed., *Indians of the Southeastern United States in the Late Twentieth Century* (Tuscaloosa, 1992).

Chapter Seven

National Expansion from the Indian Perspective

R. David Edmunds

*M*ost Americans have readily accepted the conventional view that the westward expansion of the American frontier marked a similar advance of "civilization" over "savagery." Imbued with an ethnocentric bias, textbooks throughout the late nineteenth and much of the twentieth centuries described Indian people as part of a wilderness habitat to be altered, eradicated, or pushed farther west. Indeed, in all editions published prior to the late 1960s, the most widely adopted college textbook focusing upon the history of the American westward movement discussed Indian-white relations in a chapter entitled "The Indian Barrier," while popular accounts of the American West as portrayed in movies and television emphasized the Indians' armed, if futile, resistance to the march of American "progress."

Such an interpretation is markedly simplistic and reflects an ignorance of the interaction of Indian and non-Indian peoples on the American frontier. Of course Indians sometimes resisted white expansion, but more often they interacted peacefully with white frontiersmen, shaping the region's social and economic institutions and modifying their own society in response to a challenging environment. Moreover, this interaction provides some valuable insights into the attitudes and assumptions of American society. Americans' opinions about Indians not only reflect their beliefs regarding minority groups but also illustrate their appraisal of themselves. For many nineteenth-century Americans who retained a nostalgic attachment to their agrarian past, a preconceived, romanticized conception of Indian or "savage" life provided a welcome contrast to what they envisioned as the inevitable "progress of American civilization."

Above: Detail from photo. See page 142.

During the first quarter of the nineteenth century, attitudes toward Indians probably differed between Americans on the frontier and political leaders in Washington. Most of the Founding Fathers were the products of Enlightenment philosophy; and although they viewed Indian people as lesser beings, they still had been influenced by Rousseau's conceptions of the "noble savage." More ethnocentric than racist, they believed that the Indians could be converted into small yeomen farmers and eventually assimilated into American society. Since most Indians already had been forced from the eastern seaboard, politicians ensconced in Washington, D.C., did not view them as a threat. Thomas Jefferson may have encouraged the proprietors of government-sponsored Indian factories (or trading posts) to lure the tribespeople into debt so they would be forced to cede their surplus lands, but he also supported a systematic program to provide the Indians with agents and farm implements so they could learn to be farmers.

American settlers were less willing to assimilate the Indians. Although American historians continue to argue over the reasons frontiersmen moved west, most scholars agree that economic opportunity was of primary importance. Many frontiersmen were economic opportunists, eager to better their lot, and they had no qualms about seizing every advantage that furthered their aspirations. If some of those advantages came at the expense of the Indian people, so be it; it was of little concern to frontier entrepreneurs willing to ride roughshod over any group denying them access to riches. To many frontiersmen, the lands and the resources controlled by Indians were "plums ripe for the plucking." At worst, Indians were a threat; at best, they were a nuisance.

Conflicts over Indian policy spurred considerable disagreement between local, state, and federal governments. Many of these disputes reflect a theme familiar to most American historians: the federal government's inability to maintain effective control over its western citizens. Between 1795 and 1809, federal officials signed seventeen treaties with the tribes of Ohio, Indiana, Illinois, and Michigan, but the agreements were honored more in their violation than in their adherence. Imbued with a sense of their own self-righteousness, American frontiersmen ignored the treaty regulations and regularly crossed over onto Indian lands to hunt, trap, or establish homesteads. Although federal officials in Ohio and Indiana made desultory attempts to protect Indian interests, they could not stop the tide of American aggrandizement. White trespass upon Indian lands reached such proportions that in 1808 William Henry Harrison, the governor of Indiana Territory, complained:

> The people of Kentucky . . . make a constant practice of crossing over onto Indian lands . . . to kill deer, bear, and buffaloe [*sic*]. . . . One hunter will destroy more game than five of the common Indians.

And, in response to a more serious problem, Harrison added, "A great many of the Inhabitants of the Fronteers [*sic*] consider the murdering of the Indians in the highest degree meritorious." Federal lawmakers in Washington might be willing to differentiate between Indian and white lands, but for many frontiersmen the western territories were a vast cornucopia to be exploited, without regard to Indian claims to the land and its resources.

American aggression caused considerable problems for the Indian people of Ohio, Indiana, and Illinois. Not only were their homelands overrun by frontiersmen, but the invaders severely depleted the surrounding areas' game animals. Moreover, Indian attempts to seek justice brought little recourse since white juries systematically freed most Americans accused of crimes against Native Americans. Not surprisingly, resentment swelled and the tribes struck back at the intrusive white settlers. Unwilling to admit that they were the authors of their own misfortune, American frontiersmen in the first decade of the nineteenth century blamed the British, whom they charged with inciting the Indians against them. Although the British did exercise considerable influence among the tribes, a close examination of these events indicates Indian resistance to American expansion was a natural, indigenous act. The British did attempt to manipulate Indian resentment of the Americans for their own purposes; however, in most instances the tribesmen were more militant than the Crown, and British Indian agents often attempted to restrain the warriors rather than precipitate a general conflict with the United States. In these instances, the Indians welcomed the technical and logistical support of the Crown, but their decision to resist the Americans was their own.

Ma-ke and Kun-zan-ya,
St. Louis, 1848. Courtesy, The
Newberry Library.

Traditionally, historians have championed Tecumseh, the Shawnee war chief, as the architect of the Indian resistance that coalesced prior to the War of 1812. Both British and American authors have been eager to point out that from 1809 through 1811, the Shawnee statesman traveled among the western tribes attempting to enlist the warriors into a pan-Indian political and military organization designed to defend the remaining Indian land base east of the Mississippi. In contrast, Tecumseh's brother, Tenskwatawa, known as the Prophet, usually has been portrayed as a religious charlatan who rode Tecumseh's coattails to a position of minor prominence. Yet throughout American history, during periods of significant stress, Indian people traditionally have turned to religious leaders or revitalization movements for their deliverance. Spiritual spokesmen such as Neolin, the Delaware prophet who emerged prior to Pontiac's rebellion; Handsome Lake of the Senecas, a contemporary of Tenskawatawa; and the Paiute Wovoka and his Ghost Dance are good examples of holy men who arose to meet their people's needs.

It appears from recent scholarship that Tenskwatawa was more instrumental than Tecumseh in forging the Indian coalition in the years preceding the War of 1812. Upon examination of all the primary materials focusing on these events, it is clear that for four years, from 1805 until 1809, the religious teachings of the Prophet were the magnet that attracted thousands of Indians, first to Greenville, in Ohio, then to Prophetstown, in Indiana. Although there are extensive references to the Prophet and his movements in documents from this period, there is no mention of Tecumseh prior to April 1808, when British officials in Canada mention that "the Prophet's brother" visited Amherstburg. William Henry Harrison, Tecumseh's primary antagonist, does not mention the Shawnee chief until August 1810, and then Harrison also refers to him only as "the Prophet's brother," since he evidently had not yet learned Tecumseh's name. Indeed, Tecumseh did not challenge his brother for leadership until after the Treaty of Fort Wayne (1809), which transferred extensive Indian landholdings in Indiana to the United States. The Shawnee war chief then used his brother's religious movement as the base for his ill-fated, political-military confederacy.

White historians have probably championed Tecumseh as the author of the Indian resistance movement since his concepts of political and military unity seemed more logical (by white standards) than the Prophet's religious revitalization. In retrospect, white historians had little understanding of Indian religious doctrines, but they believed that if *they* had been Indians, they also would have attempted to forge the tribes into a multitribal confederacy. Yet the Prophet's doctrines had more appeal to the Indians than did his brother's manifesto. Americans have idolized Tecumseh because they believe that he fits their concept of the "noble savage"; since his death both folklorists and historians have enshrouded the Shawnee chief with extensive apocrypha.

Recent inquiry has also illustrated that different socioeconomic groups on the frontier reacted to the Indians in different ways. Historians have indicated, for example, that much of the violence between Indians and whites that occurred in the Far West during the middle decades of the nineteenth century was triggered by miners and other more transient workers, not farmers. Many white farmers who saw themselves as permanent residents of a region were interested in promoting peace and stability between their communities and local Indian populations. In contrast, miners were eager for the maximum exploitation of mineral resources and had little interest in the long-term development of a region. Preferring to make their "stake" and then retire to more comfortable surroundings, miners and other transients viewed Indians as impediments to their success and were quite willing to eliminate them. In addition, since many miners and other transient laborers often were unemployed, they sometimes welcomed the opportunity to draw rations and wages for service in militia or paramilitary units that were formed to suppress "Indian uprisings." Such earnings hardly matched the riches of a bonanza strike in the gold fields but, for destitute laborers, payment for military services offered ready cash.

The notion that frontier transients formed the backbone of frontier militias suggests an explanation for other Indian-white confrontations. In 1774 Lord Dunmore's War was precipitated when frontier riffraff murdered innocent Shawnees and Delawares along the Ohio. Almost sixty years later, on May 14, 1832, the Black Hawk War probably would have terminated without bloodshed if the drunken militia partially composed of miners from Wisconsin's Fever River District and commanded by Major Isaiah Stillman had not attacked Black Hawk's envoys as the old Sauk war chief prepared to surrender. The resulting Battle of Stillman's Run ended any chance for the hapless Sauks and Foxes to withdraw peacefully to Iowa. On November 28, 1864, ill-trained and drunken militia were also responsible for the slaughter of more than 150 Cheyennes and Arapahos at Sand Creek in Colorado. Many of the volunteers making up this force were unemployed miners lured west by the Colorado gold rush of the late 1850s. Illegal trespass by miners onto Indian lands in the Black Hills also triggered the last of the Sioux wars, culminating in Custer's defeat at the Battle of the Little Big Horn. Other miners organized the mob who murdered 144 Apaches at Camp Grant, near Tucson, Arizona, in April 1871.

In retrospect, if Indian lands held valuable resources, those treasures were exploited. Although the federal government might promise to protect the inviolability of Indian real estate, such promises often were broken. The consequences of this repeating cycle should have a profound message for tribal communities holding valuable mineral or water resources in the twentieth century.

Disputes between Indians and whites over Indian lands in the Southeast also offer some interesting insights into the conflict between frontiersmen and federal officials while illustrating the entrepreneurial values of the

Jacksonians. By the 1820s, many Americans were dissatisfied with the established organic economic system that emphasized careful centralized planning (a national bank, tariffs, federal support for internal improvements, etc.), and new entrepreneurs emerged who argued that "the powdered wig set" (the federal government) controlled the nation's resources for their own benefit. After the adoption of the cotton gin spread cotton production across the Gulf plains, Indian lands in the region became the focus of local land speculators. Their complaint was not that the federal government had failed to purchase Indian land holdings (indeed, by the 1820s much of the former tribal holdings already were in the public domain) but that the government did not immediately buy all Indian lands remaining within their respective states and send the tribes packing across the Mississippi.

In contrast, many officials in Washington, as exemplified by President John Quincy Adams, still gave at least lip service to the civilization programs that had been in force since the beginning of the century. In theory, the Indians were to adopt white values and be assimilated into American society. In actuality, Adams also may have favored some type of removal program, but he championed carefully planned and legalistic procedures through which the changing status of the Indians and their tenure of tribal lands could be delineated.

Any delays necessitated by long-term planning were unacceptable to local expansionists. In Georgia a group of these expansionists, led by Governor George M. Troup, negotiated the Treaty of Indian Springs with a faction representing a minority of the Creek Confederacy. The treaty was signed by federal officials, but these men were clearly acting on behalf of Troup. After the treaty was ratified by the Senate in March 1825, the Creeks executed William McIntosh, the leader of the treaty faction. In response, Troup threatened to overrun Creek lands with the Georgia militia. Federal officials interceded, nullifying the Treaty of Indian Springs, but signed the Treaty of Washington with the Creeks one year later. The new treaty also called for the cession of Creek lands in Georgia (already a fait accompli, since settlers had moved into the region); but the terms were more favorable for the Indians, and the federal government promised to guarantee the remaining Creek lands in Alabama. In theory at least, federal officials had interceded to partially protect Indian interests from expansionists at the state and local levels of government.

Whether the Adams regime would (or could) have honored its promises remains doubtful, but in 1828 Andrew Jackson was elected to the presidency—now a spokesman for the frontier entrepreneurs was in the White House. Jackson's election also marked an increase in federal pressure to remove the tribespeople to the trans-Mississippi west. Although previous administrations had counseled the Indians to remove, they had appraised the problem from an ethnocentric rather than a racial perspective. Presidents such as John Quincy Adams believed the Indians to be inferior, but from Adams' viewpoint they were inferior because they had not attained the socioeconomic-political level of Europeans or Americans. If Indians would adopt white ways and become civilized, they could be assimilated into American society.

The Jacksonians had no intention of assimilating the Indians into American society. Regardless of the tribespeople's adoption of American institutions, frontier entrepreneurs wanted them removed from their lands and forced beyond the frontier. The Cherokees' "civilization" program, for example, afforded them little protection from white Georgians. After gold was discovered on Cherokee lands, white Americans ignored the tribe's constitution, newspaper, and pious Protestant congregations. Tribal lands were overrun. Regardless of how "civilized" the Cherokees had become, other Americans still saw them as "Indians" and, therefore, not encompassed in the protection that the Constitution extended to white people.

Ironically, however, by the 1820s many of the Cherokees, Choctaws, and other southern tribes were of mixed Indian-white descent. The emergence of these mixed-blood communities on the frontier indicates that considerable acculturation already had transpired. Still, frontiersmen considered such individuals, regardless of the minority quantum of their Indian descent (one-half blood, one-quarter blood, etc.), to be Indian. On the southern frontier this infusion of white lineage often had occurred in the middle and late eighteenth century, when British and sometimes French traders had married Indian women. The mixed-blood children of these marriages often exerted considerable influence in tribal affairs; and since they were the products of both cultures, they sometimes served as cultural brokers, representing tribal interests (as they defined them) in mediating with the federal government.

The Choctaws provide a telling illustration of the key role that mixed-bloods played in this interchange. Although the Choctaws originally had sustained themselves through hunting and horticulture, by the middle of the eighteenth century they had become so enmeshed in the European trading system that much of their economy was based on their ability to supply deerskins to British merchants. After the American Revolution they shifted to Americans, but by 1800 they had so depleted the deer population in Mississippi that they no longer could provide enough hides to purchase necessities. Meanwhile, they had grown increasingly in debt to American traders who constantly clamored for payment.

Aware that the deer herds had diminished and that they could no longer maintain their old lifestyle in Mississippi, some of the traditional Choctaw leaders were willing to exchange the tribe's lands in Mississippi for similar regions in Arkansas. In contrast, many mixed-blood Choctaws opposed such a removal. Adapting to a market economy, they began to raise cattle and eventually to plant cotton on their old Mississippi lands. Although many rank-and-file Choctaws no longer could sustain themselves in Mississippi, they still retained an emotional attachment to their homeland and rallied to the mixed-bloods' leadership.

An Englishman named George Winter captured this scene near Vincennes, Indiana, in September 1838. Winter was an itinerant artist who had been trained in New York, and who arrived in Indiana just as the state's Indians were being removed to the West. Here, he portrayed Bishop Bruté of Vincennes preaching his last sermon to the Potawatomis. It was, Winter wrote, "a grand and imposing scene." Courtesy, Tippiecanoe County Historical Society.

In response, the mixed-bloods portrayed themselves as Choctaw patriots attempting to defend the tribe's homeland. Federal officials preferred to negotiate with the older, more traditional chiefs, but their leadership was usurped by the mixed-bloods who brought further changes to the tribe. Allying themselves with Protestant missionaries, the mixed-bloods encouraged the work ethic, thrift, the accumulation of capital, and sobriety since they asserted that these qualities would enhance the tribe's ability to retain their homelands. Under the mixed-bloods' leadership, much of Choctaw society was transformed, and growing numbers of tribesmen began to raise cattle and grow cotton. In addition, the political structure of the tribe was altered as mixed-bloods such as Peter Pitchlyn, David Folsum, and Greenwood LeFlore emerged as the new leaders of the Choctaw Nation.

A parallel but different blend of cultures also occurred in the Old Northwest. In 1827, Commissioner of Indian Affairs Thomas McKenney traveled among the tribes of Michigan, Illinois, and Wisconsin. Discouraged over the Indians' lack of "progress," he reported back to Washington that the tribes should be removed beyond the Mississippi because they had rejected federal attempts to transform them into small yeoman farmers. McKenney charged that they still followed the lifestyle of their fathers: "They catch fish, and plant patches of corn; dance, hunt, and get drunk when they can get liquor, fish and often starve." From McKenney's perspective, tribes such as the Ottawas, Miamis, or Potawatomis seemed hopeless: they still clung to their tribal values and had rejected all tenets of "civilization."

Yet McKenney and most other Americans failed to understand that many of these Indian people had also made great changes from the traditional cultures of their forefathers. Although they generally had rejected American attempts to foster western forms of agriculture among them, they had adopted a lifestyle that resembled that of whites with whom they had the closest contact: the Creole French whose ancestors had settled in the region during the previous century. Like the Indians, during the first decades of the nineteenth century many of the Creoles also continued to hunt, trap, and fish; and, like the Indians, they too were seen as improvident and even "uncivilized" by Anglo-Americans. American officials newly arrived at Vincennes, Indiana, described the Creole population as "a rabble whose appearance caused us to doubt whether we had not actually landed among the savages themselves," and at Detroit, Governor Lewis Cass charged that Creole traders:

> spend one half the year in labor, want, and exposure, and the other half in indolence and amusements. Associated with the Indians, they contracted their manners, and gained their confidence. As a necessary consequence, their farms are neglected. . . .

In retrospect, if American observers had been less biased, they would have noted that by the 1820s many Miami, Potawatomi, and other tribesmen were active in the fur trade, working as porters or laborers, or selling merchandise to both whites and Indians. In 1816, when Indiana entered the union, the wealthiest man in the state was reputed to be Jean Baptiste Richardville, a mixed-blood Miami trader. During the 1830s, when frontier artist George Winter painted Miami, Delaware, and Potawatomi residents of the Wabash and Tippecanoe valleys, his portraits indicate that many of these people dressed in ruffled shirts, frock coats, and other clothing similar to that of white frontier residents. Of course not all Indians were as acculturated as Richardville, or the Burnett or Coquillard families among the Potawatomis, but neither were they living in the manner of their forefathers. Indeed, many of these Indians already had adopted tenets of European culture; however, from the American perspective, it was the wrong culture: the Creole French. Ironically, American frontiersmen were almost as biased in their attitudes toward the Creoles as they were toward the Indians. Since the tribespeople had acculturated toward the "wrong" ethnic group, American observers refused to admit that the Indians had made any significant changes. They were not yeoman farmers, so they should be removed to the West.

The importance of the Indian trade to the economy of the American frontier has often been underestimated. By the third decade of the nineteenth century, almost all of the tribes east of the Great Plains were enmeshed in the American economic system and were dependent upon traders, both Indian and white, for many of the necessities of life. In addition, because of their annuity payments (annual payments received by the tribes from the previous sale of lands to the government) and other sources of income, Indians provided an important source of revenue for frontier communities, especially for the merchants. Historians have begun to explore the nature of this relationship, and their inquiries indicate that the Indian trade, if properly manipulated, was so lucrative that frontier merchants vied among themselves to gain a greater share of it. In 1821 John Crowell resigned his seat as the lone congressman from the state of Georgia to accept an appointment as agent to the Creek Indians. He promptly issued trading licenses to members of his family, and Crowell and his kinsmen amassed a fortune.

Because most tribesmen were illiterate, they had little control over the distribution of treaty and annuity payments; and there were few checks upon the traders' practice of selling the Indians goods on credit, then padding the accounts when the payment was due. Sometimes the fraud reached phenomenal proportions. In 1833 treaty goods worth $20,000 and destined for the Ottawas, Chippewas, and Potawatomis were pilfered from government storehouses at Chicago. In another instance, Governor George B. Porter of Michigan Territory was charged with illegally validating over $100,000 in claims against the tribes for a trading firm composed of his friends. Although federal officials attempted to investigate the frauds, Porter died of cholera and the proceedings were abandoned. Three years later, other bands of Potawatomis in Indiana were alleged to have accumulated debts to frontier merchants totaling over $160,000. Another federal investigation subsequently proved that almost half of these claims were fictitious. Nevertheless, in many other instances the funds were deducted from the Indians' annuities. If the Age of Jackson was a time of economic opportunism, Indian people and their resources played a significant role in the development of the economy in the West.

Not surprisingly, many frontier merchants exercised considerable influence over the tribes. Indian traders such as the Ewing brothers of Indiana, the Kinzie-Forsyth partnership at Chicago, or the Chouteau brothers at St. Louis dabbled in tribal politics and sometimes attempted to prevent the removal of tribes that allegedly owed them money In 1837 George Ewing warned government officials that certain tribes in northern Indiana would never remove unless he was paid what he claimed the Indians owed to him. In some instances federal agents negotiating for the purchase of tribal lands were forced to work through the traders to ensure the success of the proceedings. Ironically, some traders then removed west with the tribespeople, following the source of their revenue across the Mississippi.

Although much has been written about the hardships encountered by the Indians during the removal process, there is another facet of this forced relocation that we often overlook: the role played by the Indians in bringing changes to the trans-Mississippi West. Ironically, those eastern tribes seeking new homes on the fringe of the Great Plains were agents of the very socioeconomic system they were fleeing. Moreover, their entrance onto lands previously dominated by tribes indigenous to the region posed a substantial threat to western peoples. In many cases the western tribes opposed the resettlement of eastern Indians, and bitter conflicts emerged over hunting lands in Iowa, Kansas, Missouri, and Oklahoma.

The emigrant warriors usually emerged as victors in these conflicts. Although the popular press has touted the military skill of the Plains tribes, the eastern warriors had experienced over a century of intertribal conflict generated by European and American confrontations. Cherokee, Shawnee, and Delaware warriors steadily pushed the Osages from their lands in Missouri and Arkansas, while tribes from the Old Northwest usurped the hunting lands

These portraits of a Cherokee girl and Chickasaw boy who were removed from the Southeast to Indian Territory suggest the cultural distance between the western Indians and those who were forced across the Mississippi. Courtesy, The Newberry Library.

of several Plains tribes in Kansas. Potawatomi, Sauk, and Fox tribesmen may have feigned pleas to federal agents asking for protection against the Sioux, but when the two sides met on the prairie, the newcomers (the Potawatomis) formed ranks and, firing from horseback, easily repulsed the Sioux and their allies. Seeking revenge, one year later another large war party of almost seven hundred Plains warriors attacked about two hundred Sauks and Foxes who were hunting buffalo on the Smoky Hill River in Kansas. In this instance, the Sauks and Foxes dismounted, again formed ranks, and repulsed their enemies' repeated charges. When the Plains Indians withdrew, they had suffered over one hundred casualties. The Sauks and Foxes lost only a handful of warriors.

In frontier Oklahoma, the occupation of the eastern part of the state by the five southern ("civilized") tribes created an oasis of sophistication in an area not known for its gentility. Although full-blood traditionalists may have moved west intending to recreate their old way of life free from American influence, the acculturated mixed-bloods who had dominated the tribes in their ancestral homelands reasserted themselves. Centered around communities such as Atoka, Tahlequah, Muskogee, and Tishomingo, the Choctaws, Cherokees, Creeks, Chickasaws and, later, the Seminoles carved out plantations, planted fields of cotton, and erected fine antebellum homes. Indeed, their adherence to southern values was sufficiently pervasive that during the Civil War so many fought for the Confederate cause that they formed an effective barrier to any Union expeditions against Texas.

The emigrant tribes made significant achievements in other fields. The Cherokees established perhaps the best rural school system west of the Mississippi during the antebellum period. Financed by the tribal government, both male and female seminaries sent their graduates back to the eastern states to attend college, from which they returned to help build the Cherokee Nation. Modeled after Mount Holyoke College at South Hadley, Massachusetts, the Cherokee Female Seminary, established near Tahlequah in 1851, provided its students with a "progressive" nineteenth-century education featuring instruction in subjects ranging from English literature and geography to proper manners.

Further north, in Kansas, acculturated Potawatomis at St. Mary's Mission operated ferries across the Kansas River and sold produce and other supplies to both military expeditions and settlers traveling west to Colorado and California. One western emigrant commented that the Indians at St. Mary's were as "civilized" as most whites on the border, but added that "their head gear ran much to feathers." Other travelers expressed surprise at the Potawatomis' degree of sophistication and described the prosperity of their villages. In 1854 these Potawatomis purchased and operated the first McCormick's reaper utilized in Kansas (although they refused an offer by the McCormick Company to provide them with a retail franchise); and when dignitaries visited their mission, they entertained them with band concerts and piano recitals. By any standard, these Indian emigrants did as much to "tame" the frontier as did most non-Indian pioneers.

The economic success of the five relocated southern tribes created another phenomenon that also proliferated in Oklahoma: the continued intermarriage of Indians and whites. Since all members of the tribe or their spouses were eligible to claim potential farmland within tribal territories, many white men married Indian women. Such marriages were celebrated for other reasons; most frontier whites in Oklahoma were from relatively low socioeconomic classes. When these men married the often more sophisticated, more financially secure Indian women, they were marrying "up." It is not surprising that so many modern Oklahomans claim Cherokee grandmothers. Maternal ancestors such as these Cherokee women were proud additions to non-Indian families struggling to improve themselves on the frontier.

There is another facet of the American experience in the first half of the nineteenth century in which Indians played an important, if sometimes unwitting, role: the attempt by a new nation to establish its own intellectual identity. In this instance, Americans used idealized or popular conceptions of Indians to define their own "progress," or as foils to rationalize American expansion. Indeed, the dual image of the Indian that emerges during this period offers interesting insights into the intellectual life of the new nation.

The concept of the Indian as a "noble savage" did not become popular in the United States until the nineteenth century. Eager to develop a national literature, authors along the eastern seaboard turned to the Indian as a subject uniquely American. Since all Indians had been removed from the region and, therefore, were associated with the past, it was easy for writers to romanticize the tribesmen. Indian leaders such as King Philip (Metacom), Hiawatha, Tecumseh, and Pocahontas emerged from nineteenth-century literature in images that were larger than life. Moreover, the depiction of Indians in heroic, if sometimes tragic, terms also enhanced most Americans' self-esteem, for in their victory over such champions Americans could assure themselves they were worthy to inherit the tribesmen's kingdom.

Other Americans envisioned Indians in less heroic terms. In the decades following the War of 1812, the United States was eager to take its rightful place among the "civilized" nations of the Western world. Although most Americans seemed to be pleased to have broken with a decadent Europe, others were uncertain of the nation's status and sought reassurance that American society had come of age. For Americans unsure of their standing, the triumph of American civilization over the Indian population of the United States seemed to provide one favorable measure of their country's progress. Not only did their "republican virtue" separate them from European corruption, but their achievements assured them that they no longer were "primitives" like the Indians. The Indians symbolized a wilderness that was being transformed and conquered, and the tribespeople's demise was indicative of the "grand dame of progress" sweeping westward across the United States.

THE FIRST READER.

LESSON 13.
This is a little sail boat.
De śina watopekiyapi wata cistinna.

It looks nice on the water.
Mini akan owanyag waśte ĥinca.

John is in the boat.
John wata kin en yanka.

Is John afraid? John kokipa he.

John knows how to steer the boat.
John iyupse yuza onspe.

*A page from Rev. Stephen Riggs'
Model First Reader, published in
1873 for use at the Santee Training
School operated by the Presbyterian
Church. This lesson must have been
especially puzzling to children who
had grown up on arid plains.
Courtesy, The Newberry Library.*

Finally, the "civilization" programs fostered by the Bureau of Indian Affairs also offer some useful insights into the value systems of American society. Since many Americans continued to champion small yeoman farmers as the American ideal, federal Indian policy attempted to remold Indians in the yeoman image. Although many tribes had a rich agricultural heritage, such labor traditionally was performed by women; but these individuals were excluded from the government's efforts. In American society, farming was dominated by males, and federal programs expected Indian men to adopt similar roles. Since white Americans did not encourage their wives or daughters to till the soil, Indians were forced to follow a similar pattern.

Viewing the early frontier experience from an Indian perspective enriches and enlivens the story of America's national expansion. Discussions of the "Indian problem" demonstrate that there was a considerable gap in understanding between Washington, D.C., policymakers and enterprising frontiersmen, and that the nation's new federal institutions were exceedingly fragile.

Moreover, the interaction of Indians and whites on the moving western frontier was both fluid and multidimensional. Contacts did not simply involve white male yeomen and befeathered chiefs, but also mixed-blood politicians, fur traders, miners, local merchants, missionaries, tribal religious leaders, war chiefs, and ordinary citizens. The Indian experience on the American frontier both illuminates powerful themes in our past—racism, nationalism, and economic development—and demonstrates the variety of people and interests who contributed to the process we have come to call the "settlement" of the West.

For Further Reading

Students interested in further reading will find that Reginald Horsman's *Expansion and American Indian Policy, 1783–1812* (East Lansing, 1967) contains a good discussion of the impact of western expansion upon American Indians and those officials who formulated federal policy, while Colin G. Calloway's *Crown and Calumet: British-Indian Relations, 1783–1815* (Norman, 1987) focuses upon British influence among the tribes and the Crown's response to American-Indian relations in the Old Northwest. In *The Shawnee Prophet* (Lincoln, 1983) and *Tecumseh and the Quest for Indian Leadership* (Boston, 1984), R. David Edmunds emphasizes that the Indian resistance that emerged prior to the War of 1812 was initially a religious revitalization movement to which Tecumseh added a political and military dimension. Gregory Dowd's *A Spirited Resistance: The North American Indian Struggle for Unity, 1745–1815* (Baltimore, 1992) argues that the pan-Indian activities that emerged between the American Revolution and the War of 1812 were part of a larger pattern of such activity that had developed earlier in the eighteenth century; while Joel Martin's *Sacred Revolt: The Muskogee Struggle for a New World* (Boston, 1991) analyzes the religious conflicts that developed among the Creeks in these years and discusses the Creeks' involvement in hostilities during the War of 1812 period.

For a broad survey of American Indian policy in this period see Francis Paul Prucha's *The Great Father: The United States Government and the American Indian* (Lincoln, 1984). Prucha's encyclopedic study of American Indian policy generally examines such activities from the federal government's perspective. Also see Bernard Sheehan, *Seeds of Extinction: Jeffersonian Philanthropy and the American Indian* (New York, 1973); James P. Ronda, *Lewis and Clark among the Indians* (Lincoln, 1987); and Ronald D. Satz, *American Indian Policy in the Jacksonian Era* (Lincoln, 1975).

Creek acculturation and the tribe's attempts to retain their homelands have been analyzed by Michael D. Green in *The Politics of Indian Removal: Creek Government and Society in Crisis* (Lincoln, 1982), while Richard White's *The Roots of Dependency* (Lincoln, 1983) provides valuable insights into acculturation and the rise of mixed-blood leadership among the Choctaws. Many scholars have examined cultural change among the Cherokees. Theda Perdue's *Slavery and the Evolution of Cherokee Society* (Knoxville, 1979) analyzes the adoption of chattel slavery among the tribe, while the late William McLoughlin has written or edited five volumes, including *Cherokee Renascence in the New Republic* (New Haven, 1986) and *Cherokees and Missionaries, 1789–1832* (New Haven, 1984), which examine the impact of Christian clergymen upon Cherokee culture in the early nineteenth century. McLoughlin's

After the Trail of Tears: The Cherokee Struggle for Sovereignty, 1839–1880 (Chapel Hill, 1993) focuses upon the Cherokees' attempts to establish an autonomous society in the Indian Territory in the post-removal period.

Acculturation and the role of mixed-blood or metis people among the tribes of the Old Northwest are analyzed in Richard White's *The Middle Ground: Indians, Empires, and Republics in the Great Lakes Region, 1650–1815* (Cambridge, 1991), and in Sarah E. Cooke and Rachel B. Ramdhyani, *Indians and a Changing Frontier: The Art of George Winter* (Bloomington, 1991). The pervasive influence of traders upon these tribes is described in Robert Trennert's *Indian Traders on the Middle Border: The House of Ewing, 1827–1854* (Lincoln, 1981), and in Gary C. Anderson's *Kinsmen of Another Kind: Dakota-White Relations in the Upper Mississippi Valley, 1650–1862* (Lincoln, 1984).

The struggle between newly removed eastern Indians and tribes indigenous to the trans-Mississippi West is discussed in Grant Foreman's *Indians and Pioneers: The Story of the Southwest Before 1830* (Norman, 1936); Willard Rollings' *The Osage: An Ethnohistorical Study of Hegemony on the Prairie-Plains* (Columbia, 1992); and in Stanley Hoig's *Tribal Wars on the Southern Plains* (Norman, 1993).

Chapter Eight

How the West
Was Lost

William T. Hagan

*I*n a remarkably brief period—the thirty-eight years from 1848 to 1886—the Indians of the western half of what is today the United States lost their fight against the white invaders and had most of their land taken from them. Some groups of western Native Americans already had a history of contact with white men that went back several generations. Indians of the Southwest and California had been trying to cope with the Spanish, the Mexicans, and the Americans recently settled in Texas. Other tribes had dealt with English, Russian, and American explorers, trappers, and traders. As a result, since their first contact with whites, most of the tribes of the West had, by the mid-nineteenth century, had a great deal of time to make some adjustments and to acquire new tools, weapons, and even—particularly in the case of the Pueblo groups—new crops and livestock. Therefore, while some Indians already had suffered badly at the hands of the white invaders, many others had seen an improvement in their standard of living since first meeting the newcomers.

In 1848 the West was populated by hundreds of flourishing, autonomous Native American societies enjoying cultures that had evolved over many centuries. In hardly more than a generation, however, these same societies would have most of their territory wrested from them, and their religious, social, and political practices subjected to attack. There must be few instances in history when people of a comparably sized region suffered such violent dislocation, physical and cultural, in such a brief period of time.

The major difficulty in presenting the story of "How the West Was Lost" is that it was not a single story, but rather literally hundreds of stories, as many

Above: Detail from photo. See page 160.

as there were groups of Indians in the region in the 1840s. The individual unit could have been as small as a few hundred people or as large as several thousand. Nor did the many different groups suffer equally. The Pueblos suffered relatively less, as they were farmers and had managed to retain much of their land. The Plains Indians suffered most because continuation of their life as nomadic buffalo hunters became impossible. But each Pueblo's experience differed somewhat from that of their neighbors, and the Plains bands, which were the focus of the loyalties of their members, each had its own story. As a result of this political fragmentation, the narrator of "How the West Was Lost" is compelled to approach the subject by regions, in the process lumping together many disparate Indian experiences.

It is logical to begin, both geographically and chronologically, with the Plains Indians. In the early 1840s these Indians were living testimony to how Native Americans had been altered by contact with Europeans. The acquisition of horses had given them the mobility that by the mid-nineteenth century was the principal characteristic of their lifestyle. Ownership of horses had been sufficiently diffused so that the nomadic life of the Plains people had evolved to its highest state and provided a challenging and deeply satisfying life for thousands.

But already these people were being forced to cope with intruders. In the late 1820s, it was the fur trappers ascending the Missouri River with whom the warriors occasionally clashed. By the 1830s, wagon trains were appearing on the Santa Fe Trail and the southern Plains tribes were reacting angrily. In the next decade, thousands of whites crossed the Plains en route to Oregon and California, killing game and destroying scarce timber resources as they went. The Plains tribes had staked out and maintained their hunting grounds against other Indians by force of arms, resulting in what were by the 1840s traditional enmities among tribes. Long accustomed to defending their territory, Plains warriors were not prepared to stand meekly aside for the white invaders. Moreover, Plains societies honored the man who demonstrated his courage in combat and friends and relatives were expected to seek revenge for band members lost in battle.

Closely following the settlement of the Oregon question in 1846 and the Mexican cession to the United States two years later was the discovery of gold in California. All had momentous consequences for the Plains tribes, which had to try to cope with a rapidly escalating scale of invasion. Now white men seeking precious metals were ignoring Indian territorial claims to search every nook and cranny of the West. Tribespeople also had to contend with the intrusions of stagecoach operators and of railroad and telegraph-line construction crews. Warriors struck back at the encroachers, but in an unsystematic and relatively ineffective fashion.

The nature of Plains Indian society, with its emphasis on the rights of the individual and its absence of political centralization, made effective resis-

Prairie Chicken,
Pawnee Scout, 1868. Courtesy,
The Newberry Library.

tance difficult if not impossible. Moreover, tribes that were traditional enemies did not close ranks in the face of the greater threat. The absence of fixed
tribal authority meant that even the several bands of a particular tribe would
have difficulty uniting for a campaign against a common foe. Those qualities
that made Indian society so attractive to the individualist diminished its capacity for organized resistance.

Beginning in the 1850s, the Plains Indians were introduced to the com-
plexities of treaty negotiation with the United States. In 1851 the northern
tribes, and in 1853 the southern tribes, participated in councils that resulted
in pieces of paper which, according to the white man, roughly delineated the
boundaries of the principal tribes and secured permission for Americans to
maintain military posts on Indian land and to traverse it on specified trails.
But in these and subsequent negotiations there was no guarantee of participation by all the bands concerned, nor any real machinery by which a handful of
chiefs and headmen could bargain away the property of all members of a
tribe. For the average Indian, the negotiations were significant only to the
extent that he or she shared in the distribution of gifts that were held out to
attract a certain tribe to the council site. The resulting treaties also usually
provided for annual distributions of goods, and the government-issued annu-
ities that would become such bones of contention. These, nevertheless, usually did not amount to more than the equivalent of a few dollars worth of
shoddy merchandise per individual.

As the frustration of the Indians mounted, they sometimes vented it by attacking outlying ranches, wagon trains, and stagecoaches. The Americans responded by establishing more military posts in the area, which in turn attracted more settlers, further alarming the Indians and driving them to additional efforts to protect their land. By the 1860s, the fighting had intensified to the point that the white man often said wars were occurring. For the Indians, it was simply more of the same. Raiding parties, usually as few as thirty or forty warriors, would ride from their camps seeking revenge for casualties suffered in an earlier raid, or simply the opportunity to count the coups that gave a man status or to increase his pony herd at the expense of some rancher or army post. Prisoners might also be taken who could then be held for ransom. If successful, the raid would probably lead to troops trying to run down the perpetrators, and another cycle of violence would be underway.

The Indians seldom had much trouble eluding the army detachments pursuing them. Entire camps, including women, children, and the elderly, proved elusive targets in terrain where an unobserved approach by an army column was extremely difficult. If the troops pressed too closely, the Indians would disperse, forcing the officer in command to either give up the pursuit or persist against a steadily diminishing target.

While the Plains warriors held their own in the initial skirmishing, a new series of treaties with the United States in 1867 and 1868 provided the framework for their ultimate undoing. These treaties, negotiated at councils to which the Indians were attracted, as usual, by the promise of food and presents, contained terms of far-reaching significance. By treaties such as that negotiated on Medicine Lodge Creek in 1867 with the Kiowas, Comanches, and Apaches, many tribes were committed to selling to the United States most of their land and settling on reservations. On these they were then supposed to begin farming and to send their children to school. And there even was provision in the treaties for the ultimate division of the reservations into family-sized farms, with the implication that the Indians would over a thirty-year period abandon their communal lifestyle and fully adopt the white man's customs.

It is highly unlikely that the average Indian appreciated that such treaties committed him to changing an entire way of life. Indeed, it is unlikely that even the chiefs and headmen whose marks appeared on the treaties completely comprehended their terms. Nevertheless, the Indians soon would discover that the Americans considered the treaties to be their authority to force them onto reservations and to keep them there.

During the decade after the negotiation of the 1867–68 treaties, the Plains were in turmoil. In the face of U.S. demands that they give up their freedom, and seduced by the promise of further rations, which became more and more appealing as the buffalo herds melted away under the relentless killing by the white hide hunters, bands began to trickle into the agencies. But others clung desperately to the old life. Every summer those who held out would be joined by reservation Indians who had tired of the scanty rations provided them and resented the constant pressure to substitute the white man's way of life for their own familiar and cherished customs. The whites' insistence that they begin farming was particularly objectionable to men who regarded such activity as, at best, fit only for those tribes not capable of no-madic plains life and, at worst, a gashing of the earth's surface that bordered on sacrilege.

But each year it became more difficult to live the old life. The buffalo herds were rapidly disappearing, and army patrols were more numerous. The soldiers seldom were able to overtake the more mobile Indians, but they could harass the warriors and their families and keep them moving. It reached the point that all tribesmen off a reservation might be considered hostile and subject to attack without warning. Camp equipment and tipis abandoned by fleeing Indians were destroyed at a time when it was becoming much harder to get new buffalo hides to make tepee covers. Nor could a warrior hope to quickly replace the pony herd seized by U.S. troops. These animals, which

"On the Canadian." Drawing by Cheyenne artist Bear's Heart depicts white hunters and settlers disrupting life in Indian Territory in the 1870s. Courtesy, Museum of the American Indian, Heye Foundation.

had made the Plains life possible, were either shot—and herds of as many as a thousand animals were so disposed of—or given as rewards to other Indians serving the army as scouts. Not only were traditional enemies happy to play the role of scout, but even members of bands that had settled on the reservation were persuaded to trail other members of their own tribe who were trying to preserve their free way of life.

By the late 1870s, the Plains Indians were worn down. In a decade of fighting they had, however, scored some successes. The Sioux and Cheyennes, following such able leaders as Crazy Horse, Red Cloud, and Two Moon, had forced the abandonment of the Bozeman Trail forts in 1868. In 1876 they first drove the army soldiers from the field at the Battle of the Rosebud and then killed over half of the Seventh Cavalry Regiment on the Little Big Horn. In hundreds of skirmishes, the warriors demonstrated their ability to inflict losses disproportionate to their own and to outmaneuver the more heavily armed enemy.

By the decade's close, however, the Plains Indians' capacity to resist steadily declined. They faced a growing enemy strength while theirs eroded. As mentioned, a lack of racial, even tribal, solidarity meant that at no time was all Indian manpower arrayed against the white invaders. Indeed, at any given time the enemy columns were most likely being guided by other Indians, and not necessarily from tribes hostile to those being pursued by the troops. Crazy Horse of the Oglala Sioux, Horseback of the Comanches, and Grey Beard of the southern Cheyennes were typical of Plains chiefs whose final surrender was hastened by the aid provided the troops by their fellow tribesmen. Finally, the slaughter of the buffalo by the hide hunters in the 1870s struck at the mainstay of the Plains Indians' existence: without the buffalo the Plains Indians' cherished lifestyle was impossible.

The experience of other western tribes that attempted to defend their homelands was depressingly similar. In 1846 the Navajos suddenly found themselves being told by American officers that they were now under the jurisdiction of the United States and should give up immediately their long-standing custom of raiding Pueblo and Mexican villages. At the time the Navajos lacked any semblance of a tribal government, and their less than ten thousand people lived in many small communities, seldom larger than two hundred people. The Navajos subsisted by farming and grazing sheep and horses on the open range—and by raiding. The last was an important part of their economy and provided them with additional sheep and horses, as well as captives who might be sold, ransomed, or assimilated.

The Navajos had difficulty comprehending American proscriptions against raiding. The Indians had been at war with the Mexicans for generations, and the Americans had been so recently. That the Americans wished peace with the Mexicans seemed little reason for the Navajos to give up a long and profitable practice.

Nevertheless, a few Navajos were found to affix their X's to the white man's treaties calling for a cessation of raids against Pueblos and Mexicans. Most Navajos were not even aware of the existence of the treaties, and few of those who were felt themselves bound by them. The raiding continued under leaders like Manuelito, only now the Navajos had to avoid patrols and punitive expeditions operating from new American posts established deep in Navajo territory. On their rounds, the American soldiers frequently were guided by Utes, Pueblos, and even Navajos.

As the fighting accelerated, Navajo losses rose. In 1860 an attack on the principal U.S. post in Navajo country by an unusually large force of one thousand warriors was unsuccessful. Navajos also were losing people to other Indian raiders, with hundreds of Navajos ending up as slaves in Mexican and Pueblo settlements. Then, in 1863 and 1864, the Navajos had to contend with soldiers who penetrated to the heart of Navajo country, invading Canyon de Chelly where they destroyed the cornfields and peach trees upon which the families depended. Intimidated by this show of strength, thousands of Navajos gave up further resistance and submitted to a 300-mile trek east, the notorious Long Walk, to confinement on a reservation on the Pecos River. For three years they suffered under military rule, and more than two thousand died from a smallpox epidemic. Meanwhile, some managed to elude their guards and make it back to Navajo country. They were joined in 1868 by survivors of the Pecos River ordeal, after the Navajos had pledged to live on a reservation and abandon their raiding.

The Navajo resistance had not been as protracted as that of the Plains warriors. As more or less stationary farmers and herdsmen, the Navajos had been more vulnerable to attacks by the U.S. Army than were the buffalo hunters. And like the plainspeople, the Navajos suffered from a lack of tribal cohesion, and their long-standing hostilities with neighbors ensured that the American soldiers had no difficulty recruiting Mexican and Indian guides into their ranks.

Other tribes in the Southwest had their homelands invaded by the whites in the 1840s and 1850s; some resisted only briefly, although others defied the Americans into the 1880s. The Apaches provide examples of both extremes; Jicarilla resistance ended in the 1850s, while some western Apaches were still fighting as late as the 1880s. In general, the Apaches persisted longer in their struggle to maintain their independence than did the Navajos for several reasons. For one thing, the Apaches had never developed the Navajo's dependence on agriculture and stock raising that, while raising the Navajo standard of living, tied them to one place and made them more vulnerable to hostile armies. For another, Apacheria, the Apache homeland, comprised terrain even more rugged than that of Navajo country, which discouraged its attack. Moreover, Apacheria's proximity to Mexico offered the Apaches further opportunities for refuge if hotly pursued by U.S. troops.

The Apaches had not been as disturbed by the long Spanish presence in the Southwest as they would be by the relatively recent American presence. No permanent Spanish settlements had been established in Apache country, and the number of Spaniards in the Southwest was nothing compared with the relative flood of Americans in the 1850s and 1860s.

The initial contacts of the Apaches with the Americans resembled those of the Navajos. The Apaches likewise considered themselves at war with the Mexicans and were evaluating the Americans as potential allies. By 1850 the usual treaties had been drawn up and the Apaches began to learn that the United States not only would not join them against the Mexicans but expected them to give up the raiding that was a part of Apache lifestyle. The Apaches were willing to recognize that the Americans had defeated the Mexicans and therefore had the right to dictate to Mexicans. They could not comprehend, however, how that gave the United States the right to dictate to Apaches.

Then the Apaches became acquainted with that most persistent of intruders, the white prospector. Reports of gold in Apache country attracted those men who knew no boundaries and respected no rights. When Mangas Coloradas of the Mimbreño Apaches protested their incursions, he was badly beaten.

As the Plains wars wound down, it became common practice to bring delegations of tribal leaders to Washington for the negotiation of peace treaties. This portrait of Old Crow and his wife was taken in 1880 while he and other Crow leaders were on one such trip. Courtesy, The Newberry Library.

The prospectors, however, were only the beginning. The Apaches also had to contend with ranchers who began to operate on Indian land without so much as a by-your-leave. And government agents displayed the usual facility for obtaining pieces of paper complete with the marks of Indian leaders that purported to give the Americans the right to develop lines of communication through Apache territory.

It was the beginning of more than thirty years of Apache efforts to protect their homelands from white trespassers. As always, the level of violence ebbed and flowed, and at no time were the many bands of the several western Apache tribes able to combine against the common enemy. Apache heroes of that long war included Mangas Coloradas, Cochise, Victorio, and Geronimo.

Mangas Coloradas was a big, powerful man whose intelligence was as impressive as his physical attributes. He had convinced Mexican authorities of his military skills long before the Americans asserted their claims to the Southwest. When American miners stormed through the country of the Mimbreños in the early 1860s, Mangas rallied his fellow tribesmen and drove most of the prospectors out. Subsequently, however, he failed in an effort to ambush a U.S. Army column in the fabled Apache Pass, near the boundary of southern Arizona and New Mexico, and within six months Mangas would be dead. According to an eyewitness, a white man, Mangas had been captured by soldiers violating a flag of truce and then tortured into sufficient resistance for the soldiers to rationalize shooting him.

Apache Pass was in the territory of the Chiricahua Apaches, whose chiefs included Cochise, an ally on occasion of Mangas. Cochise was driven to hostilities against the Americans by a matter of mistaken identity. Americans blamed his band for an attack actually made by other Apaches; when U.S. troops seized some of Cochise's people as hostages, he retaliated. Another cycle of violence was underway, one that would pit the Chiricahuas against the white intruders for the next twenty-five years. In 1872 Cochise was able to negotiate a lull in this bloody business when he agreed to locate his people on a reservation that was, at least, a part of the much vaster region they always had called home. Two years later Cochise died, and leadership of the Chiricahuas passed first to Victorio and then to Geronimo.

Throughout the 1870s, the western Apaches were under pressure to remain on reservations and undergo the American version of a civilization program. Some Chiricahuas resisted this fate more vigorously than others, and the strong willed and independent looked to Victorio for leadership. For three years he led a band, fluctuating in size but seldom exceeding 250 people, back and forth across western Texas, New Mexico, and eastern Arizona. The Apaches consistently outwitted, or simply outmarched, the troops pursuing them. If the Americans came too close, Victorio would head for the mountains south of the border. This ultimately proved his undoing when in 1880 a Mexican force trapped his band in a canyon and almost all the Apaches were killed or captured. Victorio himself died, presumably the victim of one of the Indian auxiliaries of the Mexicans.

In the early 1880s, Geronimo emerged as the most able of the Apache freedom fighters. Like many other Apaches, he had found the reservation regimen intolerable and fled to the mountains. But the odds against the Indians were mounting. The white population of Arizona doubled in the early 1880s, and the troops were not only more numerous but toughened and experienced by the constant campaigning. Moreover, Apaches off the reservation now knew that their pursuers probably would be guided by fellow tribesmen who had taken service with the United States.

During the last four years of Apache resistance, a bewildering succession of events occurred as parties of Indians were driven to the reservations, only to have some of them slip away again. Nor was Mexico the refuge it once had been now that the Americans had obtained Mexican consent to pursue Apaches deep into the Sierra Madre in Chihuahua. Nevertheless, even a small Indian force could do damage, as a party of about a dozen warriors led by Geronimo's brother Josanie demonstrated. In a month the Apaches traveled an estimated 1,200 miles, killed 38 people, seized 250 horses, and totally baffled hundreds of pursuers before retreating south of the border.

But with each campaign, those Apaches prepared to risk everything to maintain their freedom were fewer in number. Many of the bravest died in battle; others were finally forced to accept the futility of further resistance. Geronimo was in the latter category, finally surrendering in 1886. His last campaign indicated the impracticality of further resistance. Geronimo's band, including women and children, numbered only thirty some people, while pursuing them were upwards of five thousand troops with orders to kill or capture them.

The Apache wars were even more violent than most such hostilities. Fighting for their very existence, the Indians had to be implacable. Nevertheless, it was the whites, both soldiers and civilians, who were guilty of the most flagrant acts of treachery, and examples abound. The 1871 Camp Grant Massacre, in which nearly a hundred Apaches were killed and many Indian children seized to be sold into slavery, was perpetrated by a mob of Tucson settlers supported by the Tohono O'odham. The victims had been attracted to Camp Grant by the promise of rations and protection by troops. Cochise's inveterate hostility stemmed partly from the murder of Apaches who had been persuaded to appear for a peace conference. On another occasion, white settlers had invited Indians to talk peace and then killed their guests by serving them poisoned food.

The experience of tribes more sedentary than the Apaches varied. To the east, the Pueblos of the Rio Grande Valley fared better than did most Indians in the Southwest, although they too lost land. Generally speaking, the Americans agreed to recognize the village boundaries that had existed under

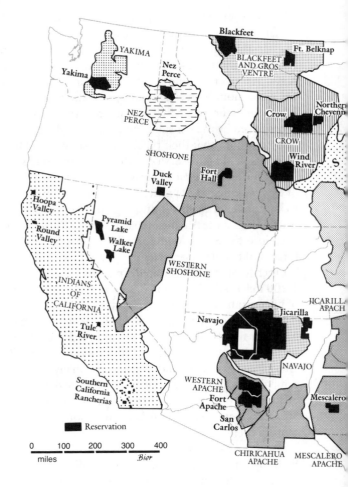

Aboriginal Territories and Modern Indian Reservations. Shaded areas indicate land areas recognized by the Indian Claims Commission (an independent tribunal established by Congress in 1946) as the "aboriginal territories" of several western tribes. Black areas represent the external boundaries of reservations where members of those tribes currently reside. The aboriginal territories (and modern reservations) are as follows: California (Hoopa Valley, Round Valley, Tule River, and the Southern California Rancherias), Yakima (Yakima), Nez Percé (Nez Percé), Blackfeet and Gros Ventre (Blackfeet and Ft. Belknap), Crow (Crow), Sioux (Pine Ridge, Rosebud, Yankton, Crow Creek, Lower Brule, Cheyenne River, Standing Rock, and Sisseton),

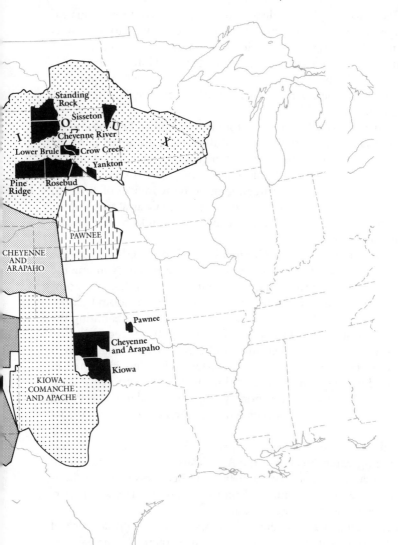

Shoshone and Western Shoshone (Fort Hall, Wind River, Pyramid Lake, Walker Lake, and Duck Valley), Cheyenne and Arapaho (Northern Cheyenne, Cheyenne and Arapaho, Wind River), Pawnee (Pawnee), Kiowa Comanche and Apache (Kiowa), Jicarilla, Mescalero, Chiricahua and Western Apache, (Jicarilla, Mescalero, San Carlos, and Fort Apache), and Navajo (Navajo). Note: Aboriginal areas were determined by the Indian Claims Commission on narrow legal grounds. In general they represent boundaries of tribal habitation at the time treaties were negotiated with the United States; they do not reflect the precontact locations of tribes or account for seasonal migrations. In short, they are suggestive rather than definitive.

Spanish and Mexican rule. The Indians, however, had traditionally grazed their livestock on large areas adjoining their cultivated fields. With the influx of Americans into the region after the Mexican War, the use of much of that land would now be denied the Pueblos. Moreover, white lumbermen's overcutting of timber in the Rio Grande watershed contributed to floods that destroyed fields that had been farmed by the Indians from the days before the Spanish entered the valley.

The legislature of New Mexico Territory had recognized Pueblo village existence, but in California the rights of the Indians were dismissed cavalierly by the new state government. In 1850 there were approximately one hundred thousand Indians in the new state of California. About sixty tribes were represented, and their cultures varied greatly, ranging from the Indians of northern California whose lifestyles closely resembled those of the Coastal tribes of the Pacific Northwest to the southern tribes with obvious links to the Pueblo cultures of the Southwest.

Several things combined to render ineffective Indian resistance to the American occupation of California. The great cultural differences among the tribes and the absence of any real tribal governments meant that Indians choosing to resist seldom were able to mobilize more than a few freedom fighters. In addition, the Indians had been demoralized by developments during the period of Mexican control of California. In the mid-1830s the secularization of the missions had cast adrift fifteen thousand prosyletized Indians, and in the interior the tribes were being pressed by Mexican settlers interested in expanding their ranchos or capturing additions to their work force. Meanwhile, diseases introduced into the region by whites were taking a heavy toll on the native population—five times the number killed by the Mexicans, according to one estimate.

Thus an already tragically weakened Native American population was faced with an even greater threat after the Americans acquired California. In 1848 the non-Indian population of California had been less than ten thousand; by 1850 it exceeded one hundred thousand, and settlers and miners were penetrating every area of the new state.

The unique California experience of bypassing the territorial stage of government only complicated matters for the Indians there. Territorial governments were directed by officials in Washington who typically took more seriously their obligation to protect the rights of the Indian population than did state officers. The white Californians, however, almost immediately obtained statehood, and they felt little compunction to observe federal Indian policy. One early state law provided that Indians could be indentured to white employers for extended periods of time. The result was at best peonage, and for those Indian women and children who were kidnapped and sold to white settlers, little better than slavery.

Indian resistance to this and other white abuses was sporadic. They would burn a barn here, steal cattle there, and occasionally kill a settler or a miner.

These acts of defiance would be met by punitive expeditions that would exact revenge out of all proportion to the alleged crime. Frequently these operations were conducted not by disciplined forces of the U.S. Army but by militia units or local posses whose members had the typical citizen's contempt for Indians and a complete disregard for their rights.

Those Indians who were willing to locate on the few reservations hastily established in California did not find there the peace and security they had been promised. Settlers, with the connivance of reservation employees, were constantly encroaching on the land set aside for the Indians. Rations and supplies designated for the reservation inhabitants were diverted to other channels by corrupt agents. Meanwhile, disease was taking a terrible toll on the remaining Indian population.

Under multiple blows, the fabric of Indian political and social life gave way. A half century of American control saw the California Indian population steadily decline until it was less than one-fifth of what it had been in 1848. "Genocide" is a term of awful significance, but one which has application to the story of California's Native Americans.

North of California, the Indian populations initially welcomed the white traders because the newcomers brought with them tools and other goods that improved Indian living standards. By 1800, the tribes had developed regular commercial relations with the "Boston men," as they referred to the Yankee traders, and with their rivals, the "King George men." Within two decades the interior tribes also had been brought into contact with traders and trappers, and their societies began to show some of the same improvement in standards of living as had that of the Plains tribes after their acquisition of horses and firearms.

The Chinooks discovered the dangers of the new relationships. For many years they had flourished as middlemen between American and British traders and tribes more remote from the coast. But around 1830 the Chinooks fell prey to one of the diseases imported by the whites and were virtually exterminated as a tribe.

The situation changed abruptly for the worse for all the tribes of the Northwest in the 1840s. First Americans began to occupy the Willamette Valley and move north towards Puget Sound. Then the Indians had to contend with the whites lured to the region by reports of gold.

The first tribes to be attacked were those in southern Oregon, after they were mistakenly blamed for depredations committed by people to the south of them. In 1853 Indians from the Rogue River area resisted briefly and then were required to accept a treaty locating several of the tribes on a single reservation. As some of these tribes were traditional rivals, few people actually took up residence on the reservation.

Indians who found themselves within the newly established Washington Territory had problems of their own. They quickly became acquainted with the peremptory demands of a territorial governor that they sign treaties, surrender most of their land, and gather on designated reservations. These reservations were usually located east of what had been the tribal homelands and comprised land less well watered and timbered and not as plentifully supplied with game and fish. Moreover, the tribes again were expected to share a few reservations, regardless of longstanding intertribal rivalries. At the treaty councils, the Indians seldom spoke with one voice. Among the Nez Percés, for example, most tribesmen strongly opposed assignment to a reservation, and Old Joseph and Looking Glass were among the resistors' most effective spokesmen. Other Nez Percés, however, accepted the leadership of Lawyer, who was convinced that resistance was not a viable option. As usual, the whites finally obtained treaties that purported to show that the tribes had ceded large areas of land and had agreed to move to reservations.

Pressure on the Indians to move coincided in 1855 with new gold strikes in the Northwest. More whites began to invade the area, and some Indians were driven to resist. Native peoples from the Rogue River area fought until overwhelmed, whereupon the survivors were forced onto a reservation. Concurrently, the Yakamas and their allies put up a real battle to hold their homelands, although the steadily mounting white power in the region soon proved too much for them. Pressed by the brutal local militia, which was backed by U.S. Army regulars armed with rifled guns that outranged the muskets and bows and arrows of the tribesmen, the Indian resistance faded. In the process, the tribes lost some of their best leaders, among them Owhi, chief of the Kittitas, and his son, Qualchan.

Owhi was a chief whose prestige extended beyond his own tribe, and his determination not to give in to the whites helped mobilize other Upper Salishan tribes in the struggle to maintain their independence. When further resistance proved futile, Owhi turned himself in only to be told that his own safety depended upon his persuading Qualchan to surrender. After Owhi accomplished this, the army officer to whom Qualchan submitted had him hanged. The betrayed and distraught father was then killed while attempting to escape.

With the exception of the Modocs and the Nez Percés, the tribes of the Northwest ended their resistance with the campaigns of the 1850s. In 1873 intolerable conditions on a reservation that the Modocs were forced to share with larger and unfriendly tribes led some of them to slip away under the leadership of Keintpoos, better known among the whites as Captain Jack. Keintpoos led his people back to their ancestral homeland, and the fugitives took shelter in a ten-square-mile area covered by lava deposits. The very rough terrain abounded in caves and ready-made trenches, making it ideal for defense. With only about sixty warriors, Keintpoos kept at bay for seven months an army that at its peak numbered nearly a thousand men. At one point hostilities gave way to negotiations, only to have the Indians kill two of the white delegates. But the whites took a terrible vengeance. When the Modocs were finally forced to surrender, four of them, including Keintpoos, were found guilty by a military tribunal and hanged. Then the heads of the four men were severed and sent to the Army Medical Museum in Washington, D.C. The surviving Modocs were exiled to Oklahoma, where the descendants of some of them live today.

The Nez Percés, who in 1877 fought one of the last Indian wars for independence, were members of several bands of that tribe that had for years refused to move to a reservation in Idaho. Under mounting pressure from the United States, they had at last reluctantly agreed to leave the land they loved. En route to the reservation, however, young men broke from the main body and killed three settlers who had committed crimes against Indians. Other warriors, assuming that the whites, as usual, would react on the premise of collective guilt, vented their spleen by additional attacks. Troops were sent against the main Nez Percé encampment, but the Indians drove them off. Undecided what to do next, the tribesmen heard conflicting counsel from their chiefs.

Looking Glass, a veteran of many expeditions to the buffalo country east of the Rockies, urged the Nez Percés to head in that direction with the object of seeking refuge among the Crows or retreating north to Canada as Sitting Bull had done the previous year.

With severe punishment and banishment to a reservation as the alternative, the eight hundred Indians began a 1,500-mile retreat that took them over some of the most rugged trails in the Northwest. Pursued by four detachments of U.S. troops, the Nez Percés, under the leadership of chiefs like White Bird, Young Joseph, and Looking Glass, managed to beat off their attackers in several early engagements. The discovery that Crow scouts were serving with one of the army columns ruled out refuge with that tribe as a Nez Percé option. That left retreat into Canada. The Indians were about thirty miles from that sanctuary when they were surrounded by troops led by Cheyenne scouts. During intermittent fighting over a period of a week, Looking Glass and many other Indians were killed. About three hundred Nez Percé, including White Bird, managed to slip through enemy lines and escape into Canada. The remainder of the Indians who had survived the long retreat were surrendered by Joseph, who concluded the negotiations with his poignant, "From where the sun now stands, I will fight no more forever."

There remained only one major effort by Indians to resist by armed force the domination of the United States—the 1879 struggle of the White River Utes. In 1868, Utes had been subjected to one of the treaty proceedings with which the Plains tribes were becoming so familiar. Seven bands gave up all their land claims and received title to a reservation that covered the westernmost third of Colorado Territory. There were the usual provisions for the Indians to begin farming, to send their children to school, and otherwise to transform completely their mode of living.

For a few years the Utes continued to hunt and roam over the area much as their ancestors had done. Then prospectors infiltrated the reservation and found silver in the San Juan Mountains. Other white men poured in

A group of Ute chiefs photographed soon after the 1879 White River conflict. The group consists of Ouray (front, center), who negotiated an end to the fighting, and four others: Guero (front, right), Shavano (rear, right), Warency (rear, left), and Ankatosh (front, left). Courtesy, The Newberry Library.

and, unable to keep its own citizens off Indian land, the United States extorted another land cession from the Utes. By 1878, the Utes at the White River agency had settled onto a smaller reservation. During that year, this northernmost of the two Ute agencies had to contend with a new agent, Nathan Meeker, who proposed an immediate transformation of the Utes from hunters to farmers. In the space of a year, Meeker had driven the White River

Utes to the brink of armed rebellion. When Chief Canavish protested the agent's having ordered a plot of grazing land prepared for plowing, a pushing match ensued and Meeker reported he had been "assaulted." He called for troops to be sent to the agency. Ute warriors, understandably frightened at the prospect of what the troops might do, fought them to a stand still when they approached the agency. Meanwhile, other Utes vented their fury on Meeker, his family, and other agency employees. The white men were killed, the women and children taken captive.

Within a few weeks the army had mobilized almost four thousand troops, some arriving from distant posts by railroad, to contend with the less than one thousand Ute men, women, and children enrolled at White River. Utes from other bands, including the celebrated Ouray who had represented the tribe in earlier negotiations with the white men, interceded and helped arrange a surrender, thus avoiding even more bloodshed. The ending was as familiar as the events that had led to it: the Utes were forced to cede almost all of the reservation in Colorado and retire westward to a less desirable tract in Utah Territory.

The Ute War of 1879 was the last major reenactment of a tragic scenario played out many times in the period from 1848 to 1886. First the Indians of a region would be subjected to invasion of their territory by small parties of whites who killed the game upon which the Indians depended, or drove the tribesmen from the best fishing sites. Other whites would appear to seize land for farming settlements. When faced with Indian resistance—threatened or actual—the United States would arrange treaty negotiations. What almost always resulted was a document that few Indians involved could understand, but which nevertheless committed them to surrender most of their ancestral homeland and relocate on a reservation where they could count on being badgered to give up cherished ways.

Such treaties were powerful weapons in the hands of whites who used them to give an aura of legality to the dispossession of the tribes. Time and time again these scraps of paper were invoked to justify policies abhorrent to the Indians. If the Indians then resisted, they were portrayed as violating agreements freely agreed upon.

Indian resistance, when it did occur, was usually doomed to defeat for the variety of reasons previously mentioned. Indian societies produced an abundance of individual heroes prepared to die in defense of their homes and families, and many tribal cultures assigned the highest status to the warrior. Nevertheless, the tribes lacked effective political unity, and their members were unwilling to submit to the discipline that would enable them to carry on protracted campaigns. Indians paid more than lip service to individual freedoms; the latitude given tribal members, however, meant that rarely would all those capable of fighting be willing to do so at any given time. There was no machinery by which a majority could commit all to a course of action. Chiefs could only lead by example; they did not have real authority over members of their bands. They held their positions of honor on the sufferance of their fellows and had little power to discipline. A common response of chiefs to complaints of whites about the conduct of their warriors was the plaintive, "We cannot control our young men."

If individual tribes had difficulty mobilizing all their bands on a particular course of action—and band chiefs rarely could produce all their warriors to meet a threat—it is not surprising that all tribes of a region would be incapable of closing ranks against the white invader. In such a situation, traditional rivalries with neighboring tribes took precedence over what was the much greater threat of the white man. As mentioned, U.S. Army troop columns commonly went into battle led by scouts from rivals of the tribe the troops were fighting. Nor was it rare for members of one band of a tribe to take service against other bands of the same tribe. This phenomenon of Indians supporting U.S. soldiers against other Indians was as old as the first wars of the seventeenth century.

Other factors also contributed to the losing of the West. The Indians' capacity to resist was eroded, as the example of the Plains Indians dramatically illustrated. The whole nomadic way of life of those Indians, which made them such elusive targets for the troops, became impossible with the mass slaughter of the buffalo. Life could be just as desperate for Indians driven from traditional fishing or gathering sites, thereby drastically diminishing their capacity to resist.

Wars are determined by more than weaknesses, however. The ultimate victor brings strengths to the contest that cannot be matched. Population was a major factor, and the disparity between the numbers of whites and Indians steadily widened with the passing years. To impress chiefs and headmen with

Spotted Tail, the Brule Sioux leader who fought bravely against the U.S. army in the 1850s but who later concluded that military opposition to American expansion was futile. Courtesy, The Newberry Library.

the futility of opposing the millions of whites, with their more advanced technologies, the United States pursued a policy of taking Indian leaders on junkets to major cities in the East, particularly to Washington. Spotted Tail of the Brule Sioux and Ouray of the Utes were only two of many chiefs who returned to their tribes convinced that successful resistance was impossible.

The enemy also strove to deny the Indians the means to continue to fight. Disarming and dismounting the hostiles was standard policy for the army in this period. The thousand ponies killed by troops in 1875 helped end one Comanche resistance. Requiring the surrender of ponies and weapons by Crazy Horse's people when they came into the reservation in 1877 severely restricted their chances of fleeing again to the plains.

Finally, the rapid expansion of the railroad network multiplied the effectiveness of the available U.S. troops. The speed with which forces were mobilized against the White River Utes in 1879 demonstrated that.

Again, what is remarkable is how quickly the West was lost, given the individual abilities of the warriors and the willingness of so many to give their all for freedom. Few people have had a better cause for which to fight than did the inhabitants of the West from 1848 to 1886, but the odds against them were too great.

For Further Reading

The best general history of the wars in the West is to be found in two volumes by Robert Utley. They are *Frontiersmen in Blue: The United States Army and the American Indian, 1848–1865* (New York, 1967) and *Frontier Regulars: The United States Army and the Indian, 1866–1891* (New York, 1973). Dee Brown, *Bury My Heart At Wounded Knee: An Indian History of the American West* (New York, 1970) was a pioneer effort at integrating Indian perspectives about the wars. For the role of those Indians who acted as scouts and auxiliaries for the U.S. troops, see Thomas W. Dunlay, *Wolves for the Blue Soldiers* (Lincoln, 1982). The influence of the military on Indian policy is explored by Robert Wooster, *The Military and United States Indian Policy, 1865–1903* (New Haven, 1988) and Jeffrey Ostler, "Conquest and the State: Why the United States Employed Massive Military Force to Suppress the Lakota Ghost Dance," *Pacific Historical Review* 65 (May 1996), 217–248. Sherry L. Smith, *The View From Officers' Row: Army Perceptions of Western Indians* (Tucson, 1990) provides a useful overview.

The Plains wars were not the most protracted, but they have been the most widely covered. There are a number of valuable studies of particular Indians or particular tribes. Father Peter John Powell's *People of the Sacred Mountain: A History of the Northern Cheyenne Chiefs and Warrior Societies, 1830–1879* (San Francisco, 1981) is a Cheyenne view of their past. A Cheyenne perspective on the battle of the Little Big Horn may be found in John Stands in Timber and Margot Liberty, *Cheyenne Memories* (New York, 1967). Mari Sandoz, *Crazy Horse* (Lincoln, 1961) is a successful effort to recreate the life and times of that great Oglala Sioux chief. His rival for primacy among the western Sioux is the subject of a new biography by Robert Larson, *Red Cloud* (Norman, 1997). For the Indian role in the southern Plains, a good starting point is Donald J. Berthrong, *The Southern Cheyennes* (Norman, 1963).

A valuable survey of the history of the tribes of the Southwest is Edward H. Spicer, *Cycles of Conquest: The Impact of Spain, Mexico, and the United States on the Indians of the Southwest, 1533–1960* (Tucson, 1962). For discussions of Navajo resistance and rebuilding, see Frank McNitt, *Navajo Wars* (Albuquerque, 1972), and William Haas Moore, *Chiefs, Agents, and Soldiers: Conflict on the Navajo Frontier, 1868–1882* (Albuquerque, 1994); Navajo oral historical accounts are Tiana Bighorse, *Bighorse the Warrior* (Tucson, 1990), and Ruth Roessel, ed., *Navajo Stories of the Long Walk Period* (Tsaile, Ariz., 1973). Dan L. Thrapp, *The Conquest of Apacheria* (Norman, 1967) and Donald Worcester, *The Apaches: Eagles of the Southwest* (Norman, 1979) are standard overviews of their subjects. Eve Ball, *Indeh: An Apache Odyssey* (Norman, 1988), is informed by oral history. Two well-regarded biographies are Angie Debo, *Geronimo: The Man, His Time, and His Place* (Norman, 1976), and Edwin R. Sweeney, *Cochise: Chiricahua Apache Chief* (Norman, 1991).

For the California Indians, a good point of departure is Edward D. Castillo, "The Impact of Euro-American Exploration and Settlement," in vol. 8 of the new Smithsonian Institution *Handbook of North American Indians* (Washington, D.C., 1978). The volume also contains articles on the culture and history of the state's individual tribes. Albert L. Hurtado, *Indian Survival on the California Frontier* (New Haven, 1988) furnishes another helpful perspective on economic and social change.

An excellent introduction to Northwestern Indian communities is Robert H. Ruby and John A. Brown, *Indians of the Pacific Northwest* (Norman, 1991). For the Modocs and the Nez Percés, two widely used sources are Keith A. Murray, *The Modocs and Their War* (Norman, 1959), and Alvin M. Josephy, Jr., *The Nez Percé Indians and the Opening of the Northwest* (New Haven, 1965). The standard work on the Ute War of 1879 is Robert Emmett, *The Last War Trail: The Utes and the Settlement of Colorado* (Norman, 1954).

Chapter Nine

The Curious Story of Reformers and American Indians

Frederick E. Hoxie

At ten o'clock on the morning of September 28, 1887, Albert K. Smiley stood in the parlor of the Lake Mohonk Mountain House and called an unusual meeting to order. Smiley, the Quaker proprietor of this fashionable Catskill resort, faced a group of men and women who had come to New York from as far away as South Dakota to discuss the future of the American Indians. Among the assembled were Massachusetts' Senator Henry L. Dawes, recently reelected to a third term in Washington; Lyman Abbott, editor of the influential *Christian Union;* the presidents of Vassar and Swarthmore colleges; editorial writers from the Hartford *Courant,* the Springfield *Union,* and Boston *Journal;* the Reverend F. F. Ellinwood of the Presbyterian Board of Foreign Missions; the superintendent of public instruction for the state of New York; and Harvard Law School professor, James Bradley Thayer. From their opening prayer to the closing hymn, sung together two days later, Smiley and his guests talked about people who were not there and wrestled with a "problem" that had no direct impact on any of them.

One can hardly imagine a less likely spot for a discussion of Indian affairs than the sitting room of the Mohonk lodge. Perched on a peak overlooking the Hudson Valley, built for weekend tourists from New York City, and proud of its fine cuisine and rustic luxury, Mohonk represented everything American Indians lacked in late-nineteenth-century America: wealth, security, and supreme confidence in the future. On the other hand, the resort's distance from the daily reality of Indian existence symbolized the revolutionary changes these reformers had in mind for their Native "friends." The men and women who gathered at Mohonk wanted to destroy traditional Indian life by dissolving all

Above: Detail from photo. See page 194–195.

tribal bonds, ending the practice of communal land ownership, overthrowing Native religions, and eradicating traditional social customs. They wanted to eliminate the distance between Mohonk and the Indian world by "raising up" the Indians to Christianity and "civilization." Thus the conferees did not notice the absence of Indians from their meeting. They were far too enthusiastic about the Native Americans' rosy future to dwell on the bizarre present. "Out of shadows of night the world rolls into light," the closing speaker intoned, "it is daybreak everywhere. . . . [L]et us go from this meeting . . . as we have never gone from it before, inducing all philanthropical bodies to stand shoulder to shoulder and help us solve this problem, until these remnants of tribes are prepared for citizenship in that better country which is in heaven."

The Mohonk meetings, first held in 1883 and continued with the support of the Smiley family into the twentieth century, are significant in the history of Indian reform. While efforts to devise humane policies towards Native Americans began in the colonial era, it was not until after the Civil War that reformers generated sufficient influence to affect a broad range of federal programs. During the late nineteenth century, political reformers, missionaries, and educators—each of whom had previously been involved in Indian affairs—combined forces to make Native people conform to Anglo-American standards of "civilization." Their efforts culminated in the passage of a variety of new laws and the expansion of the Indian Office's social service apparatus. Despite their victories, however, the reformers' agenda proved disastrous for Indian people, and the nature of reform agitation changed drastically in the twentieth century.

The Mohonk reformer's single-minded desire to "raise up" the absent Indians to citizenship and Christianity raises in turn a number of historical puzzles. Why were the Indians of such concern to these genteel easterners? The tribes numbered less than 1 percent of the national population in 1887, and they were far less visible than the recently freed slaves or the thousands of hapless immigrants who were, at that time, cascading into eastern cities. The fervor at Mohonk is also puzzling when one considers that freed slaves and greenhorn immigrants were eager for the reformers' assistance while the Indians were not.

It is also difficult to explain how the Mohonk participants managed to attract such an illustrious audience for their Catskill speechmaking. The 1887 meetings took place in a deeply conservative political climate. In the South, for example, all-white state governments had long since reestablished a racial caste system modeled on the antebellum world. At the same time in the West, politicians had managed to slam shut the door to Chinese immigration in 1882 as well as to segregate both schools and factories so that Anglo-Saxons need never rub shoulders with their nonwhite brethren. In the Midwest, the seven convicted Haymarket "conspirators" awaited execution in a Chicago jail, and the public seemed pleased with the government's vigorous campaign

Three students wearing the uniform of the Carlisle Indian Industrial School, ca. 1890. Pictures like these often were used to win support for the school by demonstrating its success in "civilizing" Indian children. Courtesy, The Newberry Library.

of red baiting and union bashing. President Grover Cleveland suited the age well with his repeated calls for a balanced budget and his frequent ceremonial appearances with his new, young wife. And there was little variation from this vacuous piety in Congress where legislators aimlessly exercised their lungs over the tariff and the gold standard. It was not a visionary age.

Explaining both the existence and the influence of the Indian reformers gathered at Lake Mohonk in 1887 requires unraveling at least two puzzles: first, why Indians? and, second, why so much success? Answering these queries requires recognizing first that the 1887 meeting was not unprecedented. From the time of the American Revolution, political leaders had focused at least part of their attention on American Indians. This interest stemmed from the symbolic association of Indians and the new nation itself. The colonial seal of Massachusetts, for example, had featured an Indian at its center who proclaimed, "Come over and help us." Painters and sculptors in the revolutionary age often used Indians along with indigenous animals and plants to represent the promise of the new nation. Significantly, George Washington argued that peaceful relations were preferable to Indian wars because peace "would be as honorable to the national character as conformable to the dictates of sound policy." For men like Washington and Jefferson, treating Indians well was a republican virtue to rank with promoting husbandry and defending natural rights.

As time passed, and Euro-American settlement spread across the eastern mountains, American leaders also began to equate the westward movement and American destiny. Within this process, the subversion of Indian culture came to be understood as a regrettable, but necessary, consequence of civilization. Thus, Thomas Jefferson wrote to a friend in 1824 that if someone were to travel east from the Rocky Mountains, he would first see "savages . . . living under no law but that of nature." Next he would find Indians living "on our frontiers in the pastoral state, raising domestic animals to supply the defects of hunting." The traveler would then discover "our own semi-barbarous citizens, the pioneers of the advance of civilization, and so in his progress he would meet the gradual shades of improving man until he would reach . . . our seaport towns." Jefferson's evolutionary perspective neatly defined Indians as both objects of public concern and opponents of progress. Their movement away from traditional lifeways would prove the young nation's claim to being the instrument of human advancement.

The attraction of Indian culture to Americans was also reflected in social values and practices. Racial taboos enforced against blacks, Jews, and even Catholics did not always apply to Indians. Indians were admitted to bastions of Protestant privilege such as Harvard College (although few stayed very long), and were largely exempt from antimiscegenation laws. The celebrated marriage of John Rolfe and Pocahontas in Jamestown in 1614, for example, typified the Indians' exceptional status, as did the rise of a significant mixed-blood population in the Great Lakes area during the seventeenth and eighteenth centuries. The product of contact between fur traders and their Indian customers, these *Métis* (as they were called in Canada) became an important factor in the lives of many Indian communities. Thus, while discrimination against Indians was complete and cruel in many areas, Indians were never relegated to a permanent, racial caste.

When the Mohonk reformers discussed what they called "the Indian question," they were addressing a subject that was unlike any other. Indians were indigenous to America, and their fate was inevitably linked to the progress of American civilization. It should not surprise us, therefore, that Indians generally had a prominent place in patriotic celebrations and ceremonies. One of these, marking the centennial of the adoption of the U.S. Constitution, took place in Philadelphia only a few days before the meetings at Mohonk. Five hundred Indians were a part of it. *Harper's Weekly* called the writing of the Constitution "one of the most important events in the history of the world," and therefore covered the centennial celebrations extensively. The centerpiece of those celebrations was a fourteen-mile-long parade up Broad Street on September 15. Near the head of the parade was the float from the Carlisle Indian school, a display that demonstrated the Indians' imminent

The Philadelphia parade held to celebrate the centennial of the U.S. Constitution included this entry from the students of the Carlisle Indian School. Their float was intended to demonstrate the Indians' passage from the tipi to modern industrial life. Courtesy, The Newberry Library.

transformation from nomadic hunters to regimented citizens. Students in gray military uniforms pulled a wagon carrying a tipi and costumed Indians who represented the old life. Other students displayed "civilized" tools and books. Thus, just as patriotic citizens applauded the centennial of the Constitution and the "taming" of the national landscape, they could also endorse the effort to "raise up" the Indians so they might participate in the nation's progress.

But even granting the public's interest in Indians, why were these Mohonk reformers so influential? How could men like Senator Dawes, Reverend Ellinwood, and Lyman Abbott be drawn to a mountaintop hotel to discuss federal Indian policy? Here as well, the answer to the puzzle begins with historical precedents. Just as interest in Indians was long-standing in America, so the involvement of reform politicians, missionaries, and schoolmen in Indian affairs had been evident throughout the previous century.

General Henry Knox, who served as secretary of war under both the Articles of Confederation and the first years of the Constitution, was the first politician to outline a "reform" policy towards the Indians. It was he who originated one of the reformers' principal themes: rooting Indian affairs in law rather than force. Knox argued that peace was preferable to Indian war from the standpoint of both cost and security (wars would be expensive and might bring on foreign intervention). He argued that long-term peace between the United States and the continent's original inhabitants would best be served by adopting explicit rules of conduct and fair dealing. "It is presumable," Knox wrote in 1789, "that a nation solicitous of establishing its character on the broad basis of justice would not only hesitate at, but reject every proposition to benefit itself, by the injury of any neighboring community. . . . The Indians," he added, "possess the right of the soil. It cannot be taken from them unless by their free consent, or by the right of conquest in case of a just war. To dispossess them on any other principle, would be a gross violation of the fundamental laws of nature, and of that distributive justice which is the glory of a nation." It was largely through Knox's efforts—supported by his old comrade President Washington—that Indian treaties became the basis for federal dealings with Indian groups. These agreements, which contained explicit statements of mutual obligation and respect, represented Knox's concern for justice and his desire to avoid armed conflict with tribal groups.

The formal, legal relationships established between Indians and whites by treaties also served as a foundation for the reformers' ongoing commitment to bringing Native people under American law. Thomas Jefferson, for example, envisioned the treaty relationship leading the tribes to trade with the majority society and gradually to emulate the customs of the young republic. While never specific regarding the timetable for this evolution of Indians into yeomen farmers, Jefferson was consistently optimistic about the possibility of Indian assimilation. In an atmosphere of trade and fair dealing, Jefferson wrote in 1803, "Our settlements will gradually circumscribe and approach the Indians, and they will in time either incorporate with us as citizens of the United States, or remove beyond the Mississippi."

Jefferson's admission that Indians might "incorporate with us" was even a theme—albeit a minor one—in the rationale for removing eastern Indians to the West in the 1830s. Andrew Jackson himself defended these removals as the fulfillment of "the moral duty . . . to protect and if possible to preserve and perpetuate the scattered remnants" of the Indian race. This theme persisted. In the aftermath of the early-nineteenth-century relocations, officials such as Indian Commissioner William Medill argued, for example, that removed tribes were fortunate to be progressing toward "a point at which they will be able to compete with a white population, and to sustain themselves under any probable circumstances of contact or connexion with it." Such arguments also lay behind the creation of reservations in the West in the 1850s. Here, faced with the uncontrolled violence that accompanied initial Anglo-American settlement of California, Oregon, and Washington, officials proposed the creation of special preserves as, in Robert Trennert's phrase, "alternatives to extinction." Such reservations, one commissioner observed, were the only way "the great work of regenerating the Indian race may be effected."

Following the Civil War, general support for Indian survival and regeneration evolved into advocacy of Indian citizenship. This occurred first because general interest in Indian affairs increased during the Reconstruction era. With the precedent of the freed slaves before them, politicians argued that legal rights and the franchise were the instruments that would bring Native communities into the nation. The wrongs committed against Indians, one former abolitionist wrote in 1865, "have been almost equal to those of the black race; and the government ought to be made to feel that the eye of the people is on them." Following a Boston rally in support of Indian citizenship, another, younger reformer wrote a friend that "I think I feel as you must have felt in the old abolition days."

In addition, it seemed that Indians were no less prepared for citizenship than the freedmen and were equally in need of legal protection. A number of incidents occurred in the postwar period to emphasize these beliefs. Efforts to improve the quality of Indian Office personnel and upgrade the government's "civilization" program under President Grant—the so-called Peace Policy— were undermined by nagging corruption and continued conflict between Indians and whites. During the 1870s, violence in the West reached a new peak. The Sioux wars moved towards the climax on the Little Big Horn, while smaller conflicts flared up in Colorado, Arizona, and California. The problem seemed to be both the dishonesty of federal administrators and the wisdom of the reservation policy they were charged to implement. It seemed time for something new. In this setting, new organizations, modeled loosely on the abolitionist societies of the prewar period, began to appear. The Women's National Indian Association was organized in Philadelphia in 1879; the Boston Indian Citizenship Committee appeared in 1880; and the largest group of all, the Indian Rights Association, was founded in 1882. All of these organizations were concerned with ending frontier conflicts by extending legal protection to the Indians.

As in the abolition campaign, the advocacy of Indian citizenship involved reformers in efforts to mobilize general public opinion. Helen Hunt Jackson produced *A Century of Dishonor* (1881) in a fever of anger at the corruption of the Indian Office and conviction that citizenship would empower tribesmen to resist arbitrary government action. She followed that book with a novel, *Ramona* (1884), which was set in southern California and intended to be the "Uncle Tom's Cabin of the Indian reform movement." Other writers joined the effort. Among these were Thomas H. Tibbles, who produced *The Ponca Chiefs* (1880), and William J. Harsha, who wrote two novels, *Ploughed Under* (1881) and *Timid Brave* (1886). These books—which were often serialized in the new, large-circulation weeklies—succeeded in attracting broad sympathy for a change in national policy.

The citizenship campaign received an added boost in 1884 when the Supreme Court decided the case of John Elk, a "civilized" Indian who had attempted to vote in Omaha, Nebraska, and was turned away because of his race. The Court announced that because Indians owed allegiance to an "alien" power, their children, while born within the limits of the United States, were no more subject to the jurisdiction of the Fourteenth Amendment than were "children of subjects of any foreign government born within the domain of that government." In other words, the civil rights amendments to the Constitution did not protect the rights of John Elk, and Indians could not become citizens without formal naturalization. In the aftermath of the *Elk* decision, groups like the Indian Rights Association and the Boston Indian Citizenship Committee redoubled their efforts to win the franchise for Native people, and they found a ready audience among Republican stalwarts like Henry Dawes and legal scholars like Professor Thayer. Dawes had been an early leader of the Massachusetts Republican party and Thayer was active in a number of the American Bar Association's reform activities. Men like these were committed to the idea that the rights of citizenship would dissolve racial barriers and counteract the growing inequities of late-nineteenth-century American life.

The culmination of the reformers' efforts on behalf of Indian citizenship was the passage of the General Allotment Act in February 1887. Sponsored by Senator Dawes, but supported by a broad group of congressmen, the bill had been endorsed by the 1886 Mohonk conferees and all the major Indian rights organizations. It set up a procedure for dividing reservations into individual homesteads and assigning these to tribal members. Once they received these farms—their allotments—Indians would become citizens. The Dawes Act, one speaker at Mohonk declared, "has given us what Archimedes wished for, that he might test the power of his lever to lift the world, and now we have a standing place, an opportunity to test the power of our civilizing influence to lift the Indian."

Despite their legislative victories, the men and women gathered at Mohonk in the fall of 1887 did not view their mission as purely political; for them the enterprise was also deeply religious. When they spoke of "a new day" for the Indians, or when they rose to sing the "Coronation Hymn" at the conference's final session, the reformers were simply affirming something that for them was axiomatic: "civilization and the Gospel go hand in hand." That belief had long been a part of the non-Indian concern for Indian welfare. Religious societies, missionaries, and church officials were, after all, among the very first groups to develop permanent ties to tribal communities. Franciscans in New Mexico, Jesuits in New France, and individual Protestant missionaries such as John Eliot and David Brainerd in New England had made the "salvation" of the Indians a central part of the Christian mission in America.

In the early nineteenth century, as the United States struggled to develop a consistent policy towards Indians, missionaries became actively involved in government action. Congress established a civilization fund in 1819 to spread agricultural and literary education, but because there was no bureaucratic mechanism available for distributing the money, it was turned over to the churches to spend. By 1830, fifty-two schools and more than fifteen hundred students were benefiting from the fund. In addition, several denominations sponsored special institutions such as the Choctaw Academy in Kentucky (administered by Baptists) and the Presbyterian and Congregationalists' school for the Santee Sioux at Lac qui Parle, Minnesota. During the 1820s and 1830s, missionaries were also prominent in the controversy concerning the removal of eastern tribes to the West. The Reverend Isaac McCoy, a Baptist, was an outspoken supporter of the idea. He believed the West offered Indians both the time and the space necessary for the modernization of their governments and the education of their people. The Reverend Samuel Worcester, on the other hand, was a Presbyterian who went to prison rather than surrender his claim to Cherokee sovereignty within the state of Georgia. He subsequently followed the tribe to Oklahoma and spent another two decades there, developing tribal schools and preaching the Gospel.

In addition to their involvement in government programs, churchmen in the early nineteenth century established tribal missions among Indians in all parts of the country. The Congregationalists and Presbyterians organized the interdenominational American Board of Commissioners for Foreign Missions (ABCFM) in 1810. This group sponsored missions overseas as well as in the United States, but fully half of the early budgets went to "saving" the American Indians. The ABCFM founded a mission at Brainerd, Tennessee, in 1816 and another a few years later in Mississippi. The Baptists also sent missionaries to the Southeast, dispatching Humphrey Posey to the Cherokees in 1817; the Methodists quickly followed suit. Following these early efforts, all

Boarding schools often emphasized athletics and introduced students to new forms of recreation. Olympic medalist Jim Thorpe was the most famous Indian athlete of the early twentieth century, but there were many others who participated in baseball, track, and football. In this photograph from about 1915, James Bad Marriage makes an end run at the Bureau of Indian Affairs boarding school at Fort Shaw, Montana. Courtesy, Montana Historical Society.

the major denominations spread their mission work into new areas. The Presbyterians became active in the Great Lakes region and in Oregon; Anglicans established outposts in Minnesota and the Dakotas; and the Methodists set up missions in the Pacific Northwest. Among the smaller denominations, the Quakers and the Moravians (who had both been active in the colonial era) were particularly prominent.

Catholic missionaries were most visible around the Great Lakes and in the Far West. Associated for over a century with the fur trade and the Frenchmen who pioneered it, "black robe" priests had considerable experience among Native Americans. In the nineteenth century, the great Catholic missionary was Pierre Jean DeSmet, a Jesuit who traveled to the Rockies in 1840 and founded a mission among the Flatheads in Montana's Bitteroot Valley. While DeSmet's original mission declined during the 1850s, other men followed his lead; by the Civil War, Catholic missions had been established among the Sioux, Blackfeet, Kalispels, and Coeur d'Alenes. Together with the previously organized churches in the Spanish Southwest and in California, these western missions confirmed the preeminence of Roman Catholicism west of the Mississippi.

Both mission activity and church involvement in federal policy dovetailed in the aftermath of the Civil War when President Grant announced his "Peace Policy." Under this program, Grant planned to turn over reservation administration "to such religious denominations as [have] heretofore established missionaries among the Indians." In addition to replacing political appointees with missionary agents, the administration created the Board of Indian Commissioners (BIC), a body made up of men who were both business leaders and eager Protestants. This group would oversee the awarding of contracts and monitor the activities of the Indian office. The Peace Policy promised to place the administration of Indian affairs in the hands of churchmen devoted to the Natives' "uplift." Grant promised his scheme would end corruption, undermine the influence of war chiefs within the tribes, and hasten the day when Indians would "live in houses and have schools and churches." Under his administration thirteen denominations gained control of seventy-three agencies, and the Board of Indian Commissioners began investigating shady administrative practices. The Peace Policy was not long-lived, however. Catholics complained that they had been excluded from both the BIC and a number of jurisdictions (such as the Dakotas) where they had been active for many years while groups like the Methodists (President Grant's denomination) had more reservations than they could handle. Politicians complained that the new policy endangered a rich source of patronage, and the Indians themselves were generally unimpressed by the incoming tide of "approved" agents. By 1880 the Board of Indian Commissioners had proven ineffective and the status quo had returned with the sole exception that the Catholics, miffed by their treatment under the Peace Policy, had created their own missionary board, the Bureau of Catholic Indian Missions, with headquarters in Washington, D.C.

The religious overtones of the Mohonk meetings, then, are not surprising. Called by a prominent Quaker activist, attended by representatives of both the ABCFM and the major Protestant denominations, and kept to order by the gavel of Clinton B. Fisk, chairman of the Board of Indian Commissioners, the conference was in many ways a carry-over from the days of Grant's Peace Policy. Those attending shared an assumption that political and religious goals in Indian affairs were compatible and that churchmen could offer guidance in policymaking as well as in spiritual affairs.

The third group prominent at Mohonk—professional educators—was relatively new in American reform circles. In the 1880s the separation of religion and public education was not as clear as it is today. Protestant churchmen saw schools as "civilizing" institutions that would foster patriotism, Christianity, and literacy. They also saw public education as a weapon for combating the influence of Catholicism that was beginning to proliferate in the nation's eastern cities. Nevertheless, the growth of public schools and the emergence of a cadre of professional educators had produced the beginnings of a self-conscious group that believed in modern schools as fundamental institutions in a well-integrated, industrial nation.

Education had been an important goal of federal Indian policy throughout the nineteenth century, so it was natural for members of the new educational profession to be active in discussions of Native welfare. Two additional factors help account for their presence at Mohonk. First, schools were traditionally a central focus of missionary and reform activity. Early missions such as Cyrus Kingsbury's ABCFM-sponsored outpost at Brainerd, Tennessee, had been schools, and every mission had had an educational component. In the years immediately preceding the Mohonk conferences, reformers had been particularly active in organizing two new educational enterprises, Hampton Institute and the Carlisle Indian Industrial School. Hampton had been founded in 1868 for the education of newly freed slaves, and it had the support of both private philanthropists and the American Missionary Association. In 1878 the school accepted a group of twenty-two Indians who had previously been held as prisoners of war at Fort Marion, Florida. These new students confirmed the educators' argument that good schools could "raise" Indians to civilization. Their success inspired Congress to bring additional students to Hampton (the program continued there until 1912) and led to the creation of a new school in Pennsylvania, one that would be devoted exclusively to Indian education. Carlisle opened its doors in the fall of 1879, and for the next four decades served as the flagship of the government's Indian school system.

The second factor that encouraged educators to become active in Indian affairs was the opportunity the government schools provided for trying out modern educational methods. While Carlisle was directed by Captain Richard H. Pratt, a former cavalry officer, its focus on industrial education reflected the very latest thinking among educators. These men and women argued that practical application was as important as rote memorization and that manual skills would teach students self-reliance, punctuality, and self-pride. In 1889 a professional educator, Thomas Jefferson Morgan, became commissioner of Indian affairs. Morgan epitomized the new breed. He was both an ordained Baptist minister and a former head of the Nebraska, New York, and Rhode Island state normal schools. He believed deeply in the ability of public education to instill common values in an increasingly diverse public, and his efforts while in office reflected this faith. Morgan brought a professional educator's perspective to Indian affairs. He organized the sprawling and uncoordinated federal educational effort into a system that began with reservation day schools and culminated in off-reservation boarding schools like Carlisle. Morgan also began the process of developing a uniform curriculum and a set of approved textbooks for the government schools. Finally, Morgan called for higher standards for government teachers and civil service protections to prevent political patronage from undermining the quality of school staffs.

The meeting rooms at Lake Mohonk thus contained the major groups involved in efforts to "reform" the government's treatment of Indians in the nineteenth century. Politicians, churchmen, and educators, each with their own agendas, saw the conference as an opportunity to promote their concerns and rally support for their policy goals. From Senator Dawes to Reverend Ellinwood to Professor Thayer, these individuals saw citizenship, humanitarian treatment, and education as compatible tactics, separate efforts towards an overarching goal: the "elevation" of the Indians and their eventual assimilation into the majority culture of the United States. By achieving this goal, the reformers believed, they would be fulfilling their destiny as Americans, affirming their Christian faith, and demonstrating the power of their nation's political and educational institutions to dissolve racial and cultural barriers.

In the decade following the 1887 Mohonk meeting, it seemed that the reformers would have their way. Government schools proliferated so that by 1900 more than twenty thousand Indian children were attending their classes and being exposed to the lessons of "civilization." The Dawes Act distributed land and citizenship at dozens of reservations, and missionaries extended their efforts to convert Native people to Christianity. The Indian Office responded to this new level of activism by expanding its ranks and increasing civil service protection for its employees. Long a dumping ground for political hacks and election-day legmen, the office began to see itself in professional terms. School personnel came under civil service regulations in 1891, and other employees followed suit later in the decade. Yet another aspect of the "Indian problem" was addressed during the first decade of the twentieth century when the sad state of Indian health became a public concern. The Indian office responded with the appointment of a medical supervisor for government programs, and Congress began appropriating special funds to fight trachoma, tuberculosis, and other infectious diseases. Once again, men of good will seemed poised to roll back Indian "backwardness."

With their record of achievement before us, however, we are left with still another puzzling question about the reformers: Why did their influence evaporate so completely in the twentieth century? Why do the Mohonk meetings tell us so much about nineteenth-century reform and so little about reform in the century to follow? What happened?

Two facts became evident in the decades following the Mohonk meetings that rendered the men and women gathered there in 1887 both obsolete and irrelevant. First, the policies they advocated—citizenship, Christianity, and education—failed in themselves to eradicate the boundaries between Indian and white society. Second, there emerged in the early twentieth century a significant group of articulate Indian leaders who called for something quite new: the protection (rather than the destruction) of tribal culture. The presence of these Indian leaders, and their rejection of the Mohonk agenda, altered the course of Indian reform for good.

The nineteenth-century reform program failed to achieve the "new day" promised at Mohonk. Citizenship proved to be no guarantee of equality. Just as freed slaves in the South found themselves bound by Jim Crow laws and the cruel economics of sharecropping and debt peonage, so the newly enfranchised Indians of the West discovered that citizenship eliminated neither prejudice nor economic weakness. Anglo-Americans generally recognized Indian citizenship, but the Native Americans' continuing status as federal wards was used—sometimes with humanitarian intent—to limit their rights. As a result, Indians were prohibited from buying and selling alcohol, barred from attending public schools without federal subsidies, excluded from local juries, and often prevented from voting. The last restriction applied differently in different states, but in general every jurisdiction with a significant Indian population limited Indian voting to some extent. These restrictions ranged from the stipulation that Indians be "citizens" (citizenship was not universal for Indians until 1924) to the requirement that they reside off the reservation and pay local taxes.

More significant than their legal problems, however, were the Indians' economic burdens. Citizenship did not prevent the Dawes Act from transferring 90 million acres of Native-owned land to white ownership. Rather than shepherding Indians into "civilization," the allotment law granted the newly minted citizens titles to homesteads that attracted the attention of local farmers and speculators. The Dawes Act provided for a twenty-five-year "trust period" during which allotments could not be sold. Following the removal of this restriction, some Indians were able to retain their lands, but many more could not resist the blandishments and ready cash of real estate investors.

Those with restricted lands could lease their allotments to ranchers and large agricultural enterprises. Leasing land was often the only way for it to be farmed efficiently. Leaseholders with adequate resources could consolidate Indian homesteads and organize large-scale operations on rented land. Once this occurred, it was difficult for Indians to regain control of their property.

Finally, the convolutions of federal policy made it nearly impossible for Indian landowners to pass on their land undivided to their children. Government agents instead carved up the allotments of deceased tribesmen in a mindless, mathematical exercise that often left heirs with tracts of land so small they could not be put to any economic purpose. Rather than transporting Indian homesteaders to self-reliance, the Dawes Act carried them swiftly to poverty and economic dependency. The fact that they were American citizens once they arrived at this new destination did little to alleviate their suffering.

Continuing economic inequality also belied the "good news" often reported by Christian missionaries. Indeed, growing numbers of Indians identified themselves as Christians, but the label seemed to do little for their spirit or income. During the twentieth century, tensions with local whites remained, exploitation of Indian resources continued, and the goals toward which the Mohonk reformers had bent their efforts seemed as far away as ever.

The final portion of the reformers' program to fall short of its goals was Indian education. Indians schools remained a fixed feature of federal policy, but the general uplift envisioned at Mohonk was not to be. Increasingly in the twentieth century educators called for vocational training for Indians and an abandonment of the idea that schools could be vehicles for Indian assimilation. Ultimately, the government boarding schools were so hampered by budget cuts that even vocational skills were abandoned in favor of laundry, cooking, and cleaning. Students became the maintenance crews for boarding establishments staffed by underpaid, dispirited instructors. These schools were an empty remnant of the reformers' original design. As the early commitment to government schools declined, thousands of Indian students began attending public institutions. On the surface it would seem that this trend would fulfill the reformers' call for assimilation, but in fact local public schools were reluctant to admit students without a federal per capita subsidy, and the Indian office made no effort to oversee the Indian students' education. Native pupils thus became a kind of voucher that could be cashed in for federal dollars and tolerated in the classroom.

The failure of the reformers' nineteenth-century dreams was verified scientifically in 1928 when the Institute for Government Research published *The Problem of Indian Administration*. Commonly known as the Meriam Report, this well-publicized study was carried out by an impressive group of social scientists and Indian professionals. It documented rates of illiteracy, poverty, disease, and early death among Indians that were several times the national average. The Meriam Report captured the attention of policymakers who had long been told that conditions were gradually improving in Indian America. They learned instead that at the height of "Coolidge prosperity" two-thirds of all American Indians earned less than $100 per year.

The second fact to undermine the Mohonk reformers' preeminence was the emergence of a cadre of educated Indian leaders. The men and women who arose in the first decades of the twentieth century to articulate Indian concerns were like flowers that push their way up between the cracks in city sidewalks. Emerging from situations of intense hardship and deprivation, these individuals came from a variety of tribes. They had tried out their voices in churches, tribal council chambers, and village meeting halls before turning their attention to national policy. By 1900 every reservation had a group of spokesmen, from boarding school alumni who were often outspoken on reservation affairs, to Indian ministers who defended their communities, to young chiefs who used their traditional standing in a modern setting. On the national level, the most prominent Indian leader of the early twentieth century was Dr. Charles A. Eastman, a Santee Sioux whose family had fled to Canada following the Minnesota Indian war of 1862 and who, in his own words, had traveled from the "deep woods to civilization." Eastman had attended mission schools as a boy and eventually made his way to Dartmouth College and the Boston University medical school, where he received his M.D. degree in 1889. Between 1900 and 1920 Eastman published several popular books, became a popular public speaker, and served as an official of both the YMCA and the Bureau of Indian Affairs. Dr. Carlos Montezuma was another active

physician and community leader. He had been enslaved as a boy and eventually sold to an itinerant Italian photographer who passed him off to a series of
missionaries. After graduating from the University of Illinois and Chicago
Medical College, Montezuma began a medical practice and published his own
newsletter on Indian affairs. Other national Indian leaders of this era were
Henry Roe Cloud, a Ho-Chunk graduate of Yale; Laura Cornelius, a social
worker from the Oneida tribe of Wisconsin; Gertrude Bonnin (Zitkala-Sa), a
Sioux writer who attended Carlisle and Earlham College; and Sherman
Coolidge, a Northern Arapahoe priest in the Episcopal Church. These men
and women banded together in 1911 to form the Society of American Indians (SAI). Their first president was Arthur C. Parker, a Seneca anthropologist
who devoted his life to collecting and preserving the wisdom of his Iroquois
forbearers.

The Society of American Indians had a relatively short history. It appeared in 1911 and had dissolved into ineffectiveness by the mid-1920s. Its
leaders divided over a variety of issues: the abolition of the Bureau of Indian
Affairs, the condemnation of peyote as a religious sacrament, and the role of
non-Indians in the group. Nevertheless, the rise of the SAI signaled the end
of the period when white reformers could discuss the Indians' future in the
isolation of a mountaintop resort. To be sure, there would continue to be
people who believed that they knew what was "best" for Native Americans,
and there would always be intense debates over what the Indians *really* wanted,
but there could no longer be policymaking in a vacuum.

The final mark of the nineteenth-century reformers' fall from power was
the rise of John Collier to prominence in Indian affairs. Commissioner of

*The Society of American Indians' American Indian Quarterly Journal often urged
native people to become educated and prosperous. These two photographs, labelled "The
Difference Between Education and No Education," appeared in a 1913 issue.
Courtesy, The Newberry Library.*

Indian affairs under Franklin Roosevelt (1933–1945), Collier typified the new realities of the twentieth century. A critic of assimilation, he acted out of a distinctly secular vision of human progress. He was not concerned primarily with extending legal or political rights to Indians, and his idea of Indian education carried none of the "uplifting" rhetoric of Thomas Morgan. John Collier developed his policy agenda during a career as a professional social worker in the immigrant neighborhoods of New York City and from travels among the Pueblo Indians of the American Southwest. Instead of eradicating traditional cultures and "raising" them to civilization, Collier called for their "regeneration" through economic development, political reorganization, and legal protection.

John Collier became a major figure in Indian reform in 1922 when he led the opposition to a congressional proposal to confirm non-Indian claims to Pueblo lands. While some of these claims were legitimate, the bill (introduced in the Senate by New Mexico's Holm O. Bursum) would have made it difficult to separate good-faith settlers from squatters and would have led to significant losses of tribal land. Supported by the General Federation of Women's Clubs and the Indian Rights Association (now nearly fifty years old), Collier campaigned against the Bursum bill at public gatherings and in print. As support for his position grew, he organized the Indian Defense Association to orchestrate the fight.

Collier served as executive secretary of the IDA from 1923 to 1933, when he left it to become commissioner of Indian affairs. His work during that decade defined the new reform vision: he attacked allotment and the old assimilation agenda, and he called for Indian involvement in federal policymaking. As a frequent witness before congressional committees investigating reservation conditions, he never failed to point out the educational and economic failures of the past. At the same time he became a master at bringing Indian delegations to Washington to state their own cases. The first of these was the All Pueblo Council, which entered its protests against the Bursum bill in 1923 and contributed substantially both to its defeat and to the passage of the Pueblo Lands Act in 1924.

John Collier did not act alone. He was supported in his campaigns by a variety of other groups. The General Federation of Women's Clubs was an important source of funds and political influence as was the New York–based Association on American Indian Affairs and smaller associations of social workers, educators, and churches. The Indian Rights Association and the Board of Indian Commissioners, both still active but far less influential than they had been in the nineteenth century, also endorsed some of the work of Collier and the IDA. Nevertheless, the young reformer's idea that Indians required defense rather than civilization was revolutionary. Critics later attacked Collier for failing to listen carefully to Indian concerns or for trying to manipulate Indian public opinion, but in the 1920s and 1930s he stood virtually alone

Delegates to the Society of American Indians' 1913 annual meeting posed at Wildcat Point, near Denver, for this formal portrait. Courtesy, The Newberry Library.

among policymakers in his insistence on programs that would fit the interests and needs of tribal groups.

The centerpiece of Collier's efforts was the Indian Reorganization Act, a law passed in 1934 at the height of the New Deal and intended to be the cornerstone of federal policy for years to come. By prohibiting further allotments, empowering tribes to organize their own businesses, and recognizing the Indians' right to develop constitutions and modern governments, the bill made it clear that the old reformers' agenda had failed and that Indian tribes would be a permanent part of American life.

In the decades since the New Deal, Indian reform was increasingly an Indian enterprise. Major policy initiatives such as the development of tribally controlled schools or the emergence of tribal housing and social welfare agencies came in response to active community lobbying. Other innovations such

as bilingual education programs, the legal recognition of Indian religious free-doms, and the growing practice of allowing tribes to contract with the Bureau of Indian Affairs to provide their own services rested on the viability and persistence of tribal cultures. While the Indian Rights Association and the Association on American Indian Affairs continued to function, their agendas were now set by tribal, rather than non-Indian, concepts of civilization or progress. At least as important today are the reform groups organized and led by Indians themselves. These include the National Congress of American Indians (NCAI), formed in 1944, the National Indian Education Association, the American Indian Movement, and smaller groups that have arisen to advo-cate a single political issue or represent a particular region or group of tribes.

A fitting coda to the curious story of reformers and American Indians occurred in the summer of 1986 when television news programs and weekly magazines carried stories about the century-old land dispute between the Hopi and Navajo tribes. The dispute arose over the partition of land that had been occupied jointly for decades by members of both groups. As part of this partition, several hundred Navajo families were relocated to another part of their reservation. While the relocation was largely complete by 1986, it had been carried out in a clumsy and inefficient manner, and several of the Navajo families who remained on "Hopi" land refused to leave. Church groups, environmentalists, and others quickly entered the scene to defend the remaining Indians who were scheduled for removal. A national defense group was formed and sympathetic stories began to appear in the media. Public attention peaked when a documentary film on the plight of the relocated Navajos won an academy award and began to play in movie houses across the country. In the midst of this rising tide of concern, the Navajos' tribal newspaper published an editorial. Rather than express appreciation for the support they were receiving from non-Indian reformers across the country, the editors of the *Navajo Times* wrote that the activists should "find another whale to save and move on." They argued that reformers were polarizing the situation on the reservation and preventing the Indians from reaching a peaceful resolution of the land dispute. The paper's editor called instead for further negotiations by the parties involved.

The Navajo editorial made it clear that in the century since Albert Smiley called his Mohonk guests to order, the center of reform activity had moved from eastern sitting rooms to western reservations, and that the activists were no longer non-Indian visionaries. The modern Indian reformers were the Native people themselves.

For Further Reading

The principal source for the history of reform in American Indian affairs is Francis P. Prucha's monumental two-volume work, *The Great Father* (Lincoln, 1984; also available in an abridged, single-volume edition from the same publisher). A different view of this general history can be found in Harold E. Fey and D'Arcy McNickle, *Indians and Other Americans* (New York, 1959).

For studies of reform in the antebellum period, see Bernard Sheehan, *Seeds of Extinction: Jeffersonian Philanthropy and the American Indian* (Chapel Hill, 1973); Francis P. Prucha, *American Indian Policy in the Formative Years* (Cambridge, 1962); Robert Trennert, *Alternative to Extinction* (Philadelphia, 1975); Robert F. Berkhofer, Jr., *Salvation and the Savage: An Analysis of Protestant Missions and American Indian Response, 1787–1862* (Lexington, Ky., 1965; reprinted, New York, 1972); Christopher Miller, *Prophetic Worlds: Indians and Whites on the Columbia Plateau* (New Brunswick, 1985); and William G. McLoughlin, *Cherokees and Missionaries* (New Haven, 1983).

For the late nineteenth century, see Robert W. Mardock, *The Reformers and the American Indian* (Columbia, Mo., 1971); Francis P. Prucha, *Ameri-*

can *Indian Policy in Crisis: Christian Reformers and the Indians, 1865–1900* (Norman, 1976); Frederick E. Hoxie, *A Final Promise: The Campaign to Assimilate the Indians, 1880–1920* (Lincoln, 1984); Robert H. Keller, *American Protestantism and United States Indian Policy, 1869–82* (Lincoln, 1983); and William T. Hagan, *The Indian Rights Association* (Tucson, 1985).

The failure of the reform agenda and the rise of new Indian leaders in the twentieth century are covered in William T. Hagan, *Quanah Parker, Comanche Chief* (Norman, 1993); Peter Iverson, *Carlos Montezuma and the Changing World of the American Indians* (Albuquerque, 1982); Raymond Wilson, *Ohiyesa: Charles Eastman, Santee Sioux* (Urbana, 1983); Dorothy R. Parker, *Singing an Indian Song: A Biography of D'Arcy McNickle* (Albuquerque, 1992); and Stephen Cornell, *The Return of the Native: American Indian Political Resurgence* (New York, 1988).

Reform in the Collier era and its aftermath is the subject of Thomas Biolsi's *Organizing the Lakota: The Political Economy of the New Deal on the Pine Ridge and Rosebud Reservations* (Tucson, 1992), which traces the New Deal in one community; Lawrence Kelly's *The Assault on Assimilation* (Albuquerque, 1983), a study of Collier's early career; Vine Deloria, Jr., and Clifford Lytle, *The Nations Within: The Past and Future of American Indian Sovereignty* (New York, 1984). For a vivid case study of the relationship of reform, Indian leaders, and tribal traditions, see Edward Lazarus, *Black Hills/ White Justice: The Sioux Nation Versus the United States, 1775 to the Present* (New York, 1991).

Chapter Ten

Modern America
and the Indian

Alvin M. Josephy, Jr.

In May 1934, during a hearing on the Roosevelt administration's proposed Indian Reorganization Act, the chairman, Senator Burton K. Wheeler of Montana, got into a testy discussion with John Collier, the New Deal's formidable commissioner of Indian affairs. The question was how to define the blood criterion for an Indian who lived off a reservation. Collier, the principal architect of the proposed bill, suggested that anyone having at least one-fourth Indian blood be recognized by the government as an Indian. Objecting, Wheeler insisted that recognition be accorded only to those with at least one-half Indian blood. "If you use one-fourth, then all sorts of people are going to come in and claim that they should be put on tribal rolls," he lectured Collier. "What we are trying to do is get rid of the Indian problem rather than add to it." Wheeler had his way, and the final bill carried his one-half blood criterion.

Although Wheeler had previously been an ally of Collier in condemning the deplorable economic and social status of American Indians and in acknowledging the need for drastic governmental reform, his remark about getting rid of an "Indian problem" reflected a political and philosophical point at which he—and undoubtedly the overwhelming number of non-Indian Americans of that day—parted way with Collier. Whether so characterized or not (and it often was), to most non-Indians since the time of Jamestown and Plymouth, Indians and their destiny had constituted a continuous and ever-frustrating problem—or, to be more precise, a maze of problems. Resisting a multiplicity of policies designed to dispossess them of their lands and other resources while eliminating them as Indians, Native Americans and their nonmainstream cul-

Above: Detail from photo. See page 207.

198

Lewis Plenty Treaties, Blackfeet, ca. 1930. Photo by Peter Red Horn.

tures, values, lifestyles, and religious and social organizations, together with a residue of their properties, had persisted into the twentieth century—a discordant element in an otherwise ordered dream of a homogenous melting-pot nation with a compact of constitutionally based relationships among the federal government, states, and the people. It was true that, in many ways, Indians and their institutions and cultures had changed and adapted through the years. But Indians had refused to vanish or to meld so completely into the rest of the body politic as to end problems occasioned by their uniqueness. Reservations, which to many twentieth-century non-Indians represented a jarring and nonconstitutional phenomenon and a withheld source of wealth; treaty rights that involved seemingly unwarranted special privileges; trust protections; taxpayer-borne services; and numerous unique and thorny situations made the vast complex of interrelationships among Indians, the federal government, states, and the non-Indian population a source of unending controversy and confusion.

From far back in time until well into the second half of this century, it was widely believed that the Indians and the problems generated by their

presence would ultimately vanish—if not by disease and war, then by assimilation and attrition on the reservations. Especially in the half century following
the end of the Plains wars, most policymakers, molders of public opinion, and
reformers worked hard, and often fanatically, to hasten the process of assimilation. Inevitably, they were helped by aggrandizing anti-Indian interests, those
who coveted Indian lands and resources.

To most non-Indians during that period, contemporary Indians were
largely out of sight and out of mind. Save in reservation areas in the West,
where frequent contact continued, the popular culture of the United States—
reflected in history texts and schoolroom learning as well as in such vehicles of
mass communication as museums, magazines, newspapers, books, theatrical
presentations, movies, and other forms of expression and art—dealt almost
entirely with Indians of the past, and then most often in unreal and stereo-
typical fashion. The images they created were demeaning, disparaging, and
dehumanizing as well as grossly inaccurate. Most Americans actually did believe that Indians were disappearing, if not physically, then as identifiable Indians. Even the disappearance became romanticized in such powerful cultural
symbols as Richard Dix's movie of the 1920s, *The Vanishing American*, and
James Earle Fraser's much-celebrated statue, *The End of the Trail*.

In the 1920s a series of governmental and private inquiries into the
status and condition of Indians, occasioned by the eruption of conflicts in
which John Collier and a new breed of reformers took the Indians' side, brought
the nation—or at least many of its opinion makers and public officials—up
short. The Indians, it was discovered, were still far from vanishing or assimilating. Moreover, reservation conditions—the product of a combination of
government policies and government neglect—were revealed, particularly by
the encompassing Meriam Report of 1928, as a national scandal. In many
quarters it was perceived, and agreed, that attention and reform were urgently
required.

It is important, nevertheless, to understand just how far the American
people of that time were willing to allow Indian reform to go. The hardships
and misery of reservation life, the poor health, ill housing, lack of sanitation,
poverty, deprivation of education, unemployment, and isolation from capital
and other means to share in the American economic system touched the hearts
of those who paid attention. If only because the Indian survivors were Americans too, and Americans who had plenty of cause to complain over treatment
in the past, fair play was demanded. But most non-Indians still knew precious
little about Indians and still clung to the belief that the only way to end "the
Indian problem," with all its currently seen manifestations and ramifications,
was to do whatever new might have to be done to revive the assimilation
process and hurry the Indians into the mainstream of American life. There,
like everyone else—as most non-Indians still believed—Native Americans would

have equal opportunity to share in whatever blessings the American system provided to all its people.

The initial reform proposals of the 1920s offered little more than piecemeal tinkerings; they barely, if at all, called the goal of assimilation into question. In 1934, however, John Collier introduced something different. A social worker with experience as a leader in reform movements among non-Indian groups on the East and West coasts, Collier first "discovered" Indians in New Mexico, thrilled to their age-old values and cultures in a somewhat idealistic burst, and settled down to help them in their struggles against rapacious and bigoted white men. Angry, fearless, naive, self-righteous, logical, contentious—this extraordinarily complex man had all kinds of adjectives applied to him. But he was a battler for right and justice as he saw it; he had a wondrous ability to gain publicity and mobilize public support for the Indians; and—influenced by anthropologists who adhered to the somewhat new ideology of cultural pluralism, or relativism—he formed a philosophy and theoretical framework for an Indian policy that envisioned a break with prevailing attitudes. It was his fortune, too, to arrive on the scene when he did. An inheritor of the populist and progressive reform movements—personified by such old Bull Moosers as Harold Ickes, who as secretary of the interior gave him steady support—Collier was able to ride the winds and currents of the New Deal. His arrival in Washington coincided with the launching of a variety of New Deal reforms and social experiments. Innovations and breaks with the past were in the air, and to some extent at least Collier's new Indian policy was a significant part of the changes that were refashioning America.

The original Indian reorganization bill was intended to give Indian communities a new lease on life. It did not say explicitly that the government would no longer push or coerce them toward assimilation, but its provisions pointed in a new direction by encouraging Native Americans to revitalize their cultures, traditions, and institutions and choose their own destiny for themselves. The bill would allow Indians to assimilate at their own rate of speed if they wished to become assimilated, or to remain distinct if they preferred.

In a number of ways Collier was ahead of his time. Most important, perhaps, he struck a blow against the reigning melting-pot concept of assimilation. The nation's leaders were still strongly wedded to this concept, as a glance at almost every school reader and textbook of the period will attest. It was another three decades before large numbers of Americans would share Collier's conviction—much of which they acquired from a new and more realistic familiarity with Indians in the 1960s—that America was, and should be, a plural society.

There were those, of course, who agreed with Collier at the time and supported his original bill. But the underlying concept of the right of Indians to be Indians, and the aims of many of the original bill's provisions that were to give that new policy meaning and strength, were not shared by Senator Wheeler, by most members of Congress, or by the general American public whom they represented. Nor, indeed, were these aims accepted at the time by many Indian-interest organizations such as the Indian Rights Association, which still believed that the melting pot was the best place for Indians. Even some Indian leaders opposed Collier's bill, having been persuaded that all Native Americans should shed their Indianness and make every effort to enter the mainstream of American life.

In light of the opposition, particularly that of Senate Indian Affairs Committee Chairman Wheeler, it is remarkable how much Collier achieved in the final version of the bill. Wheeler, in effect, took the original bill out of Collier's hands, struck out parts and modified others. The finished document was a compromise. It appeared to get the Indians back on the road to assimilation by assisting their economic and social development. Nevertheless, in many instances Collier argued successfully that achievement of economic and social "progress" depended on, or would be furthered by, provisions protecting the Indians' political or cultural freedom. Aided sometimes by pressure from President Roosevelt or Secretary Ickes, Collier got much of what he wanted.

The final bill, sometimes called the Wheeler-Howard Act after its sponsors (Wheeler in the Senate and Representative Edgar Howard of Nebraska in the House) was enacted on June 18, 1934. Without enumerating all of its provisions, we may note some of its principal points. It brought an end to the devastating allotment policy that since 1887 had stripped Indians of some 90 million acres of their lands. Although Wheeler scrapped Collier's original title that would have set the stage for the acquisition of far-ranging and meaningful powers of self-government by the tribes, it gave tribes the opportunity to organize themselves for limited self-government, authorizing them to write tribal constitutions, elect tribal councils, and incorporate tribal institutions. It established a $10 million revolving credit fund to help tribes; fostered educational and medical improvements; provided for the acquisition of land, water, and surface rights for tribes to consolidate or increase their holdings and assist their economies; restored freedom of religion to the Indians; and promoted a revival of Indian arts, crafts, and cultures.

Soon after the bill's passage, Collier and his solicitor, Nathan Margold, prepared a paper to assist the implementation of the act by clarifying and elaborating on its wording. Their memo proved to be an important addendum, for it enumerated a host of inherent powers, not spelled out in the act, which the commissioner and his solicitor maintained were authorized by the act. Together, the act and the clarifying memo—which the otherwise preoccupied New Deal Congress barely noticed—went far toward meeting Collier's original goals. The final act had not ended assimilation as a national objective, but its provisions gave the Indians opportunities and encouragement to choose their own destiny and to continue as Indians with their own institutions, cultures, and self-government.

The implementation of the Indian Reorganization Act during Collier's regime as commissioner was difficult, often stormy, and not without serious opposition from members of Congress, dissenting bureaucrats within the Bureau of Indian Affairs (BIA), aggrandizing whites in the states, various tribes, traditionalist Indians, and organizations of "progressive" Indians. Chronic inadequate funding by Congress, together with BIA shortcomings and bureaucratic opposition, hobbled and crippled many of Collier's aims and efforts. On occasion some tribal groups resisted Collier's policy and programs. To this day Navajos have not forgiven him for a stock-reduction program that he forced on them as a conservation measure designed to save their limited rangeland. Most annoying, some assimilationist Indians fought the commissioner viciously in meetings and in the press, charging that his policy was a Communistic plot to thwart Indian progress.

Nevertheless, many tribes established governments in conformity with the provisions of the Indian Reorganization Act, or IRA, as it was known. To help meet financial shortfalls resulting from inadequate congressional appropriations, Collier adopted the revolutionary approach of letting Indians share in specialized New Deal assistance programs passed by Congress for the benefit of non-Indians. Heretofore all benefits and monies for Indians had come through appropriations to the BIA; other agencies and their programs were customarily for everyone but Indians. Now Collier made arrangements with such agencies as the Civilian Conservation Corps, the Farm Security Administration, and the Public Works Administration that put Indians to work and made funds available for Collier's Indian programs. With such help, between 1934 and 1947 the Indian land base increased by 3.7 million acres, the first increase since 1887. During the same period Indian-owned livestock increased

During the Collier years, Indians were encouraged to organize new tribal governments. Here, Stabs Down By Mistake addresses the Blackfeet tribal council. Photo by Helen M. Post.

from 171,000 to 361,000 head, and the total agricultural income received by Indians grew from $1.85 million to $49 million. At the same time advances were made in Indian education and health; new emphasis was given to raising the standard of living on reservations; arts, crafts, and traditional cultures were revitalized; and official restraints on the practice of Indian spiritual life were removed.

In practice, facets of the IRA were not without blemishes and deficiencies. Some of the act's provisions, together with the precedent-setting implementation carried out by the sometimes self-righteous Collier, led to conflicts and controversies that have still not quieted. The methods and practices of voting to accept IRA, tribal constitutions, and tribal governments frequently aroused or exacerbated intratribal conflict. Because of the opposition of Congress, which had refused to entertain possibilities that might have led to governments of the Indians' own choosing or to a fuller and more meaningful Indian rule of themselves, the act's provisions for self-government fell short of Collier's original hopes. Despite Margold's and Collier's memo, the IRA-authorized tribal governments were by and large seriously circumscribed in asserting their inherent powers. Subject to veto by the secretary of the interior in fiscal, resource, and other key matters, they were susceptible to the authority and control of reservation superintendents and their staffs who sometimes colluded with, and helped to maintain in office, pliant cliques of professional Indian politicians. In addition, a Court of Indian Affairs, which Collier had proposed in the original bill to ameliorate and settle intratribal and community conflicts, was eliminated in the final act.

It should also be noted that although Collier had sought, received, and in some instances accepted Indian criticism and changes—for the first time in history taking proposed Indian legislation to meetings in the field for Indian consideration and input—the recognition by most Americans of the right of Indians to self-determination was still far in the future. The guardian-ward relationship, though not articulated as frequently as in the past, was still strongly felt, believed in by whites and accepted passively by many Indians. Indeed most whites still thought it their duty and right to think, speak, and act for Indians, in effect to impose upon them what they, the whites, deemed to be in the Indians' best interests. Not surprisingly, what was deemed best for the Indians often turned out to be what was best for the non-Indians' interests. There is no doubt that Collier meant to enable and encourage the growth of Indian self-determination, looking toward a day when assimilation, in another sense of the word, would reflect an accommodation without coercion between the dominant society and Indians who were managing and running their own affairs. But Collier himself, along with such aides and supporters as the anthropologist and author Oliver LaFarge, still practiced a paternalism that considered the Indians too untutored in the white man's ways to be able to cope with the dominant society on an equal basis. Thus, falling within the context of its times, the IRA was a white man's document, devised and written by whites for Indians. As such, it could not be perfect, since Indians inherently knew better than whites what they needed and desired and what they would welcome and be able to make work successfully within the framework of their cultural backgrounds and contemporary life. It would be years before most whites would learn this lesson.

At the same time, as the late Indian anthropologist D'Arcy McNickle pointed out, some of Collier's innovations were precedents in U.S. governmental administration. Collier's creation of an anthropological unit in the BIA, and his enlistment of anthropologists and social scientists foreshadowed similar developments in antipoverty and other government agencies working in later years with members of American subcultures or peoples of other cultures overseas. "It was a breakthrough," McNickle observed, "that later on led to technical assistance programs all over the world."

During World War II, some twenty-five thousand Indians served in the nation's armed forces, a number of them in communication teams where they used their own languages on telephones and radio equipment to confound enemy interceptors. It was the first time that most of them mixed with non-Indians in the non-Indian world, and cultural influences and impacts ran both ways. Among the honored flag raisers on Iwo Jima was Ira Hayes, a Pima Indian from Arizona. After the war, returning Indians were anxious to bring more of the white man's material traits to the reservations. Others found little to do on the reservations and went back to the white man's world to try to make a living. At the same time, other Indians who had left the reservations during the war to work in defense plants and shipyards preferred to remain in their new environments, gradually adapting to non-Indian life.

Both the IRA and the reservations were severely hurt by the war. Indian budgets were cut drastically, and the implementation of IRA policies and programs was all but stalled. The departure of many of the best-educated Indians for military service and war work crippled and ended hopeful new tribal enterprises. In addition, the atmosphere of unity engendered by the war subjected Collier and the IRA, with their perceived philosophy of perpetuating Indians as separate and different from other Americans, to new criticism. Congress turned angrily against the IRA, charging it with having hampered assimilation. Seeking economies, the lawmakers demanded that Indians be taken off the backs of the taxpayers and "freed from the reservations" so that they could make their own way like all other Americans. Prominent among the complainers were the aggrandizing interests that still coveted Indian lands and resources. They urged the end of reservations, tribes, treaties, and trust protections and the turning over of Indians and their possessions to the jurisdiction of the states.

Buffeted by the criticism, Collier finally resigned in the spring of 1945. In his wake, reaction took over in Indian affairs. In 1946 the government established an Indian Claims Commission. Its function was avowed to be the settling of all Indian claims of unjust land dealings in the past by hearing whatever evidence tribes wished to bring before it and awarding payments to tribes that proved their case. Its more realistic purpose became clear in 1952, when Dillon Myer, then commissioner of Indian affairs, revealed that it had been established to provide "the means of removing a major Indian objection to any move in the direction of Bureau withdrawal" from further relations with the tribes. Nevertheless, through many congressional extensions, the special court lasted until 1978, heard hundreds of cases brought by the tribes, and awarded many millions of dollars in claims.

In 1953, the passage of two measures—Public Law 280, authorizing states unilaterally to assume jurisdictions over criminal and civil matters on reservations, and a resolution declaring Congress's intent to end federal relations with the tribes at the earliest possible time—ushered in a new era marked by a destructive effort to terminate federal involvement in Indian affairs. Impulsive and radical in the extreme, it served notice that support no longer existed for the pluralist philosophy of the IRA. In one sense, the new policy was part of the nation's Cold War turn toward conformity, most dramatically exemplified by McCarthyism. In another sense, the policy reflected one of the most cherished tenets of American liberalism, which in the optimistic aftermath of World War II held that everyone, including minority groups, should receive equal treatment. Still ignorant of Indian needs or desires, non-Indians generally accepted the devious argument that the segregation of the reservation system, together with the continuance of tribal institutions, Indian cultures, and BIA rule—all alleged anachronisms in modern-day America—were holding the Indians back and had to go. In all, termination stemmed from many motives but it added up to the return of enforced assimilation.

Termination, imposed on tribes whether they wished it or not, meant the withdrawal by the federal government of all relations with them, including the observance of treaty and trust obligations and the delivery of services. Terminated tribes were to be incorporated into the states in which they were located, and their resources placed in private hands. One by one a number of tribes, ranging from large ones like the Klamaths of Oregon and the Menominees of Wisconsin to small ones like the Alabamas and Coushattas in Texas and bands of Paiutes in Utah, were terminated. Trusteeship of tribal property was shifted from the federal government to trust officers of private banks who knew or cared little about the Indians' needs. The hurried process soon produced scandals. Indians and their resources were subjected to renewed fraud, robbery, and other injustices; tribes were demoralized by confusion and economic disaster; and states were confronted with huge welfare burdens.

Simultaneously with the implementation of the termination policy the federal government gave increased emphasis to a relocation program aimed at easing economic pressures on the reservations and accelerating assimilation.

In the aftermath of the New Deal, government officials were more willing to override the wishes of tribal governments. In 1950, Secretary of the Interior J. A. Krug signed a contract selling 155,000 acres of reservation land to the government for the construction of the Garrison Land and Reservoir Project. The project would cause large portions of the Fort Berthold reservation to be inundated. Here, the secretary signs the order before weeping members of the Fort Berthold Tribal Business Council, led by George Gillette, third from the left. Photo, courtesy Wide World Photos.

Indians considered best able to accommodate to the white man's world were sent from reservations to large cities where they were provided with housing and jobs. Some made the change successfully and settled permanently among the non-Indians, joining those who had preceded them during the war. Together they gave rise to a new category of "urban Indians," possessing their own special off-reservation needs and problems. Others became homesick, could not adjust to an alien culture and society, lost their jobs and homes, and landed on skid row or returned home.

The termination policy and the relocation program left broad wakes of human suffering and tragedy. Both also had historic consequences for Indians and non-Indians. Feared and opposed by virtually every tribe, termination gave strength and purpose to the Indians' leading national organization, the National Congress of American Indians (NCAI). Founded in 1944 and based in Washington, D.C., the NCAI helped mobilize the tribes, as well as non-

Indian organizations such as church groups, to oppose the new federal program. To the non-Indians, the injustice of a unilateral policy that brought widespread disorientation and new problems to the tribes was self-evident. But the crusade was also an educational process, for it spread new awareness and understanding of Indians and their need for a strong reservation land base among large non-Indian constituencies. Most important, the resistance to termination caused many whites to recognize the right of Indians to be Indian. This enlightenment, dawning first among longtime reformers and self-styled friends of the Indians whose churches and Indian-interest organizations had traditionally been assimilation oriented, heralded a fundamental change that would soon affect a large part of American society.

The opposition, the distress and dislocations brought to the tribes, and the financial and social loads placed on the affected states—all combined to persuade the Eisenhower administration finally to reverse itself, and in September 1958 it halted the implementation of termination without a tribe's consent. Although the policy remained on the books as a continuing threat to the Indians, actual termination came to an end. But enduring damage had been done to the progress of the Indians and to the future of federal-Indian relations. Not only had development under the IRA been aborted, but a confrontational environment had been created between the Indians and the federal government. For a long time afterward, tribes were suspicious of the motives of government actions and programs and resisted anything that risked opening the door to a renewal of termination.

At the same time, in their fight against termination Indians had gained strength in standing together and self-confidence in speaking for themselves and determining on their own what they did and did not want. Seeds of Indian self-determination and nationalism that would sprout and bloom during the following decades had been planted. Moreover, Indians had begun to project realism about themselves among the non-Indian population. Large numbers of whites were at last beginning to shed paternalistic attitudes, stereotyped thinking, and opposition to the existence of reservations and separate, distinct Indian cultures alongside the dominant culture.

Among both Indians and non-Indians, reaction to the termination period became manifest in the 1960s. The Democratic administrations of Kennedy and Johnson neither endorsed nor disavowed the termination policy, but by focusing on efforts to strengthen the reservations' economies and raise the Indians' standard of living, they revived some of the spirit of the IRA. Among the avenues pursued by the Democrats were stepped-up, but largely unsuccessful, attempts to persuade job-producing private industries to locate on the reservations and the encouragement of long-term leasing of reservation lands and resources by non-Indian development and energy corporations. Some persons maintained that such long-term leasing, accompanied by large-scale corporate investments, would shield the reservations against termination. On

Grandfather Hubert Rattler (Cherokee) and his grandson, Jubal (Cherokee, Otoe, Iowa, Lakota), together in Oklahoma City. Photo by Richard Ray Whitman.

the other hand, such leases amounted practically to the sale of tribal lands and resources by putting them almost indefinitely into the possession and control of non-Indians, and many Indians began to resist leasing, fearing a more subtle "termination by corporation." Moreover, as the years went by, the terms of such leases negotiated by the government on behalf of the tribes were seen to have been financially and environmentally detrimental to the Indians. By the 1970s, the Navajos, Northern Cheyennes, Crows, and other tribes were clamoring for the cancellation or renegotiation of these leases. Dissatisfaction reached a climax when the energy crisis made clear the true value of the enormous energy reserves on many western reservations. With the assistance of government funds, a number of tribes formed a Council of Energy Resource Tribes (CERT), hiring non-Indian experts to help them control the disposition of their resources, train their own people for management and, if possible, renegotiate past leases.

In the early 1960s the Indians had made a historic turn during the fight to end termination and with increasing assertiveness they were beginning to demand the right of self-determination. At a Chicago conference in 1961, several hundred Indians hinted at what was to come by asking the Kennedy administration to allow Indians to participate in the decision-making process of policies, programs, and budgets designed for the tribes. A group of young college-educated Indians who were at the conference were more impatient. Forming a National Indian Youth Council (NIYC), they dedicated themselves to reinstilling a sense of national pride among Indians. In the coming months and years, their demands for Red Power, the right of Indians to make their own decisions and manage their own affairs, and for the observance of the Indians' treaty rights by the white man's society gained the allegiance and support of many traditional peoples on the reservations. Their influence was also felt by many of the tribal political leaders, some of whom where shamed by being called "Uncle Tomahawks" and "apples" (red on the outside, white on the inside) because they had pliantly played the white man's game against the interests of their own people. Inevitably, the growing assertiveness of both the young and old helped to bring the Indians and their needs and demands to center stage on the American scene.

A number of significant forces underlay the Indians' growing cry for self-determination. Under pressure from the Indians, the provisions of two important antipoverty agencies established in the mid-1960s, the Area Redevelopment Administration (later reauthorized as the Economic Development Administration) and the Office of Economic Opportunity, were made available to them. Both were important breakthroughs because under the mechanisms of the acts the tribes for the first time were enabled to devise programs and budgets that they felt were needed and then administer and control the programs themselves. In practice, government bureaucrats did much to guide the Indians' important decisions, and the tribes acted more as agents of the government, administering the programs they received. But on the whole, this new level of control—which the BIA had always denied them—was deemed a success and led to congressional authorization of Indian inclusion, under similar circumstances, in Great Society educational, antipoverty, housing, and health programs. As funds from these programs poured onto the reservations, Indian leaders gained experience and self-confidence in managing tribal affairs, and the demand for even more self-government and self-determination swelled.

All this, meanwhile, was keeping pace with rapid changes in the world and in the United States, which were having effects on the Indians. The spread of nationalism, the emergence of Third World nations, the civil rights revolution in the United States, particularly the struggle of the blacks, the opposition to the Vietnam War, the self-examination of ethnocentricity, the new attention paid to all American minorities, the recognition of the values of cultural pluralism, and the search by Western youth for alternative cultures and lifestyles, all formed a context in which the Indians strove for what they wanted and to which—most significantly—they in turn made profound contributions of their own. During this period, Indians were changing quickly. Mobility was increasing, and more Indians than ever before were traveling from the reservations and becoming familiar with the white man's world. Educational and other measures were helping them to go to college and graduate schools and to master the techniques of modern-day communications, politics, and industry. At the same time a proliferation of Indian newspapers, Indian-written books such as Vine Deloria's *Custer Died for Your Sins*, and Indian creative work in the arts helped make them aware and proud of their own history, cultures, and ethnic uniqueness. In powwows and conferences, Indian nationalism grew; and while tribal identity continued to be important, a Pan-Indian spirit appeared, uniting Indians behind common causes. In line with the times, this spirit took on an activist stance, aroused initially by the NIYC but spreading quickly among groups of urban Indians, culminating ultimately in the emergence of the militant American Indian Movement founded in 1968 in Minneapolis.

Protesting scores of festering grievances and injustices, and demonstrating angrily for real self-determination, governments of the Indians' own choosing, and sovereignty—ideals given lip service since the days of John Collier but still far from realization—the nationalistic-minded urban Indian activists gained followers on the reservations and, supported by Indian spiritual teachers and other traditionalists, stirred the nation with dramatic confrontations at Alcatraz, the Bureau of Indian Affairs Building in Washington, D.C., Wounded Knee on the Pine Ridge reservation in South Dakota, and other sites throughout the country. Their violence-marked militancy commanded worldwide attention for Indians and their needs but was finally quieted by the bitter repression of law enforcement agencies. Nevertheless, the activists had embarrassed and nettled the federal government, and federal-Indian affairs—like the Indians themselves—would never be the same. In 1970 President Nixon announced that self-determination had taken the place of termination as the nation's Indian policy, and in 1975 a Democratic Congress passed an Indian Self-Determination and Education Assistance Act. The former was largely rhetoric; the latter, aside from authorizing the subcontracting of federal services to tribal groups and amending certain provisions of previous educational measures, still did little to advance meaningful self-determination. But the fact was that the Indians' drive for self-determination, now fifteen years in the making, had made a great impact on the attitudes of the non-Indian American population, not only toward Indians but toward their understanding of the modern age as well.

Initially, the blacks' civil rights movement had drawn attention to all of America's minorities and helped sensitize much of the nation to the presence of Indians and their needs. But most non-Indians had learned that the Indians' special and unique historical status precluded equating them with blacks or members of other minorities. To some, it was unsatisfactorily confusing and has remained so: the blacks appeared justly to want integration, the Indians wanted separatism, seemingly "un-American." But as the Indians' political visibility grew, questions were answered for increasing numbers of non-Indians. Interest in Indians was generated not only by the Indian activists but also by the media of the popular culture and by the intellectual and creative activities of Indians and non-Indians. The new discovery was both realistic and romantic. Widespread impacts were made by best-selling books like Dee Brown's *Bury My Heart at Wounded Knee*, by the Pulitzer Prize-winning writings of Kiowa N. Scott Momaday, and—particularly among those seeking alternative cultures—by the vastly influential *Black Elk Speaks*.

At the same time, Indians became positive, though somewhat unreal, symbols for environmentalists, idealistic liberals, and the alienated. Non-Indians, especially the young, traveled in droves to reservations, as if to Shangri-La, to seek the purity of Indian values, the wisdom of Indian spiritual teachers, and the timeless beauty and serenity of Indian life. To some, the quest turned out to be a mirage; to many others, the experience was rewarding and even life-changing.

In the cities, funds were raised for Indian causes by the radical chic. Wearing Indian jewelry and fashions was "in." Museums and galleries competed to display Indian art and artifacts; collectors outbid each other for paintings by R. C. Gorman, Fritz Scholder, and other Indian artists; for jewelry by the Hopi Charles Loloma; and for photographs of Indians by Edward Curtis. Prices for sets of Curtis's photographs, unnoticed and unwanted since first made earlier in the century, shot up overnight to more than $100,000. Indian impacts were reflected all through the dominant culture—by television documentaries filmed on reservations; by movies like *Little Big Man*, which were now sympathetic to Indians although they did little to explain them; and even by a special issue of *Life* magazine devoted entirely to Indians.

The revolution, of course, had a deep influence on academic life, affecting administrators, faculties, historians, and the publishers of textbooks. Colleges and universities—not always with the purest motives, for often they simply wanted government funds—established Indian studies courses, staffing them quite frequently with non-Indians who knew little or nothing about Indians or were just starting to learn about them. Young history professors turned to writing about Indians, finding a growing number of publishers who were anxious to meet the new demand for works on the First Americans. In time, universities searched for, and found, Indian teachers for the Indian-study courses, and Indians like Edward Dozier, Alfonso Ortiz, R. David Edmunds, and Veronica Tiller began to write and publish informed and deeply felt works on Indian histories and cultures.

Simultaneously, Indian organizations like the American Indian Historical Society in San Francisco, led by a Cahuilla intellectual, Rupert Costo, shook state educational groups by condemning state-adopted texts for their false and inadequate treatments of Indians. Faced with losing state adoptions, many textbook publishers tried hurriedly to correct old texts and to lecture their authors on the need to write new ones. Firms like McGraw-Hill instructed editors to eliminate offensive words like *squaw* and to become more sensitive about ethnocentric sentences.

The Indian influences enumerated above all came to be felt in the United States during the 1960s and 1970s, making Americans aware, at last, that the nation had a capacity for accepting plural cultures and institutions. That awareness permeated all aspects of life and affected thinking about the most fundamental concerns—religion, ethics, morality, even the cycle of existence from birth to death. During the Vietnam War, the cumulative impact of the new attitudes played a role in undermining the pervasiveness and consequences of ethnocentricity in the dominant culture. For a while it became almost an article of faith that a pattern of "killing Injuns," woven deep within the American fabric, ran in a straight line from the U.S. treatment of Indians, through the imperialistic ventures against the Filipinos, to the Korean and Vietnam wars, and that America had not learned from its relations with Indians the lesson that peoples of other cultures and values could not, and did not have to, accept what Americans believed was best for them, William McKinley, Woodrow Wilson, or Lyndon B. Johnson notwithstanding. It was widely held then that America, thanks to its new appreciation of Indians, was at last learning the lesson hammered home by the Vietnam experience. Later, many Americans seemed to forget the lesson, but awareness and criticism of their ethnocentricity have never been absent from recent public controversies surrounding American involvements in undeveloped areas of the world.

In the field of law, too, one can detect the modern-day Indians' impact on recent American history. During the fight for civil rights for minorities, the question of civil rights for Indians ran smack into the tribes' quest for self-determination, making clear once again the separateness of Indians within the

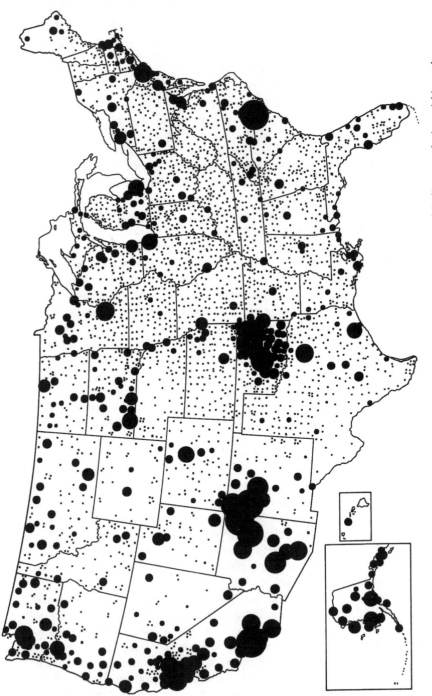

United States Indian Population as Reported in the 1980 Federal Census. Symbols represent total Indian population within each county.
Information taken from an original map by Professor F. P. Prucha.

American body politic. An Indian Civil Rights Act, passed in 1968 and extending the protection of some, but not all, of the Constitution's Bill of Rights to reservation Indians, accepted the existence of tribal laws based on cultural traditions distinct from those of the rest of the population. Avoiding interference with such laws, the act reflected a growing tendency to strengthen tribal governments, even if ultimate control over them was maintained by the federal government. To help fight Indian activists, the Nixon administration emphasized recognition and support of the tribal leaders and their own organization, the National Tribal Chairmen's Association. The trend has been apparent ever since. Court decisions, as well as legislation and executive branch actions, have underscored the tribal governments' rights to assert a growing number of police, taxation, and other powers. In 1982 a Tribal Government Tax Status Act was passed that authorized tribes to be treated as states under certain conditions.

In a way, the potential for the assertion of inherent powers of the tribes—first recognized by the clarifying memo of Collier and Margold in 1934—was at last being realized. The Tax Status Act of 1982 seemed to imply that the United States had become a nation of three types of governments—federal, state, and tribal—and, in truth, the Reagan administration began to argue that Indian affairs should rest on a government-to-government relationship. Actually, Indian tribes lacked the independence or authority of state governments since most of their funds came from the federal government and most of their important actions were still subject to approval by the secretary of the interior. When the Reagan administration cut Indian funds drastically in the 1980s, a dramatic rise in Indian unemployment and a return of hardship and suffering on reservations showed just how dependent the Indians still were on Washington, D.C.

Nevertheless, legal and political attitudes and perceptions had changed. Significant court decisions that ruled in favor of Indians against white adversaries in land, water, fishing rights, and other contentious issues produced public opinion backlashes against the Indians in the late 1970s. Sympathy for, and interest in, Indians eroded, and voices were again raised for termination. But the court decisions induced western state governments to take Indian rights more seriously than they had heretofore and, responding to pressure from the federal government, both tribes and states began negotiating with each other as if they were equals.

It is too early to assess the impact on America of the most recent developments in Indian affairs. Actions of both the executive and legislative branches of the national government have renewed Indian fears of federal termination. In the House of Representatives there is no longer a Committee on Indian Affairs, and few legislators paid serious attention to the work of the American Indian Policy Review Commission that Congress established in 1974. After two years of studies, undertaken mostly by Indians, the commission released its report in 1977. The document's 206 recommendations were largely ignored by Congress. One could almost hear again the voice of Senator Burton Wheeler: "What we are trying to do is get rid of the Indian problem rather than add to it."

During the 1970s, the Carter administration, in a somewhat confusing manner, dealt with Indians as if they were no different from the rest of the population and flirted for a while with the notion of ending the government's historic trust obligation to the tribes. The Reagan administration of the 1980s increased the confusion, acknowledging tribal governments and reservations but showing increasing signs that it would like to shed the financial burdens of Indian affairs. In addition to cutting spending for Indian services, Reaganites continued the Carter tradition of wanting to treat Indians like everyone else and warned the tribes that as the federal government withdraws from assisting them, they should turn to the states and to income-producing ventures with the private sector.

Several constants remain. It is certain that the federal government will not readily permit tribes to assume ultimate control over the disposition of their natural resources. But it is also certain that steps toward self-determination, increased self-government, and sovereignty—even some status of dependent nationhood as once articulated by Chief Justice John Marshall—will continue. It is certain, too, that the Indian presence, with its diverse heritage and cultures, will go on affecting the rest of the nation and will continue to require understanding and appreciation by all non-Indian Americans.

For Further Reading

Among works that provide valuable background overviews to recent American Indian history are *Indians and Other Americans: Two Ways of Life Meet* (New York, 1959) by Harold E. Fey and D'Arcy McNickle, and D'Arcy McNickle, *Native American Tribalism: Indian Survivals and Renewals* (New York, 1973).

The Nations Within (New York, 1984) by Vine Deloria, Jr., and Clifford Lytle is an excellent treatment of the developments leading to the Indian Reorganization Act, the history of the act itself, and many of its effects. *American Indians, American Justice* (Austin, 1983) by the same two authors, deals with the Indian judicial system.

Prominent among a large and growing literature on John Collier and the Indian New Deal are Kenneth R. Philp's *John Collier's Crusade for Indian Reform, 1920–54* (Tucson, 1977); Graham D. Taylor's *The New Deal and American Indian Tribalism: The Administration of the Indian Reorganization Act, 1934–45* (Lincoln, 1976); Donald L. Parman's *The Navajos and the New Deal* (New Haven, 1976); Laurence M. Hauptman's *The Iroquois and the New Deal* (Syracuse, 1981), and Thomas Biolsi's *Organizing the Lakota: The Political Economy of the New Deal on the Pine Ridge and Rosebud Reservations* (Tucson, 1992). For World War II and the termination period, see

Alison R. Bernstein's *American Indians and World War II: Toward a New Era in Indian Affairs* (Norman, 1991); Larry W. Burt's *Tribalism in Crisis: Federal Indian Policy, 1953–1961* (Albuquerque, 1982); and Donald L. Fixico's *Termination and Relocation: Federal Indian Policy, 1945–1961* (Albuquerque, 1986). Kenneth Philp, ed., *Indian Self-Rule: First-Hand Accounts of Indian-White Relations from Roosevelt to Reagan* (Salt Lake City, 1986) presents a helpful overview of the half century after passage of the IRA.

Various aspects of more recent history, including the Indians' quest for self-determination are dealt with in *The Indian: America's Unfinished Business* (Norman, 1966), compiled by William A. Brophy and Sophie D. Aberle; *Red Power* (New York, 1971) by Alvin M. Josephy, Jr.; *Education and the American Indian: The Road To Self-Determination, 1928–1973* (Albuquerque, 1974), by Margaret Connell Szasz; *Now That the Buffalo's Gone* (New York, 1982), by Alvin M. Josephy, Jr.; *The Return of the Native: American Indian Political Resurgence* (New York, 1988) by Stephen Cornell; *The Occupation of Alcatraz Island: Indian Self-Determination and the Rise of Indian Activism* (Urbana, 1996) by Troy R. Johnson; and *Like a Hurricane: The Indian Movement from Alcatraz to Wounded Knee* (New York, 1996) by Paul Chaat Smith and Robert Allen Warrior.

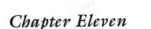

Chapter Eleven

The Struggle for Indian Civil Rights

W. Richard West, Jr.
Kevin Gover

L ike other ethnic minorities, American Indians have been subjected to discrimination by both governmental and private entities throughout the history of the United States. Unlike other minorities, however, Indian peoples' views of their rights under law extend beyond those expected by their fellow citizens to include a wide range of preferences, immunities, and prerogatives that arise not from their status as a racial minority but, rather, from their status as citizens of tribal governments.

The civil rights of Indian people are best understood, therefore, by separating them into two broad categories. The first category deals with those matters that we ordinarily think of as civil rights: the right to be free from discrimination on the basis of race; the right to vote; the right to due process of law, freedom of speech and religion, etc. And in the case of Indian people, these rights concern not only constitutional limitations on the power of state and federal governments but also limitations on the power of tribal governments. The second broad category includes the rights and disabilities of Indians as members of tribal bodies politic. The United States has established legal preferences, immunities, and disabilities that run directly to individual Indians as well as rights and immunities that flow through the tribal government. In both cases, though, it is tribal citizenship that creates the right or immunity.

In the late nineteenth century, the United States faced a critical decision in its conduct of relations with the Indian nations. The military conquest of the tribes was complete, the surviving tribes were confined to reservations comprising only small fractions of their domains, and many Indians lived on

Above: Detail from photo. See page 221.

government-furnished rations. In 1871, Congress passed a law providing that future relations with the tribes would not be conducted by treaty but, rather, by ordinary legislation approved by both houses.

The practical ability of the tribes to resist federal intrusion into their affairs having been destroyed, the exercise of federal power over Indians took an ugly turn. The federal-tribal relationship would be transformed from a solemn agreement between nations to that of a despotic guardian and a helpless ward. Ironically, Chief Justice John Marshall's description of the federal-tribal relationship would be used to ratify that transformation. Marshall had said in his landmark decision *Cherokee Nation v. Georgia* (1831) that the federal-tribal relationship resembled that between a guardian and his ward. At the end of the nineteenth century, Congress and the courts took these words to heart.

Increased federal intrusion into intratribal affairs was justified on the grounds that the tribes were dependent upon the United States for protection from hostile local populations. A telling example of this attitude is found in *United States v. Kagama* (1886), which upheld the validity of a federal statute imposing certain federal criminal laws on reservation Indians:

[T]hey are spoken of as "wards of the nation," "pupils," as local dependent communities. In this spirit the United States has conducted its relations to them from its organization to this time. . . .

. . . These Indian tribes *are* wards of the nation. They are communities dependent on the United States. . . . From their very weakness and helplessness, so largely due to the course of dealing of the Federal Government with them, and the treaties in which it has been promised, there arises the duty of protection, and with it the power.

The power of the General Government over these remnants of a race once powerful, now weak and diminished in numbers, is necessary to their protection, as well as to the safety of those among whom they dwell.

The Court's focus on the dependence of the tribes on the federal government and the duty and power arising from that dependence left the federal government with virtually unlimited power both to decide what course was best for the Indians and to act upon that decision without regard for the wishes of the Indians themselves. Under the guise of "protecting" the Indians, the government launched a full-scale assault on the most fundamental right of the Indian tribes—the right to maintain distinct political and cultural communities.

This assault took the form of the allotment policy, by which tribal lands were parceled out to adult members and "surplus" lands were opened to non-Indian settlement. The underlying philosophy of the allotment policy was that the tribal lifestyle bred sloth and dependence upon the generosity of others, while American free enterprise bred initiative and independence. Only through the pride of individual ownership of land might Indians be introduced to the benefits of American society and, ultimately, become full-fledged, church-going, tax-paying American citizens.

The tribes resisted allotment, but the United States was not about to be deterred by their protests. The government staged "negotiations" with the tribes, but the agreements that resulted were tainted by duress, coercion, forgery, and fraud. The courts participated in this charade. Although American constitutional law accorded almost sacred importance to vested property rights, Indian property rights, established by treaty, received no protection. In *Lone Wolf* v. *Hitchcock* (1903), Kiowa chief Lone Wolf challenged the validity of the "agreement" by which Kiowa, Comanche, and Apache lands were allotted and sold to whites. Despite clear evidence of fraud and the breach of the 1867 treaty with the tribes, the Court would grant no relief:

> The power exists to abrogate the provisions of an Indian treaty, though presumably such power will be exercised only when circumstances arise which will not only justify the government in disregarding the stipulations of the treaty, but may demand, in the interest of the country and the Indians themselves, that it should do so. . . .
>
> In view of the legislative power possessed by Congress over treaties with the Indians, and Indian tribal property, we may not specially consider [the allegations of fraud], since all these matters, in any event, were solely within the domain of the legislative authority and its action is conclusive upon the courts.

Theoretically, then, congressional power could be exercised only for the good of the Indians. But the Court would not second-guess Congress as to what was or was not good for the Indians. Thus, congressional power was unlimited under the *Lone Wolf* doctrine.

The racist basis of this vast congressional authority finds expression in a remarkable passage in the case of *United States* v. *Sandoval* (1913). In *Sandoval*, the issue was whether Pueblo Indians—whose sedentary, agrarian lifestyles distinguished them from the hunting nomads of the plains states—were "Indians" subject to vast congressional power. The Court found that they were:

> Always living in separate and isolated communities, adhering to primitive modes of life, largely influenced by superstition and fetishism, and chiefly governed according to crude customs inherited from their ancestors, [Pueblo Indians] are essentially a simple, uninformed and inferior people.
>
> . . . As a superior and civilized nation [the United Stares has both] the power and the duty of exercising a fostering care and protection over all dependent Indian communities within its borders. . . .

The Pueblo people had survived hundreds of years of Spanish rule, carved gardens from the desert, and created a theology so complex as to baffle anthropologists, yet were branded as "simple" and "superstitious" and, therefore, subject to Congress's plenary power.

The assault on Indian tribalism was not limited to undermining tribal patterns of land ownership. Tribal governmental institutions were ignored by federal agents, and entities based upon American modes of government were established to discredit traditional tribal leaders. Far worse was the direct suppression of tribal religious practices. Christian missionaries were imported into tribal communities and subsidized by the federal government. Tribal religious ceremonies and dances actually were outlawed by zealous federal agents firmly convinced of the propriety of their efforts to Christianize the Indians.

Far from bringing Indians to the prosperity enjoyed by white Americans, the assimilationist policies devastated the Indians, both collectively and individually. Ninety million acres, two-thirds of the tribal land base, were lost through sales of "surplus" lands, land thieves, and tax sales. A cycle of abject poverty was begun that only recently has shown signs of breaking. Sickness and ignorance were endemic. Far from showing Indians the benefits of American civilization, the assimilationist policies nurtured a firm resolve in the Indians to cling to tribal structures.

During the early twentieth century, Indians who used peyote in their religious rituals were often subjected to federal harassment and prosecution. One of the most prominent peyotists of this era was Quanah Parker, pictured here (front row, second from left) with other members of the Comanche community. Courtesy, National Anthropological Archives.

The assimilation era was the darkest hour of Indian civil rights history. Despite constitutional guarantees, Indians' rights of free speech, free exercise of religion, and property were disregarded. More significantly still, the right of Indian tribes to maintain a distinct political and cultural existence was violated intentionally and systematically. This damage to Indian well-being has yet to be repaired.

A new era, an era of reform, began in 1924 when all Indians were made citizens of the United States. Many Indians already had become citizens in the early 1900s through "competency commissions" established to determine whether particular Indians had adjusted to the majority culture sufficiently to be released from government guardianship. One might expect the Indians to have been anxious to be declared "competent." In fact, however, the declaration of competency was resisted by many, perhaps most, Indians because competency meant the end of federal protection of Indian-owned allotments. Many thousands of new citizen Indians saw their land removed from trust or restricted status, rendering the land alienable and taxable. Such lands soon were lost—taken by fraud or state tax sales.

Unlike the grant of citizenship through competency commissions, the 1924 Indian citizenship act, fortunately, did not terminate the federal duty of protecting Indians and their property. Indians thus were the beneficiaries of a unique status. They enjoyed not only the rights and privileges of American citizenship but also the rights and privileges of membership in distinct tribal political communities. The operative assumption of federal policymakers in 1924 was that the tribes eventually would disappear and Indians would be citizens only of federal and state governments. When that assumption proved false and the tribes refused to disappear, what resulted was the special dual citizenship enjoyed by Indians today.

In the 1920s, however, tribal citizenship generally meant that one was poor, ignorant, and sick. Despite all of the promises made when Indian lands were allotted, the United States failed to provide the support services necessary for Indians to make the radical transition from tribal communal lifestyles to the individualism of the majority culture. The Indians rejected the individualistic philosophy of the Americans and continued to practice and abide by tribal customs and mores. Not surprisingly, they were swallowed up by their more competitive, more greedy neighbors. By 1928 it was apparent that the allotment policy had failed miserably. A study of Indian policy was commissioned, and the resulting report, the Meriam Report, revealed to the world the pitiful condition of the Indians. The American Indian Policy Review Commission in 1977 summarized the findings as follows:

> The income of the typical Indian family was low. . . . Only 2 percent of the Indians had incomes over $500 a year. Partly as a result of this poverty the health of the Indians in comparison with the rest of the population was

bad. The death rate and infant mortality were high. Tuberculosis and trachoma were extremely prevalent. Living and housing conditions were appalling; diet was poor; sanitary provisions were generally lacking. The system of public health administration and relief work was inadequate. The educational system had no well-considered broad educational policy. A uniform curriculum was being applied throughout the Indian school system, although the different tribes were at quite different stages of development. Indian children were being fed at reservation schools on an average expenditure of 11 cents a day per child, and were being forced to do heavy domestic work actually to ease the financial burden but ostensibly to acquire training in useful industrial arts.

A new wave of humanitarian sympathy for the Indians swept the liberal community. Many felt partly responsible for these conditions, since the humanitarian organizations had backed the allotment policy.

The policy that emerged from the social activism of the 1930s was based on the proposition that there was a place for Indian tribes in modern America. Under the leadership of Commissioner of Indian Affairs John Collier, a policy of restoring tribal governments to their rightful place was adopted. The Indian Reorganization Act (IRA) of 1934 allowed tribes to enact constitutions for their tribal governments and renounced the allotment policy. Tribal governmental structures were recognized as the appropriate means for effecting federal policies towards Indians. The right of Indian people to maintain distinct political communities was recognized by Congress for the first time in over half a century. The assumption that tribes would disappear no longer was the basis for federal Indian policy.'

Ironically, the enthusiasm with which the federal officials pursued the new policy led to serious intrusions into the Indians' right to choose. Indeed, Collier himself led the charge for ratification of IRA constitutions that more often than not reflected some bureaucrat's notion of how traditional tribal structures might be converted to modern constitutional bodies. Many tribes had IRA constitutions foisted upon them against the wishes of a clear majority of tribal members. Most Indians remained suspicious and reluctant to be involved in any government scheme to help them.

Nevertheless, reform proceeded apace. Tribal governments were reorganized and began to reassert their authority over Indian reservations. Health and education services were improved, and Indians began to recover from the injury caused by the allotment policy. The reform movement, however, was short-lived.

With the end of the Great Depression and the beginning of World War II, America turned to other priorities. The federal Indian budget was slashed, and Collier's policy came under sharp attack from congressional critics whose constituents were unhappy with the renewal of tribal authority. Much of this unhappiness was rooted in simple racism, but some was based on the fact that non-Indian businessmen no longer had free reign to plunder reservation resources. The amount of money necessary for the administration of Indian affairs was another source of congressional displeasure. Also significant was a bizarre ideological attack born of the anticommunist hysteria of the day. Indian tribalism came to be viewed as distinctly un-American and, indeed, communistic. The stage thus was set for yet another assault on Indian tribalism.

The rallying cry for the new assault on tribalism was a familiar one. Indians, it was said, needed to be brought into the mainstream of American life, entitled to the same rights and privileges and subject to the same laws. As always, the policy was deemed to be in the best interests of the Indians, notwithstanding the almost universal opposition of the Indians themselves.

The policy was called "termination." It involved the dismantling of tribal government, the distribution of tribal assets to tribal members, and the end of federal services to individual Indians. Sponsors of the legislation spoke euphemistically of "emancipating" the Indians from federal domination. Why emancipation from federal control should require the destruction of tribal government is a question left unanswered.

The assimilationist policy took other forms as well. A program of voluntary relocation of Indians from reservations to urban areas was begun. Indian families were provided with funds for moving expenses to cities, placed in poor housing, provided with menial jobs, and then abandoned. The result was the creation of dreadfully poor urban Indian communities in such places as Chicago, Los Angeles, and New York City.

Tribal authority and federal responsibilities were weakened further by Public Law 280, a statute that transferred criminal and civil jurisdiction over Indian country from the federal government to certain states. Other states were given the option of assuming jurisdiction over reservation areas at their convenience. Responsibility for the health and education of Indians slowly was being transferred to the states through other legislation. The federal government was trying to get out of the business of dealing with Indian tribes.

Ironically, even as this assault on the Indian right of self-government was under way, the rights of Indians as American citizens were being established firmly in the courts. Despite the 1924 grant of citizenship to Indians, many states continued to discriminate against Indians for purposes of voting, jury duty, and providing testimony in court. This discrimination fell to the commands of the Fourteenth and Fifteenth amendments. Even as the NAACP carefully litigated test cases leading to the abandonment of the separate but equal doctrine in the South, activist lawyers were chipping away at state laws that discriminated against Indians on the basis of their race.

As was true for American blacks, the rights of Indians that existed on paper often were denied in practice. Racism towards Indians in the communities in which they lived was as prevalent and overt as racism towards blacks in the South. Racial epithets and petty discrimination in service establishments were a part of Indian life for the first half of the twentieth century. Indians, therefore, were to become the direct beneficiaries of the civil rights revolution of the 1960s.

By 1960, the termination policy was discredited. Those Indian tribes that were terminated fell quickly into ruin, and their members became burdens on state welfare rolls. The resources of terminated tribes were plundered by non-Indian business interests. Even the advocates of the policy had begun to question its wisdom.

As the civil rights movement gained strength, Indian-interest organizations became active participants. Indian demands were the same as those of other minorities in terms of the rights of citizenship. In another respect, however, they were fundamentally different. Indians asserted not only their constitutional rights as members of the American body politic but also their right to maintain distinct political and cultural communities. In short, Indians were asserting a right to be different.

They met with success on both fronts. This success is reflected in both the legislation and the judicial decisions of the sixties and early seventies. Indians routinely were made beneficiaries of civil rights legislation such as the Voting Rights Act, the Fair Housing Act, and the Equal Employment Opportunity Act. The Voting Rights Act, for example, not only prohibits discrimination against Indians but also creates special protections for them as persons whose primary language is not English.

Reflecting the fact that Indian rights go beyond those afforded to other citizens, however, special provisions were included in civil rights legislation. The Equal Employment Opportunity Act, for instance, excludes from its prohibition on discrimination programs granting employment preferences to Indians by employers on or near Indian reservations. On its face, this seems ripe for an attack on the grounds of reverse discrimination. In *Morton v. Mancari* (1974), however, the Supreme Court upheld a statute granting preference to Indians for employment in the Bureau of Indian Affairs and the Indian Health Service. The Court reasoned that the preference was not one based on race but, rather, one based on the unique political relationship between Indian nations and the United States. As a preference based on political status rather than race, it only needed to be "tied rationally" to the fulfillment of federal obligations to the Indians to be upheld as constitutional. It was not subject to the "strict scrutiny" applied to racial classifications under the Fifth Amendment.

The status of tribes as distinct political communities was recognized as well in much of the social legislation spawned by the civil rights movement. New Frontier and Great Society programs such as the Office of Economic Opportunity's Headstart and Community Action programs, the Elementary and Secondary Education Act, and the Comprehensive Older Americans Act

John Kennedy's 1962 meeting with tribal representatives led by the Crows' Edison Real Bird symbolized a shift away from termination. Kennedy's secretary of the interior, Stewart L. Udall, looks on. Courtesy, The Newberry Library.

all expressly included Indian tribes as governments eligible for participation. The influence of these heady days of the civil rights movement on Indian tribes and people can hardly be overstated. Aside from placing the weight of the law on the tribes' side and providing economic resources to Indian communities, perhaps the most important aspect was a renewal of Indian confidence and pride. Termination had bred a certain timidity. If a tribe had even modest economic success, it became a candidate for termination. Termination could be avoided, however, if the tribe were poor and docile. The civil rights movement changed all of this. Indians came to learn that they could assert their rights successfully without fear of termination.

An interesting aspect of the combined civil rights movement and the rejuvenation of tribal self-government was the passage of the Indian Civil Rights Act of 1968. Because of their unique political status and the absence of any express limitations on their powers in the Constitution, Indian tribes were not subject to the same restrictions on governmental action as were federal and state governments. As tribal governments began to exercise their long-dormant powers, concern was raised that Indians were unprotected from ar-

IMMIGRATION
OFFICE

" PAPERS ? "

Indian humor has always been an important aspect of Native American culture, but in the 1960s and 1970s much of that humor was aimed at white stereotypes. Here, cartoonist Robert Freeman lampoons the conventional picture of New England's pilgrim fathers. Courtesy, The Newberry Library.

bitrary and harmful actions of tribal officials. Congress decided to look into the state of Indian civil rights.

Tribal leaders were not thrilled at the prospect of having their actions reviewed by federal tribunals. Many opposed the legislation on the grounds that it represented an attempt to impose non-Indian values on tribal societies. Others believed that the act would result in costly lawsuits against the tribes by antagonistic non-Indians and dissident tribal members with no genuine complaint. Such fears were well-founded, but Congress deemed unacceptable the existence of governmental bodies without legal restraints on their exercise of official power.

The result was the Indian Civil Rights Act. The act, in essence, requires tribal governments to afford to persons under its jurisdiction the civil rights guaranteed by the Constitution. Tribal concerns, however, were accommodated in several respects. The freedom of religion provision included the right of free exercise of religion but not the prohibition on the establishment of a state religion. A number of tribal governments are theocratic, and Congress protected these governments in the act. Another difference between the act and the Bill of Rights involves the right to counsel in criminal proceedings. By 1968 the Supreme Court required states and the federal government to pay for attorneys for indigent criminal defendants. Tribal budgets could not bear such an expense. Congress, therefore, provided that criminal defendants in tribal courts were entitled to counsel, but only at their own expense.

Another difference between the act and the Constitution was a limitation on the punishments tribal courts could impose on persons convicted of crimes. The act limits criminal sentences in tribal courts to six months of imprisonment and $500 fines. The reasoning behind this limitation was that, under the Major Crimes Act of 1883, the federal government was responsible for prosecuting most felonies involving Indian offenders. The problem with this reasoning is that federal investigators and prosecutors often are less than diligent in responding to reservation crime. If federal officials fail to act, tribal officials are left to address serious crimes with minimal sentences.

Not specifically addressed was another of the tribes' objections—the fear that large numbers of federal lawsuits would be brought against tribal officials. The act was vague on the question of whether such suits were proper, and for ten years the federal courts regularly entertained them. In 1978, however, the Supreme Court ruled in *Santa Clara Pueblo* v. *Martinez* that the act did not authorize federal court suits except for those involving persons held in tribal custody. With the single exception, therefore, of petitions for writs of

Despite their civil rights victories, modern Indian communities continued to think of themselves as different from others. This group of Ute drummers at Fort Duchesne, Utah, reflects that desire. Left to right: Harvey Myanna, Billy Chapoose, Clark Tanna, Johnson Wopsock, and unidentified. Courtesy, The Newberry Library.

habeas corpus, persons aggrieved by official tribal action affecting rights guaranteed by the act must make their claims in tribal forums.

Although tribal opposition to the act was widespread, it was not universal. Many provisions of the act clearly were in the tribes' interests and encountered no opposition. States were prohibited from exerting further jurisdiction under Public Law 280 without the consent of the affected tribes, and retrocession of state jurisdiction already existing under Public Law 280 was authorized. Other provisions were directed at providing financial and technical support to tribal courts. Finally, the act required the secretary of the interior to revise certain materials relating to federal Indian law, including a revision of Felix Cohen's classic treatise *Federal Indian Law*. The inclusion of these provisions softened tribal opposition to the act and, indeed, led some tribes to support the bill.

Even as the general civil rights struggle was winding down, Indians were gearing up for an initiative that would take them beyond even the dramatic gains of the 1960s. Their rights as American citizens were firmly established, in law if not always in fact. The time now had come to assert their rights as tribal citizens, rights born of the tribes' status as domestic nations and confirmed by hundreds of treaties. Treaty rights and the right of tribal self-government would become the new focus of Indian efforts.

Perhaps the primary battleground in the field of treaty rights was a remote site on the Nisqually River in the state of Washington known as Frank's Landing. In the 1850s, the Treaty of Point Elliott was signed by Indian nations in Washington Territory and approved by Congress. Among the treaty's provisions was a guarantee that Indians would retain the right of "taking fish at usual and accustomed grounds . . . in common with all citizens of the territory." The Indians exercised this right for one hundred years before non-Indians began to challenge their fishing activities. Despite a 1963 federal court decision sustaining the Indians' rights, state courts enjoined Indian net fishing. A series of protests followed in which Indian fishermen were arrested and jailed by state officials. Allegations of police brutality fell on deaf ears. Despite continuing success in federal court, the treaty fishermen were harassed, threatened and, in one case at least, shot by local non-Indian residents.

The Indians persisted until a dramatic court decision held that they were entitled to nearly 50 percent of the annual salmon harvest. The non-Indian citizenry was enraged, but the decision survived review after review until, in 1979, the Supreme Court itself affirmed the decision in all key respects. Against all odds, the Indians prevailed in protecting rights recognized over a century earlier, and established that treaty rights do not fade with time. The allocation of resources made in the treaties was ruled binding on the descendants of the treating parties, notwithstanding the different circumstances that now exist in Indian country and surrounding communities.

Rights more than a century old were being redeemed in the eastern United States as well. Attorneys for several eastern tribes, including tribes that long had been neglected by federal authorities, discovered a startling fact. Many treaties and other documents taking land from the eastern tribes never were ratified by Congress as was required by the Trade and Intercourse Acts of the eighteenth and nineteenth centuries. Under the plain language of the acts, such transactions were void and of no effect. These cases presented a critical test of America's commitment to the rule of law. Although some claims were nearly two hundred years old, ancient rules of law established for the benefit of Indian tribes, if followed, would result in court victories for the tribes. Despite intense political pressure from the affected states and their residents, the lower federal courts ruled favorably on the Indian claims in case after case. Although many of the claims were settled out of court by the parties (and the settlements approved by Congress), others remained in court until, in 1984, the Supreme Court agreed to hear a case involving title to 100,000 acres in New York state. Finally, in *County of Oneida* v. *Oneida Indian Nation* (1985), the Supreme Court upheld the Indian claims. Thus, wrongs committed almost two centuries ago still could be addressed by the courts and lost rights restored.

Tribal rights of self-government also were redeemed in the Indians' legal offensive. State power over reservation Indians was curtailed in the areas of taxation, civil court jurisdiction, and Indian child welfare proceedings. Tribal authority over non-Indians in Indian country, though denied in criminal proceedings, was affirmed in other areas. Despite significant defeats in court, the legal offensive generally was quite effective, and the governmental authority of Indian tribes, dormant for so long, was asserted broadly and effectively.

Tribal rights of self-government were redeemed in the legislative arena as well. The termination policy was renounced formally through the restoration of the Menominee Tribe of Wisconsin in 1973 and several other tribes thereafter. The Indian Self-Determination Act of 1975 gave tribes the ability to administer federal assistance programs and wrest control of such programs from the government officials who had dominated reservation affairs for a century. The Indian Child Welfare Act of 1978 placed the welfare of Indian children squarely within tribal forums and limited state power in this critical area, state power that too often had resulted in Indian children being removed and isolated from their tribal communities. The American Indian Religious Freedom Act of 1979 recognized the validity of traditional Indian religious practices and pledged to honor and accommodate such practices.

All of these developments during the seventies and eighties resulted from the civil rights movement of the 1960s. Indians built on the progress made in the sixties to register these important legal victories in the seventies. In a very real sense, therefore, it was the civil rights movement that made these victories possible.

Still, the rights claimed by the Indians were different from those claimed by other minorities. The civil rights movement was responsible for the vindication of the rights of Indians as individuals. The vindication of tribal rights, however, could be accomplished only by the Indians themselves. Thus, while the tribal rights movement of the 1970s grew out of the general struggle for civil rights of the previous decade, the struggle for tribal rights was distinctively Indian because the rights claimed were distinctively Indian rights—rights held by no other people in the country.

No discussion of the Indian rights movement is complete without some mention of the militant wing of the movement. Although the American Indian Movement (AIM) probably never had the influence in the Indian community that the American media believed it had, it did reflect accurately the frustration and anger felt by all Indians, at least to some degree. The seizure of Alcatraz Island in 1969, the takeover of the Bureau of Indian Affairs headquarters in 1972, and the siege at Wounded Knee, South Dakota, in 1973 all served to focus public attention on the injustice of Indian life. Like all militant movements, AIM was born of the belief among young, poor people that the system that dominated them was incapable of reform from within.

Measuring the impact of AIM is difficult. Its ability to focus attention on Indian conditions was beneficial to some degree. The claims and demands of AIM, however, did not always reflect the position of legitimate tribal authorities. AIM activities frequently heightened tensions between Indians and whites and, indeed, among the Indians themselves. AIM's presence in certain

Sadie Curtis weaves a fifty-star flag on a traditional Navajo loom to commemorate the bicentennial of the United States in 1976. Photo by Jerry Jacka.

communities, particularly the Pine Ridge Reservation in South Dakota, resulted in brutal crackdowns by federal authorities that involved systematic violations of the civil liberties of persons not affiliated with AIM. Such crackdowns, of course, were not the fault of AIM; however, to the extent that such crackdowns were predictable, AIM did a disservice by choosing to agitate in particular communities.

All in all, the militant Indian movement probably was helpful, if only because it demonstrated the commitment of Indian people to the redemption of their rights and the extremes that were possible if legitimate Indian demands were not honored. Like the other militant organizations of the time, AIM's visibility and influence have diminished, in no small part because of official harassment and campaigns to discredit it.

The gains made in the sixties and seventies gave rise to an ominous tide of support for organizations dedicated to dismantling tribal treaty and governmental rights. This backlash had its roots in the philosophy of those who preach the idea of reverse discrimination. This philosophy holds that the current generation of white Americans is not responsible for past violations of minority rights and should not be made to suffer in efforts to redress past injustices. Whatever merit this idea may have in other contexts, it is intellectually bankrupt in its application to Indian treaty rights.

Indian treaty rights were not created by any act of generosity. They represent, instead, the quid pro quo for cessions of vast amounts of tribal land. The settlers who entered these lands did so on the basis of those treaties. The Indians have made no demand that those lands be returned or that the rights of non-Indians under the treaties be abrogated. Why Indians should be expected to give up their rights under the treaties is most difficult to understand. In the end, the backlash movement was troublesome and worrisome but did not score any major successes, at least in Congress.

One can say quite accurately that legally the American Indians of today are better off than at any time in the past century. Even so, much remains to be done. In its 1979 report on America's compliance with the human rights accords, the United States said that:

> Native Americans, on the average, have the lowest per capita income, the highest unemployment rate, the lowest level of educational attainment, the shortest lives, the worst health and housing conditions and the highest suicide rate in the United States. The poverty among Indian families is nearly three times greater than the rate for non-Indian families and Native people collectively rank at the bottom of every social and economic statistical indicator.

This is the legacy of past failures to honor the rights of Indian people, both as human beings and as members of distinct tribal political communities. America's treatment of Indians, even more than its treatment of other minorities, re-

Even as a growing proportion of Indians chose to live in large cities, they continued to seek out other Native Americans for social and political support. Here a crew from the Chicago American Indian Center's canoe club paddles along that city's lakefront. Photo by Orlando Cabanban.

flects the rise and fall of its democratic faith. The central issue remains the same. Whether future generations will honor the special rights of Indians acknowledged by past generations remains an open question and a challenge for all Americans.

For Further Reading

Two law school textbooks provide excellent introductions to the field of Indian civil rights: *Cases and Materials in Federal Indian Law*, 3rd ed. (St. Paul, 1993), by David H. Getches, Charles F. Wilkinson, and Robert A. Williams, Jr.; and *American Indian Law: Cases and Materials*, 3rd ed. (Charlottesville, 1991), by Robert N. Clinton, Neil Jessup Newton, and Monroe E. Price. West Publishing Company's Nutshell Series provides brief coverage of the topic; see William C. Canby, *American Indian Law* (St. Paul, 1981).

Government publications are also a good source of information regarding federal policy and the law. The most important of these are Charles T. Kappler's compilation, *Indian Affairs: Laws and Treaties*, 5 vols. (New York, 1941); the American Indian Policy Review Commission's *Final Report* (Washington, D.C., 1977); Felix Cohen's classic treatise, reissued in 1982, *Handbook of Federal Indian Law* (Charlottesville, 1982); and a publication of the U.S. Commission on Civil Rights, *Indian Tribes: A Continuing Quest for Survival* (Washington, D.C., 1981).

For commentaries on contemporary Indian rights, see the *American Indian Law Review*, published by the University of Oklahoma, and the *Indian Law Reporter*. John R. Wunder analyzes many recent issues in *"Retained by the People": A History of American Indians and the Bill of Rights* (New York, 1994). Water rights and fishing rights are considered in Daniel L. Boxberger, *To Fish in Common: The Ethnohistory of Lummi Indian Salmon Fishing* (Lincoln, 1989); Lloyd Burton, *American Indian Water Rights and the Limits of Law* (Lawrence, 1991); Fay G. Cohen, *Treaties on Trial: The Continuing Controversy Over Northwest Fishing Rights* (Seattle, 1986); Robert Doherty, *Disputed Waters: Native Americans and the Great Lakes Fishery* (Lexington, 1990); and Thomas R. McGuire, et al., eds., *Indian Water in the New West* (Tucson, 1994). Among the noteworthy commentaries on land claims and Indian rights are Thomas Berger's analysis of the Alaska native claims process, *Village Journey: A Report of the Alaska Native Review Commission* (New York, 1985); accounts of the eastern land claims process by Paul Brodeur, *Restitution: The Land Claims of the Mashpee, Passamaquoddy, and Penobscot Indians of New England* (Boston, 1985), and Jack Campisi, *The Mashpee Indians: Tribe on Trial* (Syracuse, 1991); and a presentation of the Zuni Pueblo's efforts in E. Richard Hart, ed., *Zunis and the Courts: A Struggle for Sovereign Land Rights* (Lawrence, 1995). Frank Pommersheim, *Braid of Feathers: American Indian Law and Contemporary Tribal Life* (Berkeley, 1995); Sharon O'Brien, *American Indian Tribal Governments* (Norman, 1989); and Vine Deloria, Jr., ed., *American Indian Policy in the Twentieth Century* (Norman, 1985) also contain valuable discussions of Indian legal and political issues.

Chapter Twelve

The 1970s:
New Leaders
for Indian Country

Mark N. Trahant

*F*rom the 1970s emerged a new spirit of Indian country leadership. During what can, in retrospect, be viewed as an important and distinct era, tribal governments increased their authority over people, programs, and resources. Federal paternalism was greatly diminished during this era, and the Bureau of Indian Affairs (BIA) started to shift its focus towards serving tribal governments, instead of managing Indian affairs. This was the end of the "Indian agent," now called an agency superintendent, who was for decades the BIA's local representative and sole authority on reservation governance. But by the end of the 1970s, the superintendent had become subservient, the real day-to-day authority on most reservations rested with the chairman, president, governor, or chief selected by tribal members.

Consider this era in the context of one election for a tribal council in Washington state. The Colville Tribe rejected a national policy that promoted the end of the reservation system, or termination. This community's action helped inaugurate this period as a time for new leadership.

In October 1966, the Colville Tribe polled its members on the federal policy of termination. A "yes" answer suggested ending the tribe's relationship with the United States and the eventual liquidation of tribally owned assets, distributed equally among members. The result was one-sided: more than two-thirds of the membership approved of termination. The poll occurred a year after the Colville Business Council rejected a BIA plan to build a $14 million lumber mill on the reservation. The Business Council, led by Chairman Narcisse Nicholson, Jr., said the tribe did not want to borrow money

Above: Detail from photo. See page 246.

for the project, even if it were to create new jobs. Moreover, Nicholson said it was time for the Colville people to stop taking money from the BIA and to terminate the reservation government itself. He said the case was clear because "with only a relatively few exceptions, the tribal families of today are self-supporting." He added, "Lack of employment, to the degree that it exists, is largely due to character faults which cannot be cured by paternalism." Even though he personally opposed termination, BIA Commissioner Robert L. Bennett told Congress in 1966 that he would "honor and carry out any decisions that are made by the people of the tribe, whether or not this may be in agreement or disagreement with what may happen to be particular policy of the Bureau." The U.S. Senate had passed several Colville termination bills and the House was expected to approve comparable legislation. There was, at least in 1966, overwhelming support for termination, starting with a solid majority on the Colville Business Council.

At this point, however, new leaders stepped forward to argue against termination. One of them was Lucy Covington who, representing the minority voice on the Colville Business Council, challenged every aspect of termination at every opportunity. At a 1966 tribal leaders' conference in Spokane, Covington followed Nicholson to challenge his version of Colville progress. She cited statistics that showed bleaker conditions on the reservation: only 20

Lucy Covington (right) with Emily Peone. Photograph by Corky Covington.

percent of the membership had high school diplomas, the on-reservation population was substantially below non-Indian neighbors in health, housing, and income. "The point was being made that these people would suffer immeasurably from termination," she said. Quoting from a congressional hearing record, Covington observed that of the 676 males living on the reservation only 89 had full-time jobs.

Over the next five years Covington and her allies sought to quiet what she termed "the present fever and fervor for termination." Covington published *Our Heritage,* a newspaper reminding tribal members what was at stake. The newspaper profiled candidates opposed to termination and reported on recent lobbying efforts to stop termination bills.

On May 8, 1971, those efforts were rewarded at the polls. Nicholson was defeated in his district, Omak. He was replaced by a termination opponent—and the new majority on the business council rejected termination. Mel Tonasket, thirty years old at the time, was then elected by the business council as chairman. The new business council called for more federal support, closed a reservation lake to outsiders, and voted to take back law enforcement powers that had been ceded to the state of Washington. The new council also went further, claiming the inherent power of a government through an affirmation of tribal sovereignty.

"We are a sovereignty within a sovereignty, and we must be allowed to rule ourselves," Chairman Tonasket said. "The Colvilles are not trying to get even with anyone, but are just trying to protect their rights as Indians." The election on Colville had brought an official end to the old policy of termination. From now on, the new language from Colville and from other tribal communities would speak of sovereignty.

Senator Henry M. Jackson and President Richard M. Nixon also demonstrated that times had changed. Jackson, a Democrat from Washington, had routinely sponsored termination bills. Yet in 1972, he introduced a repeal of House Concurrent Resolution 108—the termination resolution of 1952. Jackson voiced his support for the unique relationship between American Indians and the federal government, for self-determination, and for the government to protect Indian lands, resources, and cultural rights.

President Nixon sent a message to Congress on July 20, 1970, in which he formally rejected termination as national policy. "As a matter of justice and as a matter of enlightened social policy," Nixon asserted, "we must begin to act on the basis of what the Indians themselves have been telling us." The president proclaimed: "The time has come to break decisively with the past and to create the conditions for a new era in which the Indian future is determined by Indian acts and Indian decisions."

The next few years yielded a significant record. The people of Taos Pueblo in New Mexico and the Yakamas of Washington had sacred lands returned to them. The Indian Self-Determination and Education Assistance Act of 1975 encouraged tribal governments to take over federal programs and run them directly. In addition, Congress passed a host of laws designed to improve health and economic conditions on reservations.

Commissioner of Indian Affairs Louis Bruce (Mohawk-Sioux) underlined the transition. "Since I came to Washington in 1969, the face of Indian country has undergone some dramatic and far-reaching changes," he said. "Not in this century has there been such a volume of creative turbulence in Indian country. The will for self-determination has become a vital component of the thinking of Indian leadership. . . . It is an irreversible trend, a tide in the destiny of American Indians that will eventually compel all of America once and for all to recognize the dignity and human rights of Indian people."

Tribal leaders across the United States spoke of their determination that decisions would be made in tribal capitals rather than in Washington, D.C., by the BIA. Rather than seek positions within the bureau—the old route to a safe bureaucratic career—these new leaders attempted to find other means to achieve their personal goals. They understood that the BIA's power had been reduced because money from federal social programs now went directly to the tribes. The words of Vine Deloria, Jr. (Standing Rock Sioux) carried a call for leadership. "In every generation," he wrote, "there will arise a Brant, a Tecumseh, a Chief Joseph, a Joseph Garry, to carry the people yet one decade further."

Federal programs, in fact, furnished training for future leaders. At the University of New Mexico, the American Indian Law Center started a pre-law summer school funded by the Office of Economic Opportunity. A Boston law professor, Fred Hart, designed an eight-week legal boot camp. The program sought to produce successful Indian lawyers. It worked with students who wanted to become attorneys, even though many of them had yet to be accepted to law school. The law center tried both to prepare these students for and to place them in law schools.

In an article written for the *New Mexico Law Review*, director P. Sam Deloria (Standing Rock Sioux) summarized the center's achievements: "The program quickly gained a reputation among law schools for being accurate and honest in its recommendations, rather than short-sightedly running up the score with placements of students who would not be successful." At the time of the center's inception, only 25 Indian lawyers and 15 Indian law students could be identified in the United States. By 1996 the 25 had become about 1,500. Nearly half of the Native attorneys had graduated from the summer law institute. In the crucial transitional years of the 1970s nearly all of the new Indian attorneys came through the New Mexico program.

"The impact has been impossible to measure," Deloria wrote, "because it's been so great." He observed: "Indian lawyers, summer program alumni, are found throughout Indian affairs: tribal attorneys, tribal chairpersons, tribal chief judges, supreme court justices, trial judges (as well as a growing number of state and municipal judges); tribal attorney generals (and one state attorney general) and a United States attorney. Indian lawyers can be found throughout the Interior Solicitor's Office, the Bureau of Indian Affairs, the House Subcommittee on Native American Affairs, and the Senate Select Subcommittee on Indian Affairs staff."

Ada Deer graduated from the New Mexico program but did not become an attorney. She dropped out of law school to help lead the fight to restore reservation status for her people, the Menominees of Wisconsin. Deer moved to Washington, D.C., to lobby. "I talked to everyone I could," she recalled. "I held meetings with reporters. I held meetings with legislative aides. I went around to receptions. I smiled. I shook hands. I prepared bumper stickers and fact sheets and made it look like there were thousands of Indians screaming about termination. That's part of what it takes to get a bill through the Congress." In 1973 President Nixon signed the Menominee Restoration Act. Deer went on to win election as tribal chairperson and later served in the first term of the Clinton administration as assistant secretary of the interior for Indian affairs.

The quest for Native land took on a different dimension in Alaska. Oil and timber companies were demanding that Native land claims be settled so that development could proceed. The pressure for a settlement increased after a discovery of oil in 1968. Some observers called the proposed congressional settlement a new termination bill. Others labeled it the last major treaty.

"Let's turn it around and look at the real situation. The Natives are being forced to give up their land under the traditional American principle of manifest destiny and all they're asking is a fair shake," wrote Tom Richards, Jr., a Native from Kotzebue. He covered the Alaska land claims for *The Tundra Times* (then published in Fairbanks) and the American Indian Press Association. "The clincher in all this gumbo," Richards added, "is blanket termination."

This negotiation was different, Richards concluded, because it was too late to kill off the Indians before signing a treaty. "Somebody goofed," he wrote. "It was poetic justice. The country wept for its sins against Indian people, and up jumps a huge Indian land fight and Indians had the best chance of winning. Unfortunately, at the time, there were those who perpetuated the traditional means of resolving Indian issues." During the hearings, Representative John Saylor, a Republican from Pennsylvania, noted his staff had researched this country's transactions with Indian tribes. Richards quoted Saylor: "We have found that we paid Indians an average of 50 cents per acre and I suggest to pay Alaskan Natives more than that amount may be unfair to other tribes with whom we have already settled."

Fair or not, the Alaska settlement *was* different. Instead of promoting sovereign tribes in Alaska, the Alaska Native Claims Settlement Act (ANCSA) of 1971 created regional Native-owned corporations. Native people once claimed 375 million acres in the state. With one stroke of the pen that amount was reduced to 44 million acres. The December 8, 1971, signing ceremony, Richards wrote, "was the last major land treaty between the U.S. government and the aboriginal inhabitants of this country."

Canadian jurist Thomas Berger concluded that some people hailed the settlement as a "new departure" because "Alaska Natives would have land, capital, corporations, and opportunities to enter the business world. " Writing in *Village Journey,* the report of the Alaska Native Review Commission, Berger argued that Henry Jackson and other backers of ANCSA desired Natives to enter the American mainstream; they thus opposed the continuance of reservations and the empowerment of tribal governments.

The law granted nearly $1 billion to the twelve new regional corporations. The corporations were charged with making a profit from their land and resources. Each Alaskan Native received 100 shares in a regional corporation, as well as 100 shares in a village corporation. Berger called ANCSA "the result of an encounter between two very different societies." He summarized the conflict:

> ANCSA can be understood only in the context if this encounter, this conflict between two cultures. The focus of this conflict is the land. To one culture the land is inalienable. Alaskan Natives believe that the land is held in common by the tribe, a political community that is perpetual. Every member of the community in succeeding generations acquires an interest in the land as a birthright. But to a Western society, land is a commodity to be bought and sold. The Native peoples clearly understand that the land is at the heart of this prolonged conflict. The protection of the land has always been their primary concern.

The land claims, and the new corporate structures, also promoted the emergence of new leaders among Alaskan Natives. The new, well-funded corporations gave power to their spokespersons. For example, in 1970 Roy Huhndorf went to work for the Alaska Federation of Natives (AFN), the statewide coalition representing the interests of elected Native leaders. He had been a truck driver before an injury to his back forced a change in occupation. "I needed to go to school," he recalled, "and I began to think about another trade, because I was not going to do this until I was 65 years old. So I began going to college at night." He worked for AFN managing a federal program that placed underskilled workers in on-the-job training. Then he worked as a director of an Indian health program, another federally funded agency. In 1975 Huhndorf became president of Cook Inlet Regional Corporation.

He described the challenges of running a Native corporation:

> . . . we couldn't take a lot of risk, because the people who owned the corporation were poor, and it would depend on the corporations being

around for a long time, and providing those dividends . . . our shareholders . . . were not the usual shareholders, because of their . . . locked-in status. They couldn't sell stock. . . . So we took a fairly conservative approach.

Most of Cook Inlet's ventures were partnerships with natural resource companies. The corporation also invested in real estate, buying up surplus federal land and Anchorage developments. A decade after the settlement, Cook Inlet's shareholder value was greater than when it was created. Cook Inlet had made a profit, but some Native corporations reported staggering losses and others faired marginally well at best. Village corporations in more rural areas faced an even tougher challenge because they were created with fewer capital resources. A decade after ANCSA's passage, the future of Native corporations remained uncertain.

In the lower forty-eight states, many tribal governments also managed programs involving millions of dollars. Responsibility for such management required people to possess new skills and exercise new authority. The story of Joe DeLaCruz traces a common route taken by many people to positions of tribal leadership.

A Quinault, Joe DeLaCruz grew up on the reservation along the Washington coast. He was the son of a labor leader and came from a well-known family. DeLaCruz earned recognition as an athlete before leaving home in the 1950s to join the army. After college he went to work for the federal Housing and Urban Development Administration in Portland, Oregon.

At the request of tribal elders, DeLaCruz returned home. Soon he was elected president of the tribe. "When I returned home in 1967," DeLaCruz remembered, "the fisheries were pretty much down, the timber industry was in decline, the mills that people had normally worked in were all shut down, and it was pretty basically depressed, this was one of the most depressed little community, I guess you might say, in the whole state of Washington."

"The other thing that was happening," DeLaCruz added, "is that real estate speculators were coming on the reservation and buying fee land and starting to set up real estate developments and the tribe didn't like that." The Quinault reservation, with its miles of Pacific coastline, provided an ideal home—or second home—for people who could afford the vista. In fact, with the resorts, holiday cottages, and large timber companies, non-Indians owned more than one-third of the reservation.

As president, DeLaCruz began to exercise the tribe's inherent powers. He claimed sovereignty over tribal boundaries, not just the land owned by Indians. First, the Quinault Council stopped a highway that would have opened up more development and logging in a pristine stretch north of the Quinault River. Today the bridge across the river is still called "the road to nowhere" because the road ends a few hundred feet north of the bridge. The tribe also enacted stiff zoning laws that applied to non-Indian residents. These ordinances virtually prevented the creation of new subdivisions and other real estate development. Most tribal members lived in Tahola, at the mouth of the Quinault River, but, encouraged by the tribal actions, many of them started to buy the vacation houses and cottages along the coast from non-Indians.

Joe DeLaCruz's most controversial act, however, was to close the reservation beaches to non-Indians. Every spring, the Quinault Beach yielded an ideal site for digging clams. But the tribe no longer wanted the crowds nor the trash they left behind on their land. The Quinault Nation in the summer of 1969 thus officially regained control of its land through halting access by nonmembers to its beaches.

"I can recall an example where some surfers didn't believe we were serious," DeLaCruz said. "It was almost automatic, within minutes there was like a hundred pickups and cars of Indians coming down here. Those poor surfers were heading for Japan or China; one of our guys fired a rifle in the air and they came in and we confiscated their surfboards and took them down to the tribal headquarters. Of course, that got into the papers." Walter Cronkite reported the story for the CBS *Evening News* on August 25, 1969, and again on the following day. He referred to "Indians on the warpath."

The closure of the beach presented a prelude to the Native American empowerment of the 1970s. It represented action over words. Real, substantial change was taking place within many tribal governments. But most national attention was focused on the younger, charismatic leaders from the American Indian Movement (AIM), an urban Indian group founded in Minneapolis in 1968, who generally dismissed tribal government officials as BIA collaborators. Television, and to a lesser extent print media, embedded in memory the militant actions of the decade. Indian country, if not the nation, recalls the takeover of Alcatraz Island, the Washington headquarters of the BIA, and of the village of Wounded Knee in South Dakota.

What kind of memory is it? Many reminisce in a romantic haze no less thick than one generated by Hollywood filmmakers through their stories about American Indians. The Indian militancy of the 1970s may be our new myth, a theme for movies ranging from "Billy Jack" to "Thunderheart." And why not? Within Indian country, tens of thousands claim solidarity—if not actual presence—with AIM and its activities.

In their ground-breaking book, *Like A Hurricane: The Indian Movement from Alcatraz to Wounded Knee,* authors Paul Chaat Smith (Comanche) and Robert Allen Warrior (Osage) have revealed a more complicated, honest view of the era's history and AIM itself.

"AIM seemed less a political organization than a force of nature," Smith and Warrior write. "It had become a kind of prairie hurricane, wreaking havoc on one place until seemingly defeated and spent, only to inexplicably reappear weeks later somewhere else."

What Smith and Warrior call a "force of nature" was not staged by AIM. Alcatraz, a small island in San Francisco Bay, was the site of a famous federal prison. The facility was completely abandoned in 1962. Two years later an American Indian group traveled by boat to the island and claimed it for all tribes. This symbolic act was followed over the next five years by more serious proposals to build a Native American community center at Alcatraz. Then, on November 29, 1969, seventy-eight American Indians, mostly college students, arrived on the island by boat. This was an occupation force, reclaiming Native land. The island called "The Rock" became a source of pride because it showed that Indians could still defeat an enemy. The young people living there promoted ideas such as a cultural center, a university, and a home for all California tribes. But life was difficult at the crumbling prison—and dangerous. On January 3, 1971, a twelve-year-old child fell to her death from a prison stairwell. The *San Francisco Chronicle* said drunkenness and mindless vandalism had replaced the noble goals of those who had originally occupied the island. Most of the students had moved on, replaced by people who specifically came to Alcatraz for the excitement.

Some nineteen months later, when the occupation was officially ended by federal agents, Smith and Warrior write, "the symbol had become an embarrassment, a tasteless, even lethal joke and an insult to the lofty dreams of the early days." But Alcatraz had also been a lesson in what works, that "sympathetic media and guerrilla theater could generate instant attention, and place Indian issues hardly anyone in the press had ever cared about before on the front pages of major newspapers around the country and around the world."

Although Alcatraz was not an operation of the American Indian Movement, the experience, and some of the leadership, fueled AIM activities elsewhere. Smith and Warrior write: "The organization was reaching out toward a traditional Indian past, becoming a warrior society of old combined with the attitude and language of third-world rebels of the 1970s."

AIM's presence was national by 1972 when a march was organized to showcase the unfair treatment of American Indians by the U.S. government. The Trail of Broken Treaties started in three cities, Seattle, San Francisco, and Los Angeles. The protest was carefully crafted as peaceful.

However, Smith and Warrior contend that this rebellion was almost by accident. When the march arrived in Washington, D.C., planners had not found a place to stay for the arriving caravans of American Indians. "What happened was not a political conspiracy but a logistics meltdown," Smith and Warrior write. A ramshackle church proved workable as a host, and the protestors moved to the BIA building because, said one, "we own that son of a bitch." A few hours later about 500 American Indians occupied the building and, over the next few two weeks, turned it into the Native American Embassy. While living in the building, the occupiers also destroyed works of art, documents, and parts of the building itself. Eight days later, encouraged by a federal grant of "travel money," the protestors left and went home. Other than providing theater, and perhaps a trashed building, the only tangible result of the takeover of the BIA headquarters was for the Department of the

Cartoon by Charles Trimble for the American Indian Press Association.

Interior to move the agency's headquarter staff into the much larger department headquarters. What had been the BIA's building became an Interior Department adjunct facility.

The guerilla action that captured the most attention was, of course, the siege at Wounded Knee on the Pine Ridge reservation in South Dakota. Many Oglala Sioux people were early supporters of AIM, viewing the organization as a traditional alternative to the officially elected tribal government chaired by Dick Wilson. AIM was invited to Pine Ridge by one Oglala community group in 1973 as a reform agent.

Tribal factions are not unique. In any society there are almost political parties based on family ties, race (full-bloods or mixed-bloods) and philosophy. Such was the case at Pine Ridge. However, unlike previous tribal chairmen, Wilson acted as an executive—many called him a dictator—with absolute authority. He also created his own armed security force, known as the GOONs or Guardians of the Oglala Nation.

On February 28, 1973, members of AIM and their Oglala allies occupied a small trading post in the village of Wounded Knee. The site was chosen because of its historical significance, the army's 1890 attack on Big Foot's band.

Wounded Knee quickly made it to television, a major story on all three networks. AIM presented its demands based on the 1868 Sioux Treaty, and it called for federal hearings to investigate Wilson's tribal government.

The U.S. government responded to the occupation with a massive, heavily armed force led by the FBI. The government ignored or did not understand internal tribal division. Thus, Smith and Warrior write, when machine guns were set up, the government did not understand that it was taking the side of Dick Wilson. "The military played a central role in determining government strategy, concealing its presence with the simple yet brilliantly effective strategy of insisting that the colonels and generals sent to Pine Ridge wear civilian clothes at all times," write Smith and Warrior. The military called it "Operation Garden Plot."

The seventy-one-day occupation of the village captured the world's attention. But Wounded Knee, say Smith and Warrior, "proved to be the final performance of AIM's daring brand of political theater. As quickly as Indian radicalism had exploded on the national stage, it faded, disintegrating under the weight of its own internal contradictions and divisions, and a relentless legal assault by federal and state governments."

Two people died during the siege. In 1974, Russell Means and Dennis Banks, the two stars of the AIM leadership, were tried separately for their role at Wounded Knee. The two men used the media attention they received to place the U.S. government on trial, citing the harsh conditions at Pine Ridge. A judge dismissed the charges against them.

Means later told the American Indian Press Association that Wounded Knee "did not destroy the tribal government and we didn't destroy the Bureau of Indian Affairs." But Wounded Knee changed perceptions. "Little Indian girls are now writing essays in school saying Indian men are brave and great. There's a new image for Indian children. Wounded Knee bridged the gap between the young Indians and the old in South Dakota. They are together now in mind and spirit."

Many tribal leaders viewed Wounded Knee as a disaster. A few of them, however, argued that AIM and the tribes should work together for a "common Indian front." Vine Deloria, Jr., supported a coalition of the National Congress of American Indians (NCAI), the more conservative National Tribal Chairmen's Association (NTCA), and AIM. Deloria suggested the NCAI could become "an exclusive lobbying organization," the NCAI could "handle all tribal affairs with the BIA," while AIM could provide "the 'activist punch' that any solid movement needs." "At times," Deloria noted, "the bureaucracy needs a swift kick in the you-guessed it."

Despite Deloria's plea, most tribal leaders remained distant from AIM. Many of them perceived the violence associated with the occupation of the BIA offices and Wounded Knee as more damaging that helpful. Moreover, many tribal chairmen saw AIM as a movement of urban rather than reservation Indians and they distrusted the AIM leadership. The coalition could not be formed.

Perhaps the most powerful—and complicated—leader of the 1970s was Peter MacDonald, Sr.(Navajo). Like the leaders of AIM, MacDonald recognized the importance of promotion and theater. He found ways to make himself the story. MacDonald also had no love for the BIA and quickly made the agency the enemy.

MacDonald was born in 1928 near the small community of Teec Nos Pos, Arizona. His family tended sheep. The federal government's livestock reduction program in the 1930s decimated his family's herd. His family never recovered from this action, and the trauma remained a vivid memory for the young Navajo boy named Hoshkaisith Begay. Sent to boarding school in nearby Shiprock, New Mexico, he received a new name: Peter MacDonald.

When he was twelve years old, MacDonald ran away from school. Three years later he joined the U.S. Marines as an underage volunteer. After his enlistment, he attended Bacone College, a private two-year college for Indian students in Muskogee, Oklahoma. He transferred to the University of Okla-

Peter MacDonald. From the Arizona Republic, *January 15, 1989. Photograph by M. Ging. Reproduced by permission.*

homa, where he obtained a degree in engineering. He then moved to California, where for six years he worked with Hughes Aircraft as an engineer and project manager.

But MacDonald was determined to return home to the Navajo reservation, especially after seeing the way the BIA treated the Navajo tribal council in a session. "The council was engaged in a heated debate," MacDonald remembered, and the BIA official pounded on his podium and ordered the body to be quiet. "Then he said, 'if you guys continue to act like children, I'm going to throw every one of you out of this council chamber and I'm going to put a padlock on it.'" Furious, MacDonald knew he had to help change this situation. "One of these days," he told himself, "it's not going to be that way."

His public career began in 1963. MacDonald assumed responsibility for running the Office of Navajo Economic Opportunity (ONEO). Funded by the federal Office of Economic Opportunity rather than the BIA, the program built reservation infrastructure, including community centers, rodeo grounds, and offices. ONEO offered him an ideal platform from which to enter politics, because it affected the lives of so many Navajos.

MacDonald soon sought the tribal chairmanship, but his first bid for office was in 1969, when he ran for the presidency of the NCAI. Unlike most Indian communities, the Navajos did not belong to this organization. This separation mirrored the tendency of the Navajo Tribe not to be closely allied with other groups. A joke is often told in Indian country about how there are Indians—and then there are Navajos. As a youth, MacDonald said he did not think of himself as an Indian, because he didn't wear feathers like Indians did in the movies. Now he wanted to become NCAI's leader and he promised that if elected president, the Navajo Nation would join NCAI. However, Blackfeet Chairman Earl Old Person gained the presidency.

A few months later MacDonald sought office at home. He defeated the incumbent, Raymond Nakai, to become Chairman of the Navajo Tribal Council. He promptly convinced the BIA to turn over title of the council chambers and offices to the Navajo Tribe. Then he changed the locks. Never again would a BIA official threatened the Navajo tribal council in its own house of government.

MacDonald promoted himself as a new Indian leader. He was named a delegate to the Republican national convention in 1972. "Dear Peter," ran the letter he released to the news media, "it is good to know that we can count on the leadership you provided in August to help bring us victory in November." The letter was signed, "RN."

A brilliant politician, MacDonald was occasionally far ahead of his time. For example, he once announced a plan to permit gambling—dice and cards—at the annual Navajo Fair. After the press gave considerable attention to the idea, MacDonald retorted that the episode had been "exaggerated." The proposal, he suggested, was "nothing more than a large Las Vegas night."

MacDonald also spoke to the goal of Native self-sufficiency. At a news conference in Albuquerque, he announced that the Navajo Nation would be self-sufficient in ten years. For the plan to work, though, the federal government had to double its spending on Navajo programs. In fact, the federal government did more than double its spending on the Navajo reservation from MacDonald's initial election in 1970 until his defeat in 1982. Much of that money went directly to the tribal government he operated.

Federal spending opened the doors of education for thousands of Navajos. At Tsaile, Arizona, in the center of the reservation, federal funding built Navajo Community College, the first institution of higher education controlled by a tribe. Dozens of new schools were constructed on the reservation, allowing children to stay home with their families instead of being shunted off to boarding schools.

MacDonald's view of Washington differed from that of most tribal leaders. He went to the Capitol as an equal. MacDonald saw himself as equivalent to a member of Congress or a governor of a state. He often gained what he wanted in Washington, but on one matter he could not prevail. This issue involved a land dispute with the Hopi Tribe; this ongoing controversy severely harmed MacDonald's career.

The Hopis had gone to court to obtain lands they contended the Navajos had usurped from them. In 1962 the federal court ruled that both tribes were entitled to equal use of the "Joint Use Area." The court said it could not partition the property—that would have to be left to Congress. Navajo influence in Washington proved sufficient for years to kill any proposed legislation to divide the disputed estate: the Navajo Nation hired lobbyists, and MacDonald regularly appeared in Washington to plead the Navajo cause.

Though the Hopis were a much smaller community than the Navajos, they were adept at gaining public sympathy for their position. Arizona senator Barry Goldwater championed the Hopi cause. "What we have here is the richest Indian nation in the country using their muscle and downright lies to defeat the Hopis," Goldwater once alleged. Eventually the Hopis prevailed and thousands of Navajos were ordered to move from lands that had been awarded to the Hopis.

As MacDonald fought a last-ditch, unsuccessful battle, he spoke more and more about the potential for violence. He told one committee he could not "respect" anyone who did not fight for their homes. MacDonald promised to block personally the relocation of any Navajo families who lived on the lands now granted to the Hopis.

The rift between MacDonald and Goldwater continued to widen. MacDonald supported the Democratic candidate for governor, Raul Castro, in 1974; in a close election, the Navajo vote for Castro helped Castro defeat Goldwater's old friend, the incumbent governor Jack Williams. The Navajos also voted overwhelmingly for Goldwater's opponent in the same election.

In 1975 and 1976 audits of the Navajo Tribe's housing program and the Navajo Fair produced a number of indictments. Although MacDonald was not indicted, he claimed he was a target because of his past confrontations with Goldwater. Soon thereafter MacDonald did face indictment and was charged in U.S. district court with fraud and income tax evasion.

MacDonald ultimately was acquitted, when U.S. District Court Judge Herb P. Sorg of Pittsburgh ascertained the federal government had not proved that a federal crime had been committed. One of the assistant United States attorneys who had prosecuted the case expressed his displeasure with the outcome. Ken Fields charged that corruption on the Navajo reservation "ran rampant" and clearly believed that MacDonald had been guilty. According to Fields, one witness had testified that he picked up cash for the Navajo chairman. "If they wanted the business, they had to pay the price," Fields said. Defeated for re-election in 1982, MacDonald won back the chairmanship in 1986, only to be forced from office and sent to federal prison because of his conviction on subsequent charges of corruption.

Nonetheless, during the 1970s MacDonald played a major role in asserting the rights of Indian communities. He recognized the need for tribes to work together when possible to pursue a common goal. Thus MacDonald became a vital force in the Council of Energy Resource Tribes (CERT), a consortium of Indian nations seeking to obtain maximum return for the development of their minerals. While CERT offered a useful means for Indian tribes to pool the technical assistance and counsel they needed, another initiative MacDonald championed was stillborn.

In 1978 MacDonald called for the formation of the Native American Treaty Rights Organization (NATRO). He said that NATRO would be a "coordinating command post along the lines of the Allied headquarters during World War II" and equated NATRO to NATO—the North Atlantic Treaty Organization. However, few Indian leaders bought into MacDonald's call for the tribes to demand sovereignty in unison, and NATRO failed to materialize.

Nonetheless, MacDonald had ample reason for concern about the status of Indian rights. In regions where tribes competed for scarce natural resources or asserted jurisdiction, new non-Indian organizations formed in an attempt to stop the movement toward greater tribal sovereignty. Many American Indians saw this backlash as a new form of termination, and they feared that Congress would enact the extreme measures these groups started to advocate. Hopi journalist Rose Robinson expressed these anxieties:

> So strong is the threat and so pervasive is its national presence that Indians are referring to it as "the new Indian war." Its sources, most observers of the national Indian scene agree, are the results of that very progress, in particular, the long and significant train of court victories in the 1970s upholding tribal rights. . . . Whatever its sources, white backlash is, by every measure, the major concern of people today.

The backlash was promoted by organizations with names that suggested a noble calling: South Dakotans for Civil Liberties, Montanans Opposed to Discrimination, and the Interstate Congress for Equal Rights and Responsibilities (ICERR). These groups defined American Indians as "special citizens" who, because of treaty rights, were getting a better deal than other Americans. The ICERR sent a book, *Indian Treaties: America's Nightmare,* to members of Congress, the secretary of the interior, and other Washington officials. The organization charged that "The liberal treatment of minorities has reached unheard of proportions in denying equal rights to all citizens of our so-called democracy. . . . Sportsmens (sic)—organizations—fishermen—hunters—land owners—commercial fishermen and just plain tax paying citizens who have just about had it with Indian take-overs make up the membership of ICERR."

The backlash soon evolved into a national movement that threatened the very existence of tribal governments. "That the Indians' claims are being given any legitimacy at all is nonsensical," wrote a columnist in the *Boston Herald American.* Most people who took part in the backlash had emotional reasons for doing so. They were hunters or fishers competing with Indians for the same resources. Certain congressional representatives also began to speak out against Indian rights. These people tended to hail from states where the issue had become hotly debated.

Lloyd Meeds, a Democratic congressman from Washington, had been honored in 1974 by the NCAI for his legislative contributions to Native American issues. For example, he had supported the restoration of trust status for the Menominees. But when federal court judge George Boldt awarded up to half of the harvestable salmon in Washington state to Indians, Meeds changed his direction.

In 1977 Meeds wrote dissenting views for the American Indian Policy Review Commission's final report. Meeds acknowledged that "Substantial decision-making by Indians over events which control their lives should be allowed. Legislative action should come from a sincere and realistic desire to continue the special relationship between Indians and the federal government." "But," Meeds continued, "we must not legislate out of a sense of guilt or excessive zeal to cure all sins and inequities of the past. . . . Where tribal aspirations collide with constitutional values, the tribe's interests must yield. Nor can the rights of the non-Indian majority be compromised to support tribal aspirations. Doing justice by Indians does not require doing injustices to non-Indians."

During that same year Meeds introduced a resolution in Congress calling for the abrogation of treaties made with Indian tribes. He said it was time to end the "dual citizenship" of American Indians. Meeds's position gained additional attention nationally because treaty rights no longer could be considered only a western matter. Indian land claims in the state of Maine brought the matter to the fore.

In 1972, the Passamaquoddies and Penobscots of Maine asked the U.S. Justice Department to file on their behalf a claim for 12.5 million acres, or nearly two-thirds of the state. The tribes based their requests on the 1790 Non-Intercourse Act that barred states from negotiating with tribes without congressional authority. When the courts agreed that the Non-Intercourse Act could be applied to this claim, the issue suddenly became a serious one for New Englanders. The Passamaquoddies and Penobscots had lost their lands through negotiations that had not be authorized by Congress.

Most non-Indians resisted the continuing relevance of treaties or acts of Congress dating back to nearly two hundred years ago. The *Boston Herald American* decided "Whatever happened 200 years ago, the culprits were not the current land owners, so there is no justification for punishing them." Frank Trippett, in a two-page essay published in *Time,* asked: "After so many quiet years, what has got into the Indians?" Trippett essentially blamed attorneys for the situation. "The Native American Rights Fund," he observed, "the largest organization specializing in Indian law, opened its headquarters six years ago with ten cases; today it handles almost 400 cases in 40 states."

Time said Congress and President Jimmy Carter would ultimately have to decide what was fair for Indian claims. "Probably no other country would take quite so seriously land claims that propose, in effect, the impossible rolling back of history," it reasoned. "The inherent absurdity of such a proposition might be clearer, say, in a suggestion that Australia be handed back to the aborigines. . . . Congress should be able to be fair without suffering the delusion that the country can really be given back to the Indians. The time for that passed forever with the vanishing of the pioneers who took it from them." Ultimately passage of the Maine Indian Settlement Act (Public Law 96-420) in 1980 resolved the Maine land claims. The Passamaquoddies split $80 million, with the money used to purchase 300,000 acres once owned by the tribes and employed to begin new industries. The leadership of Passamaquoddy governor John Stevens, together with the efforts of able legal counsel, had resulted in an important triumph.

During much of the 1970s the courts appeared to be supportive of promoting tribal sovereignty. But late in the decade, the Supreme Court ended its support of treaty rights and began to take the side of states and other competing interests. In 1978, for example, the Court ruled in *Oliphant* v. *Suquamish Tribe* that the Suquamish Tribe of Washington did not have criminal jurisdiction over non-Indians within the boundaries of its reservation. This decision made it difficult for tribal police to enforce the law on reservations and added to an already complicated maze of questions involving criminal jurisdiction in Indian country.

The election of Ronald Reagan in 1980 also marked a significant change in federal-Indian relations. Reagan affirmed the importance of tribal governments and tribal self-determination. However, in his first budget, Reagan cut funding for non-BIA or Indian Health Service programs by more than one-third. Appropriations for legal services, housing, economic development, and job training all were slashed. The same programs that helped create a generation of Indian leaders were being dismantled.

Peter MacDonald predicted a difficult time ahead. He believed the budget cuts would push reservation unemployment to new levels. Indian leaders also decried the statements of Secretary of the Interior James Watt, who declared reservations were bastions of socialism. Reagan also made comments unveiling his limited understanding of Indian history and the contemporary problems confronting Indian communities.

As the 1980s began, the leaders who had come to the fore in the 1970s prepared for new battles over an old objective. "It is our judgment that the goal of Indian self-sufficiency is indeed a matter of over-riding importance," wrote Ada Deer, Jake Whitecrow, and Louis Bruce in the 1977 report for the American Indian Policy Review Commission. "Every single Indian tribe in this nation aspires to this goal."

For Further Reading

Unfortunately, there are few books written about Indian country during the 1970s. One good summary, both a history and a current affairs primer, is the "Final Report" of the American Indian Policy Review Commission (Washington, D.C., 1977). The report is available in many libraries in the government documents section.

Tribal Assets: The Rebirth of Indian America (New York, 1990) by Robert White is a good overview of the economic initiatives by tribes during this period. The Navajo-Hopi land dispute is chronicled by Jerry Kammer in *The Second Long Walk* (Albuquerque, 1980). Problems facing Alaskan Natives are explored in *Village Journey: A Report of the Alaska Native Review Commission* (New York, 1985) by Thomas R. Berger. The best history of Indian activists is Paul Chaat Smith and Robert Allen Warrior, *Like a Hurricane: The Indian Movement from Alcatraz to Wounded Knee* (New York, 1996). Finally, P. Sam Deloria profiles the success of pre-law students in "The American Indian Law Center: An Informal History," published in the Spring 1994 issue of *New Mexico Law Review*.

Chapter Thirteen

The Hearts of Nations:
American Indian Women in the Twentieth Century

Paivi Hoikkala

> A nation is not conquered
> Until the hearts of its women
> Are on the ground.
> Then it is done, no matter
> How brave its warriors
> Nor how strong its weapons.
>
> CHEYENNE SAYING

*I*n August 1996, Carol Redcherries, a Northern Cheyenne, rose to address the audience gathered at the Autry Museum of Western Heritage in Los Angeles for the symposium "Inventing Custer." Dressed in a stylish blue dress and wearing high heels, Grandma Redcherries, as other members of the Little Bighorn Battlefield National Monument Advisory Committee called her, spoke to the power of women in Indian communities. She talked about her life: growing up in Montana, joining the armed forces and serving in the Middle East, attending law school, and returning home where she found herself Chief Justice of the Northern Cheyenne Appellate Court—and an elder. It is the latter of these roles that Carol Redcherries sees as her most important duty: to perpetuate the stories of the past. She has been able to successfully combine that past with the present, and in doing so, attests to the central role of women in American Indian societies.

Although often invisible in historical accounts, Indian women have always been actors, not passive bystanders, in their tribal communities. Today Native American women are as diverse a group as were their foremothers

Above: Maria Martinez design. See page 260.

This pair of photographs of a group of Zuni children reflects the social roles white reformers established for Indians who entered their "humanitarian" institutions. Girls were to shed their jewelry and blankets in favor of heavy leather shoes, aprons, and sunbonnets. Courtesy, The Newberry Library.

when Europeans first reached the shores of what is now America. They live on reservations and in urban areas; many are brought up in their tribal cultures while others grow up in the mainstream. They are people of different nations, languages, and cultures. Yet, they have at least one thing in common: they are American Indian women. Furthermore, many of them continue to rely on notions of womanhood and community passed on to them through tribal tradition to rebuild their communities shattered by years of federal neglect and apathy. More than ever, women are the pillars of their nations.

Traditional Native America perceived gender roles in terms of biology, and most tribes assigned women tasks based on their reproductive and nurturing functions. However, being a wife and a mother did not preclude participation in other activities. Matrilineal tribes afforded women many opportunities in the realms of politics, economy, religion, and the family. The female figures in the creation stories of such tribes provide ample testimony of the status of women in these societies. The Cherokees tell of Corn Mother, or Selu, who cut open her breast so that corn could spring forth and give life to the people. Blue Corn Woman and White Corn Maiden were the first mothers of the Pueblo people. And the Iroquois believe that they were born into this world from the mud on the back of the Earth, or Grandmother Turtle. Patrilineal societies placed great importance on male-focused behavior, such as warfare and hunting, and their spiritual world was inhabited by male gods and spirits. Yet, they too recognized the importance of women in their societies, and women exercised power within their strictly defined maternal and nurturing roles in the community.

The arrival of Europeans altered Indian tribal societies in significant ways. Even before direct contact, many Native Americans felt the effects of the European order in disease epidemics that weakened societal structure and threatened their very survival, sometimes killing entire tribes. A growing reliance on European trade also undermined the relations of production in Indian communities. The initial emphasis on trade in furs and the European insistence on dealing with only men marginalized women's economic roles. However, the exclusion from trade transactions did not always mean immediate deterioration in female status. For example, Iroquois women's influence in village affairs initially strengthened as men's hunting and trapping expeditions increased and warfare escalated. Among the Southwestern tribes, women contributed to trade in significant ways as producers of such desired items as weavings, beadwork, and pottery. But as Indian societies became dependent on trade, traditional political and social mores began to break down. It became expedient to choose leaders favorable to Euroamerican traders, and women often lost their influence in these decisions.

The confinement of Indians to reservations in the late nineteenth century intensified the pace of change in gender relations. In these limited spaces, plagued by hunger, disease, and poverty, the missionary efforts to educate and convert Indians to Christianity had devastating consequences for tribal value systems and the status of women. The missionaries advocated Western notions of womanhood and woman's place in society, emphasizing their role as submissive housewives while discouraging their participation in the public sphere. Boarding school education took children away from their families, diminishing women's educational roles. The restructuring of land ownership in tribes effected by the Dawes Act of 1887 further undercut the foundations of women's status as it assigned men the role of family head and provider. Agents of the Bureau of Indian Affairs (BIA) also imposed their views of gender on Indian societies, dealing primarily with the men of the tribe.

Yet, reservations helped emphasize Native American distinctiveness from the mainstream society and foster a sense of community. Reservations in time became home, and despite the intense pressure to assimilate, Indians showed resilience and adaptability to the changing conditions. Women especially managed to hold on to many of their traditional tasks as mothers and nurturers. Anna Moore Shaw, a Pima, grew up on the Gila River reservation in Arizona in the early twentieth century. In her autobiography, she recalls how children used to gather around their mothers and grandmothers as they worked, "for they would tell us stories." Through these stories, women transmitted tribal values and customs to their offspring. Women often formed the core of resis-

Emma Freeman's portrait of a northern California woman. This early twentieth-century image reflects the public interest in the distinctive roles Native women played in their societies as well as the romance that seemed to constantly surround the subject. Courtesy, The Newberry Library.

tance to those aspects of American culture they saw as offensive and disruptive to their communities. Simultaneously, they showed great adaptability and pragmatism as they willingly adopted tools of that culture that simplified their work, varying from sewing machines to agricultural implements.

Education in government boarding schools during this era reinforced Western notions of womanhood. These institutions taught Indian girls "the routine of household duties pertaining to their sex," while academic learning played a subordinate role. Under the outing system, the schools placed students in American families where they would learn by association and ultimately assimilate into the mainstream society. To many young Indian women these experiences were confusing and not applicable on the reservations to which most returned after completing their schooling. Yet for others, education in the boarding schools served as an incentive to look for wage employment. The 1900 United States Census reported 14 percent of Native American women as gainfully employed; approximately one-fourth of them were in domestic or personal service, undoubtedly encouraged and influenced by their boarding school experiences. Only 2 percent of the Indian female labor force worked as professionals, usually teachers, while most women toiled in unskilled agricultural and manufacturing jobs. These figures partly reflect the occupational choices available to women in general. However, among the 16 percent of gainfully employed European American women professional work was far more prevalent, accounting for over 10 percent of employment. At the same time, nearly 90 percent of the gainfully employed African-American women worked either in agriculture or private household service, reflecting the racial divisions within the female labor force.

Two officers of the Society of American Indians, each of them Sioux. Margaret Frazier (left) was Vice President for Membership, and Gertrude Bonnin (Zitkala-Sa) served as the organization's secretary and editor of the American Indian Magazine. *This picture was taken at the 1916 annual meeting of the SAI held in Cedar Rapids, Iowa. Courtesy, The Newberry Library.*

Several Indian women excelled in their professions and became leaders and lobbyists for their people. Susan LaFlesche, an Omaha from Nebraska, became the first female Indian physician when she graduated from the Women's Medical College of Pennsylvania in 1889. Besides doctoring for the Omahas, LaFlesche was a fierce temperance speaker, recognizing the devastating effects of "demon rum" in Indian communities. She also worked for the Women's National Indian Association, a reform organization founded in 1879 to protect and further the rights and interests of Native Americans. In her later years, LaFlesche became a political advocate for her people and traveled to Washington, D.C., in 1910 to lobby the federal government for tribal and land rights.

Gertrude Simmons Bonnin, or Zitkala-Sa, perhaps best exemplifies the emerging "new Indian woman." Born and raised on the Yankton Sioux reservation until the age of eight and returning there periodically throughout the years, she received her high school diploma from a Quaker missionary school in Indiana at the age of nineteen. She then attended Earlham College in Indiana, taught at Carlisle Indian School, and studied the violin at the Boston Conservatory of Music. While working at the Uintah and Ouray reservation in Utah with her Sioux husband, Bonnin became a correspondent for the Society of American Indians, beginning what would become her lifelong work in Indian reform. The Society organized in 1911 as the first reform organization managed exclusively by Indians and requiring that full members be Indi-

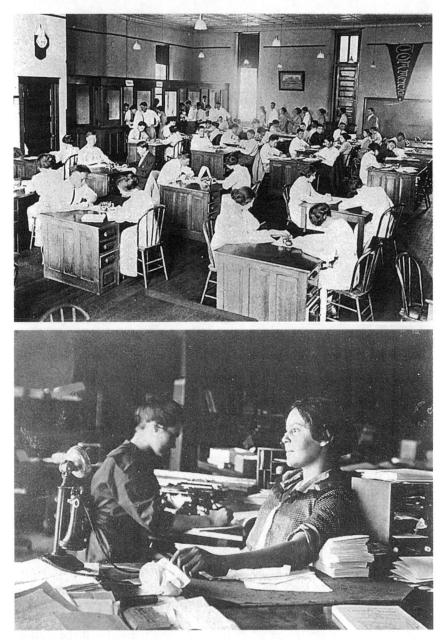

Top: *Young women who survived the shock of relocation to regimented boarding schools were expected to train for work as clerks and school teachers. This 1915 photograph shows the "commercial department" at Haskell Institute in Lawrence, Kansas. Bottom: Dora McCauley, Assistant Secretary of the Society of American Indians, dictating letters in her office in Washington, D.C., in 1913. The society, founded in 1911, advocated expanded opportunities for educated Native Americans. Both photos, Courtesy, The Newberry Library.*

ans. In 1916, Bonnin was elected secretary of the Society, and the family moved to the nation's capital. Her writings also took a turn toward political activism, concentrating on such issues as water and land rights. In 1926, Bonnin organized the National Council of American Indians, and remained in the leadership of this lobbying group until her death in 1938.

Both LaFlesche and Bonnin were part of the new Indian leadership that grew out of the boarding school experience and matured in the atmosphere of societal reform in the progressive era. Coming together for the first time, students from various tribal backgrounds realized what they had in common while their education gave them the tools to deal with mainstream society and its institutions. In the progressive tradition, many of these Indian reformers believed that education and assimilation would solve the "Indian problem," and the organizations they helped start reflected this belief. Their goals included reform of federal policies and reservation governments; their tactics were moderate, emphasizing lobbying, education, social programs, and legal defense.

The turn of the century witnessed another significant development in a Native American artistic revival. Amidst reservation poverty, many Indian communities turned to traditional arts and crafts to create marketable objects to generate necessary income. In the Southwest, the completion of the Santa Fe Railroad created a market for Indian crafts when the company began a promotional campaign, evoking the romance of the American West. Fred Harvey, a restaurateur with contracts to provision the railroad, stocked his hotels and restaurants with Native American objects to sell to visitors. These and other venues provided Southwestern Indians a market to sell craft products. The result was a renaissance of Pueblo pottery, of Apache, Pima, and Yuma baskets, and of Navajo weavings and silver jewelry.

Although both men and women participated in the production of these objects, women usually led the way. Hopi/Tewa artist Nampeyo is credited with the revival of pottery among her people. Inspired by pieces of excavated ceramics, she developed her own style based on traditional designs and elevated potterymaking to an art form. Nampeyo's popularity reached its peak during the economic boom of the 1920s, after she already had gone blind, and she continued to make pottery until her death in 1942. "When I first began to paint," she once recalled, "I used to go to the ancient village [of Sikyatki] and pick up pieces of pottery and copy the designs. That is how I learned to paint. But now I just close my eyes and see the designs and I paint them." The work of Nampeyo with that of San Ildefonso potter Maria Martinez attracted attention to Pueblo pottery, inspiring other Indian artists to revitalize and invigorate traditional forms.

Based on this foundation and the recognition of the economic opportunities inherent in the production of native arts and crafts, the Indian Reorganization Act (IRA) of 1934 established the Indian Arts and Crafts Board to promote arts as a means to self-sufficiency. The creation of the board was just one indication of the turnaround in federal policy from assimilation toward

Maria Martinez of San Ildefonso played a central role in reviving traditional pottery-making among Pueblo people in the early twentieth century. She created this design for a bowl in 1925. Courtesy, The Newberry Library.

acceptance and appreciation of Native cultures. Under the supervision of Commissioner John Collier, the act meant to give Indian tribes the tools to improve their conditions through self-government. The governmental model distributed to tribes reflected, nonetheless, non-Indian notions of civil rights and civil government. Tribal constitutions thus came to include the enfranchisement of women, but they also frequently incorporated articles that distributed property according to the ideal of nuclear family units. This notion undermined the tribal emphasis on extended family and complementary gender roles. The attempts to assign Indian women the status of middle-class, white American women also overlooked their traditional ways of influence. Despite its failings, historian Alison Bernstein points out, Collier's policy "broke new ground for Indian women from tribes with little or no history of formal public women's political participation."

Women felt the impact of the IRA most profoundly in the field of education. Increasing numbers of American Indian women entered educational institutions, receiving training in traditionally female occupations such as clerical work, teaching, and nursing. The growing bureaucracy of the BIA and its Indian hiring preference worked in favor of women. Simultaneously, the emerging tribal governmental structures added to their job opportunities on reservations. Women generally fared better on the labor market than their male counterparts because of the applicability of skills they already possessed while men continued to work unskilled, seasonal jobs in agriculture and manufacturing. Despite these advances, the vast majority of Indian women still held low-paying jobs in agriculture, manufacturing, and household service.

World War II represented a watershed in Indian communities, as it did in American society as a whole. By the war's end, some 25,000 Native Americans had served in the military, including 800 women in the military auxiliaries. In addition, by 1943 a total of 46,000 Indians had left their reservations—many for the first time—to work in agriculture and war-related industries; approximately one-fourth of them were women. On reservations, women stepped in to fill positions in tribal government and other jobs left vacant by the men who left to serve in the armed forces. The war thus expanded opportunities for women both on reservations and in the mainstream society. Although Indian women, among other groups of newly employed Americans, had to relinquish their jobs to returning veterans after the war was over, the home front experience was important in introducing large numbers of native women to wage employment and the mainstream society. The influx of women into the workforce and off the reservations thus extended into the postwar years.

Native American women continued to improve their relative position in the labor market. Between 1930 and 1960, the share of clerical work among employed American Indian women grew from approximately 3 percent to over 14 percent while their professional and technical employment increased from 4.6 percent to 9.1 percent. During this same time, the number of European American women in clerical jobs increased from 25 to nearly 35 percent while their professional employment actually declined from 16.2 to 14.6 percent. Despite their advances, two-thirds of all employed Indian women still held low-paying jobs in agriculture, manufacturing, and the service sector; their experiences reflected those of African American women, nearly 93 percent of whom worked in these sectors of the economy. Especially in the Southwest, the growing tourism industry provided numerous opportunities for women's wage work. American Indian women most often found employment as maids or as domestics in individual households. Though increasing their work load, steady income gave them a new sense of independence and power that translated into an assertiveness expressed in women's increased visibility and involvement in their communities. Many women also became the primary providers for their families while men brought in supplemental income from their seasonal labor.

Looking back at these postwar developments, some Indian women and men feel that women's sense of empowerment through wage employment may have adversely affected men's self-esteem. As a female member of the Salt River Pima Maricopa Indian Community in Arizona explained, husbands "probably felt somewhat useless because they often didn't have skills for employment. Women made men what they are, or were, in those days." This sense of displacement led to feelings of frustration and discouragement that, in turn, were expressed in the excessive use of alcohol and in apathy in general. The results were often devastating for families, and many women were left to take care of their children alone. By 1960, over 16 percent of all Indian households were headed by single mothers.

The years following the war also accentuated the political powerlessness of American Indian communities as the Truman and Eisenhower administrations moved to reverse the Indian New Deal. Assimilation and individualism again became the goals of federal policies. The efforts to end federal services to the tribes and to relocate Indians to the nation's cities epitomized these trends. Ironically, however, the threat of termination and the renewed assimilation pressures strengthened Indian tribalism and nationalism. As historian Peter Iverson contends, the decades of the 1940s and 1950s witnessed the maturation of reservation leadership. The increasing contacts with the mainstream society led many Native American leaders to realize that elements of American culture—such as the English language, new technological skills, and the legal system—could be effectively used to promote a continuing Indian America.

This shift in emphasis also was reflected in the resurgence of pan-Indian organizations. The National Congress of American Indians (NCAI) was founded in 1944 when eighty Native Americans from more than fifty tribes gathered in Denver, Colorado, to establish a broadly based, nonpartisan organization. Its goal was to work within the American political system to improve the status of indigenous people in the United States. The New Deal experience guided the group's activities, and the focus of activism thus shifted from assimilation to tribal sovereignty and self-determination. Women formed an important force within the organization, defending their cultural legacy against federal assaults on tribalism. Cherokee Ruth Muskrat Bronson served as the executive secretary of the NCAI until 1957 when she took a position as health education specialist in Arizona. Even after her retirement, Bronson continued her role as an educator, working among the Tohono O'odham and Yaqui in Arizona as representative of the Save the Children Foundation.

Helen Peterson, a Cheyenne who grew up enveloped in the Oglala Sioux culture, was appointed executive director of the NCAI in 1953. She had begun her education intending to be a teacher, but minority group relations became the focus of her life's work. Under Peterson's leadership, the NCAI took a strong stand against termination, arguing that the congressional resolution to terminate Indian tribes failed democratic principles because it had not secured the consent of the governed. The NCAI concluded that only Indians had the right to terminate federal supervision, and by 1958 the federal government accepted this argument. After Peterson's tenure with the NCAI ended, she remained committed to her belief that the recognition of tribal identity and culture forms the basis for an effective relationship with the authorities.

The threat of termination also mobilized women for action at the local level. Experiences in the workforce gave them confidence and skills to get involved in their communities, and many tribes witnessed an increase in women's political participation. Preserving the land for the children also served as an impetus for women's activism. The land for Indian mothers meant not just "a piece of land with a house on it, but the whole connection—the community, the history, the stories," explained Lumbee Donna Chavis. Reservations represented what was left of that connection, and preserving that home and its resources was central to many activist movements in the 1950s and 1960s.

This activism most frequently targeted federal water and power projects that threatened the home land and Indian survival on it. For example, the various nations of the Iroquois Confederacy resisted a series of projects affecting their lands from the 1940s into the 1960s. These resistance movements included the Seneca legal challenge to the Kinzua Dam project in Pennsylvania; Mohawk and Tuscarora resistance to the St. Lawrence Seaway project in New York; and Tuscarora armed resistance to the seizure of tribal land for a reservoir associated with the Niagara Power Plant project in New York.

In the Pacific Northwest, activist movements challenged the restrictions on Indian fishing rights beginning in the early 1960s. Ramona Bennett served on the tribal council of the Puyallup tribe when the battle over fishing rights erupted on her reservation in 1970. Holding a master's degree in education and with experience in human services in Seattle, Bennett became the spokesperson for the tribe in this conflict. She was among the thirty women and men who set up a security camp in Tacoma to protect the Indian fishers against the police and vigilantes. "In our camp, there were thirty men and women, there were teenagers and children," Bennett said, describing the extent of community participation in securing the tribe's last treaty right. But the struggle was not merely about the right to fish; it was also about the right of Puyallup culture to survive. In the words of Bennett: "Fishing is part of our art forms and religion and diet, and the entire culture is based around it." The Puyallup won the right to keep half the fish caught in their coastal waters under the 1974 ruling by federal district court judge George Boldt. Today, they continue to protest the depletion of the salmon by non-Indians, the construction of dams that block the salmon runs, and the industrial pollution that turns waters into "toxic soup." Ramona Bennett worked for these ends as the tribal chairperson from 1972 to 1978, and she continues the struggle at the national level and in many arenas. "Despite all the things that have happened to my tribe, I believe there is hope," she said, explaining her motivation. "Our children are our bright and shining stars. With each child, the promise is reborn."

Ada Deer embodies this same determination to defend Indian tribalism and sovereignty. Her tribe, the Menominee of Wisconsin, was among the most self-sufficient in the country in the early 1950s and thus considered suitable for termination of federal assistance. President Eisenhower signed the Menominee Termination Act in 1954, and the reservation became a county of Wisconsin in May 1961. However, the resources of the tribe had been depleted in preparation for termination, and by the end of the decade, Menominee county was near fiscal collapse. To raise revenue, tribal leaders began developing and selling waterfront lots to non-Indians. The reaction among the tribal members to the sale of tribal lands to whites, coupled with the possibility of losing political control over their own affairs, triggered the rise of a new tribal organization in 1970 called the Determination of Rights and Unity for Menominee Shareholders (DRUMS). DRUMS demanded that Congress reestablish its trust relationship with the Menominees, based on the recognition of their sovereign rights.

Ada Deer played a major role in restoring her people to federal recognition and trust status. She devoted her time to DRUMS and lobbied extensively in Wisconsin and in Washington, D.C., to gain support for their demands. "People said I was too young, too naive . . . I dropped out of law school. That was the price I had to pay to get involved," Deer later recalled. But her personal sacrifice paid off in many ways. In 1973, President Nixon signed legislation that restored the Menominee trust status, signaling the end of the termination policy. Ada Deer chaired the restoration committee from 1973 to 1976. She went on to teach in the School of Social Work and Native American Studies at the University of Wisconsin in Madison. In 1993, President Clinton appointed her assistant secretary of Indian affairs in the Department of the Interior.

Bennett and Deer represent a generation of Native American leaders that emerged in the activist decade of the 1960s. Influenced by the black civil rights movement, young, college-educated Indians assumed leadership positions in struggles to defend tribal rights, using the tactics of protest and civil disobedience. Encouraged by tribal elders, a group of such young activists founded the National Indian Youth Council (NIYC) in Gallup, New Mexico, in 1961. This new national organization acknowledged the role of younger Indians in setting the course for the future of Native peoples and committed itself to providing leadership to meet the challenge. Throughout the sixties, the group became particularly involved in the efforts to secure the fishing and hunting rights of northwestern tribes. In the 1970s, the organization turned its focus toward environmental issues.

Among the founding members of the NIYC was Akwesasne Mohawk Shirley Hill Witt. In addition to being an activist and taking care of her two children, Witt found time to attend the University of New Mexico, receiving a doctorate in anthropology. She taught for several years and took a particular interest in women's employment problems. She also worked for the United States Commission on Civil Rights, investigating civil rights violations in the Southwest. Although Witt's own work emphasized the challenges faced by American Indians, the research of the commission addressed all cultural groups in the United States. In the arenas of education, employment, and health, Witt found that American Indian women in the 1970s shared many difficulties with African American women, Chicanas, and the Appalachian poor. These commonalities included poor health care facilities and low education levels, resulting in jobs that did not provide enough income to take care of families. Witt further urged the recognition of commonalities between minority and majority women, "if not on a socioeconomic level, at least on a philosophic level," as an important step toward equality.

Witt herself represented a small, but growing, group of American Indian professionals. By 1970, 35 percent of all Indian women were employed, but only 10 percent of these women held professional or technical jobs. The respective figures for European American women were 40.6 and 16.3 percent, while of the over 47 percent of employed black women 11.4 percent were professionals. The most significant growth had taken place in clerical work, and 26 percent of employed Native American women worked in this sector while another 26 percent held service jobs. At the same time, the share of women employed as agricultural laborers dropped to only 2 percent while private households employed 7 percent of American Indian women. Less than 3 percent of European American women worked in these sectors of the economy while nearly 20 percent of employed African American women held jobs in private households and agriculture.

These changes in women's employment patterns also affected the structure of Indian family economies. Because they were more employable for full-time jobs than men, women's economic contributions to their households continued to grow in significance. Indian men were still concentrated in unskilled agricultural and construction jobs in which they faced seasonal unemployment. Despite their relative gains, Indian women found it hard to support families on their own. In 1980, nearly one in four American Indian families was maintained by a woman, and 47 percent of these single-mother families fell below the federal poverty line.

The 1960s and the early 1970s also saw the rise of new reservation leadership, intent on fulfilling the promise of self-determination. President Lyndon B. Johnson's Great Society provided the new generation of Indian leaders with the means to assume control over their affairs. After declaring an "unconditional war on poverty," Johnson signed the Economic Opportunity Act in August 1964, designed to eliminate poverty in the United States. While this act made no special provision for Native Americans, reservation Indians clearly comprised a rural group with a strong claim to the resources of anti-poverty legislation. In 1964, an estimated 74 percent of reservation families lived in poverty, and the median income was a mere 30 percent of the national average. High unemployment figures, low educational levels, inadequate housing, and high rates of illness and infant mortality compounded material poverty in Indian communities.

Considering the history of federal paternalism and control, the encouragement of Indian participation and local leadership in community action programs proved especially significant. As a Pima leader recalled, "community action programs helped bring about a more structural power base [and

Jaune Quick-To-See Smith was one of a new generation of Native American artists who began presenting traditional themes in contemporary art forms in the 1960s and 1970s. This image suggests the centrality of women in American Indian cultures. Courtesy, The Newberry Library.

they] involved people in the exercise to use the resources and to make decisions." Although the programs failed to eradicate material poverty, conditions on many reservations improved. New jobs also became available, providing viable alternatives for young reservation residents. Women again benefited from these job opportunities in important ways. Many programs created under community action dealt with health, education, and social services, considered part of the women's sphere of influence. Women thus expanded the boundaries of womanhood to include the public domain. The training and skills they acquired on the job allowed women to consider additional education and new occupations as options in their lives. Most of all, women gained experience and confidence in their abilities, propelling many into tribal politics and a continued commitment to community development. Pima Angela Brown reflected on her involvement as something that helped her gain "self-esteem, a sense of accomplishment, and satisfaction—a degree of power through involvement." The increasing number of women on tribal councils reflected this new sense of power; by 1980, approximately 12 percent of the nation's over 500 federally recognized tribes and Alaskan Native corporations had female leaders.

Wilma Mankiller, Principal Chief of the Cherokee Nation from 1985 to 1995 and the first female to lead a major Native American tribe, exemplifies the women leaders of this generation. Mankiller grew up in the poverty of rural Oklahoma, "raised with a sense of community that extended beyond my family." At the age of eleven, in 1956, she experienced her private Trail of Tears when the family moved to the San Francisco Bay area as part of the federal relocation program. She married at an early age and raised her family in the turbulent 1960s. After the occupation of Alcatraz, Mankiller became active in Indian causes in the San Francisco area and gained skills in community organization. She also attended college and earned a degree in social work. After divorcing her first husband, Mankiller returned to Oklahoma in 1977. She completed graduate work in community planning, spearheaded a community revitalization project in Adair County, and in 1983 was elected Deputy Chief of the Cherokee Nation. When the Principal Chief resigned in 1985, Mankiller succeeded him amid some controversy, but in the 1987 election the Cherokees gave her their support. As Chief, Mankiller emphasized indigenous solutions to develop the economy of and unity in the Cherokee Nation, maintaining that "Cherokee values, especially those of helping one another and of our interconnections with the land, can be used to address contemporary issues." Combining her Cherokee background with her experience in urban America, Mankiller thus emerged as a foremost leader in contemporary Indian America.

Mankiller is also representative of the American Indian urban experience during the 1960s and 1970s. At the turn of the century, some Native Americans already had settled in urban areas, usually close to where they had attended boarding school. By the 1920s, the Indian populations of American cities had grown large enough to merit the attention of government authorities, and the Meriam Report included a lengthy chapter on the conditions of these "migrated Indians." However, it was not until after World War II that Native Americans began to move to the nation's urban areas in significant numbers. The war years witnessed the first large-scale migration of women and men from reservations, looking for employment or service in the military. After the war, a substantial number settled in urban areas, as depressed reservation economies offered few opportunities. In the 1950s, the federal government contributed to this urbanization trend through its relocation program. Yet, most Indians moved to the city on their own, following families or friends already there or just seeking better opportunities. In 1960, 30 percent of the nation's American Indian population lived in urban areas, and a decade later that number had risen to nearly 45 percent. The 1980 census showed that more than one-half of all Native Americans had become urban.

The city offered new opportunities, but American Indian urban dwellers remained an economically disadvantaged group. Although their average income was considerably higher than that of people living on reservations, this did not translate into a higher standard of living. Not only was the cost of living—including housing, transportation, and medical expenses—generally higher in the city, but the unfamiliarity of many newly relocated Indians with the available services and with consumer affairs made them susceptible to abuses by merchants. The culture shock inherent in the move from reservation to city also added to the difficulties of adjustment. In her autobiography, Wilma Mankiller poetically recalls how she first experienced San Francisco:

> Wolves surrounded me. But my pursuers were not four-legged or fanged or covered with fur. They were a species of their own. I was nagged by anxiety, doubt, and fear that silently crept from the city's shadows with the thick bay fog to sit on window sills and hover at the door.

These conditions underscored the need for traditional support networks, but extended family units tended to suffer in the transition to an urban life and were replaced by the nuclear family. In many of these newly formed units, the mother became the center of family life and often also assumed responsibility for the economic survival of the family. While the call of the cities did uproot many different Indians from their respective reservation communities, city life did foster a sense of a common, Native American identity. This realization gave rise to intertribal networks that took on the role of an extended family. Churches often served as the initial point of contact between people from various tribes and became centers of social life in the city. In these settings, women played significant roles as "community mothers," extending their capacities for caretaking to the larger Indian community. They cooked and served meals at the socials; they took care of the children; they sang in the choir; and, they contributed their time to charitable causes. But women also assumed tasks as church elders and made decisions about the role of the church in the community. In all these functions, they formed female networks, discussing problems and concerns particular to them as women and as mothers.

Women's involvement in the Central Presbyterian Church in Phoenix, Arizona, attests to their influence in the emerging urban Indian communities. From its foundation in 1915, Central Presbyterian has been identified as the "Indian church" in Phoenix. Women participated in its functions as community mothers although they did not share in the formal decisionmaking process until 1958, when the church elected its first female elder. However, in their volunteer activities women formed a powerful network that emerged in the wake of the Great Society as a moving force behind community activism. While the church committed itself to providing for more than just the spiritual needs of the congregation, women identified family issues as their primary concern. They asked that the church apply for funding for a childcare center under the Economic Opportunity Act. The Head Start program at the church started in 1965, and women assumed a central role in running the program as employees and volunteers. Participation also aroused in them an acute awareness of the lack of Native American representation in the larger community, leading many to further involvement in community work and political activism. Reverend Joed Miller emphasized women's pivotal role in the growth of community participation:

> There never has been a sense that any of this was not women's work. You had a woman who felt something needed to be done, she would speak up . . . [T]hey were not hesitant to speak up and use their influence and their opinions and their weight, their community respect.

Besides churches, other social activities took on prominence as the number of Indians in urban areas grew. Sports proved a popular pastime and socializing activity, especially for young people. "Indian bars" assumed importance not only as drinking places but as places of contact to exchange information about housing and employment opportunities. Cultural groups formed around dancing and arts and crafts. Finally, Indian centers became significant foci of Native American urban communities. They served a socializing function, and with funding from Great Society programs, they increasingly assumed a role as the social agency for Indians in urban areas. In the early 1970s, many of these urban Indian centers became full-blown social service organizations, with programs varying from employment and housing assistance to arts and crafts to drug and alcohol abuse counseling. As with reservation community action projects, many of the services offered by the centers fell within the traditional female sphere and thus provided ample opportunities for women's employment. As a result, clerical positions at the centers became readily available, and since women often already had skills in typing, shorthand, and other office work, they were more employable than men. The training and educational programs for employees at Indian centers added to women's skills, prompting many to enroll in college programs and others to move on to new jobs. As a result, Indian women's visibility in their communities increased significantly and led many to take on more political tasks to improve the status of urban Indians.

Political activism in the urban context assumed a somewhat different character from that on the reservations. Urban Indian activists borrowed directly from other ethnic minorities, adopting the term "Red Power" as their slogan. The occupation of Alcatraz in 1969 was the starting point of this new era, culminating in the Trail of Broken Treaties in 1972 and the Wounded Knee occupation in 1973. The American Indian Movement (AIM) represented this new Indian activism, and its leaders Dennis Banks and Russell Means became the symbols of the "new American Indian." Although media concentrated on these male figureheads, as they seemed to conform to the romantic image of Plains warriors, women played a significant part in AIM as organizers of and participants in protests. Women's concerns most often reflected their roles as mothers. For example, during the Trail of Broken Treaties, Martha Grass, a middle-aged Cherokee woman from Oklahoma, stood up to Interior Secretary Morton. Mary Crow Dog, a Lakota deeply involved in AIM, recalls this incident in her autobiography:

> [She was] speaking from her heart, speaking for all of us. She talked about everyday things, women's things, children's problems, getting down to the nitty-gritty. She shook her fists in Morton's face, saying, "Enough of your bullshit!" It was good to see an Indian mother stand up to one of Washington's highest officials.

Similarly at Wounded Knee, women kept things running in the camp. They fed the occupiers and nursed the sick and the wounded. Mary Crow Dog herself gave birth during the occupation, after having refused to leave the camp during a ceasefire as requested by some male leaders. "I stayed, all the older women stayed, most of the young mothers with children stayed, the sweethearts of the warriors stayed," Crow Dog said, documenting the tenacity of the women.

Despite the lip service paid to complementarity of gender roles in Indian societies, many women activists found sexism and sexual and physical abuse to be realities. Men assumed the leadership roles in the organizations while women performed duties deemed "suitable" for them as secretaries, record keepers, cooks, and suppliers. Sexual and physical abuse have also been documented by some activist women. "Women's libber" became a derogatory term used against those women who refused to act according to the expectations of male leaders. Simultaneously though, women exerted their influence by appealing to their very feminine roles as mothers and educators. Indeed, women activists shied away from being defined as feminists or as having any particularly female agendas. They saw feminism as a white, middle-class movement with little relevance in their lives.

Navajo Annie Wauneka addressed the issue of Indian women's community participation in an article entitled "The Dilemma for Indian Women" in 1976. A longtime activist for health and education on her impoverished reservation, Wauneka pointed out that economic and cultural survival shape the realities of most Native American women. She contended that "[n]o role for the American Indian women on the reservation can be discussed without first addressing issues related to 'equal treatment, opportunity, and recognition of the Indians and the Tribal Government'." Wauneka concluded that Indian women must address their concerns within the context of those of the total group. Issues that Indian women see as critical thus include the protection of land and water rights, the strengthening of tribal governments, and the improvement of social, legal, and economic conditions among Indian peoples in the United States. Shirley Hill Witt also poignantly discusses Indian women's relationship to feminism:

> The world of the white *woman* is, for the most part, invisible to Indians. Even if it weren't invisible, it is irrelevant since the white *man's* world is the one making an impact upon Indian life and Indian individuals. It is still the Great White Father who determines the quality of life for native peoples as well as for other Americans, male and female.

In the 1970s, the "Great White Father" increasingly recognized issues facing American Indian communities, resulting in the most active period of federal legislation in the history of Indian-white relations. Women's concerns were addressed in legislation on child welfare and education as well as health issues. Women were especially active in regaining control of their children. For example, in 1974 an estimated 25 to 35 percent of Native American children were taken away from their families and placed in non-Indian foster homes or other institutions. After ten years of public hearings and pressure from Native American groups, Congress responded by enacting the Indian Child Welfare Act of 1978. Combined with increased tribal control of education and other social services, this act provided Indian nations with new tools to care for their children.

Health care was another major impetus for Indian women's activism. Ever since European epidemic diseases swept through the Americas, Native American health has lagged behind that of the general population. In the postwar years, alcoholism has become the number-one health problem among Native Americans, with an incidence over four times greater among Indians than among the general American population. For women, alcoholism is an issue not just because they, too, often succumb to the disease, but because alcohol-related physical abuse is as much a problem in Indian homes as it is in the larger society. Furthermore, the incidence of Fetal Alcohol Syndrome among Native Americans is higher than the national average. Women have taken action to fight the effects, and causes, of alcoholism by returning to traditional healing methods and emphasizing the importance of self-respect. Another aspect of the healing process is emphasis on the community. "With substance abuse, we're starting to see some changes—you have to attack it as a community, from the inside," explained Assiniboine Lois Steele.

While working to improve their communities as a whole, Indian women also became aware of the extraordinary assaults on indigenous *women*. Chippewa/Cherokee Elaine Salinas explained women's particular concerns:

> There were so many losses for women. There were cases in South Dakota where contaminated water caused abortions and premature births. A number of Indian women were sterilized—it happened in hospitals around the country. Children were taken away from their mothers. Collectively, we lost so much.

Women of All Red Nations (WARN) was organized in 1975 to address these issues. While most of these problems involved entire communities, the involuntary sterilization of Native American women emerged as a particularly female concern. According to a Government Accounting Office study, covering the years 1973 to 1976, four Indian Health Service hospitals performed nearly 3,500 sterilizations, in all but a few cases without federally required consent forms. Pressure from Native American groups led in 1978 to new regulations requiring that women indicate their informed consent before the procedure could take place. Women's groups continued to proliferate as Indian women became more involved in their communities and in the nation. For example, in 1983 a group of women from various tribes founded Ohoyo as an advocacy group for American Indian women. Among its board members were Ada Deer, Shirley Hill Witt, Cherokee scholar and author Rayna Green, and Choctaw administrator and activist Owanah Anderson.

At the local level, women also formed groups that addressed particular women's issues within the context of the larger Indian community. In Arizona, some four hundred Native women gathered at a statewide Indian Women's Conference in 1976 to discuss women's leadership in urban areas and on reservations. This group of women acknowledged their rights and responsibilities in their communities as the starting point for activism. Veronica Murdock, vice chair of the Colorado River Indian Tribes, delivered the keynote address, emphasizing women's political participation as a key to self-determination. The conference also addressed issues such as rape and sexual abuse while keeping sight of the larger historical context of Indian experiences. These Arizona Indian women clearly chose traditional notions of womanhood and community as an impetus for their activism. They also saw the teaching of those values to their children as *the* goal to bring about change. One conference participant clearly expressed this view in her comments:

> We, as mothers, have a lot to do in the upbringing of our children. Should we go on as we are, or should we revert back to our traditional ways? I strongly believe that if we revert to our traditional ways and try to instill some of the teachings that we got from our parents in the upbringing of our children . . . this would give the children a lot to think about, because after all, the old way of living to me is the best way.

One medium through which American Indian women have been able to assert effectively these traditional values is the written word. Early in the century, Zitkala-Sa wrote stories based on Indian legends and published two books of American Indian stories. Yankton Sioux anthropologist Ella Deloria played an integral role in the preservation of the Dakota language and oral traditions, beginning in the 1930s. She also moved beyond the standard anthropological approach toward literary forms based on non-Indian models. In 1944, she published *Speaking of Indians,* a nontechnical description of Indian life. During that decade, she also drafted *Waterlily,* a novel of nineteenth-century Dakota life from a woman's perspective.

Despite these early literary endeavors, it was not until the resurgence of Indian activism in the 1960s that the written word became an important form of affirming "Indianness." In 1969, Kiowa novelist and poet N. Scott Momaday won the Pulitzer prize for his *House Made of Dawn,* and since then many American Indian writers—women and men alike—have received critical acclaim for their work. The works of all these authors share certain characteristics that derive from oral forms of expression: the emphasis on event over process; the significance of language; the concern with place; and, the affirmation of tribal cultural values. In addition, the prose and poetry of female writers often focus on women's concerns, reflecting tribal notions of women's roles and status in society. Chippewa Louise Erdrich and Laguna Pueblo Leslie Marmon Silko are among the most acclaimed women authors. Their fiction and poetry affirm cultural continuity and women's roles in the face of change and transformation of Indian societies.

In their writing, as in other forms of activism, American Indian women speak out against stereotypes and articulate their own ideas of femininity and what it means to be Indian. They display strong ties to the spiritual currents of the past while keeping sight of the political realities of the present. They address issues of land and water; they deal with the historical mistreatment of their people; they discuss the struggle between tradition and mainstream values; and they speak to the ability of Indian communities to change while, at the same time, holding on to tribal values. Their motivation for writing is survival. Creek poet Joy Harjo expresses this point of view and reflects on her responsibility as a writer:

> I feel strongly that I have a responsibility to all the sources that I am: to all past and future ancestors, to my home country, to all places that I touch down on and that are myself, to all voices, all women, all of my tribe, all people, all earth, and beyond that to all beginnings and endings. In a strange kind of sense it frees me to believe in myself, to be able to speak, to have voice, because I have to; it is my survival.

In the 1990s, American Indian women are surviving and making headway in significant ways. As writers and artists, Indian women are in a position to shape the image and the awareness of Native American peoples in the larger society. More important, they can instill a positive image in the youths of their nations to help them deal with the struggle between cultures. Education is a key factor in this change, and tribally controlled education grants the opportunity to combine two cultures in an effective way. In the words of Menominee educator Carol Dodge, teaching tribal culture and language "has helped the children understand who they are, and that if they choose to be a Catholic or a Methodist, there is nothing wrong with that." Since the founding of the Navajo Community College in 1968, over twenty tribes have founded colleges to prepare Indian youth for vocational and professional careers. The emergence of Native American studies programs on campuses across the country and special recruitment efforts also have increased the number of Indian students attending colleges and universities.

The result of these developments is an emerging American Indian scholarly community, which includes a number of women. Their research has shed light on the historical roles of Native women as well as other aspects of American Indian life. Chippewa/Choctaw ethnohistorian Clara Sue Kidwell has written on Indian women as cultural mediators while Dakota anthropologist Beatrice Medicine has explored issues of mental health and education. Navajo anthropologist Jennie Joe and Cherokee ethnomusicologist Charlotte Heth are other examples of powerful women in academia. In addition, women are increasingly involved in national organizations as professionals. Ponca/Creek lawyer Yvonne Knight joined the staff of the Native American Rights Fund soon after it was established in 1970, and the Council of Energy Resource Tribes employs several influential women.

Despite the emergence of an American Indian professional class, the majority of the 55 percent of Native women in the labor force in 1990 were still concentrated in low-paying jobs. They worked in the service sector; in technical-, sales-, and administrative-support positions; and as unskilled laborers. At the same time, the number of female-headed households increased to 27 percent of the total American Indian households; the median income in these families was only about one-fourth of the national average for married couples and about 62 percent of the average for all female-headed families. As a result, one-half of the households headed by Indian women lived in poverty in 1990 while 31 percent of all Indian families fell below the poverty line. Substance abuse, poor housing, and the concomitant health problems often compound the material poverty. But even in these circumstances many Indian women are strong and manage to carry their families through difficulties. Blackfeet Betty Cooper, a mother and the executive director or the American Indian Family Healing Center in Oakland, California, explained the source of this strength:

> It is really our own cultural and traditional values that we need. . . . An Indian woman needs to know herself as an Indian woman first, then she can be better to people around her. If she doesn't know this, then something is always missing, something is not quite right. . . . I feel that when they know themselves traditionally and they know their background, their Indian identity is intact, and they are proud of who they are. And then, how do you use it? Not just one day a week; you use it in every fiber of life.

Many American Indian women today emanate this strength and sense of tradition. They serve as role models for young Indian girls in need of their own self-esteem. As professionals, artists, writers, community activists, and, most important, as mothers, women participate in shaping the images of Native peoples. Like Carol Redcherries, they exemplify the persistence of American Indians in the face of constant cultural onslaught. The hearts of these women are not on the ground—and the Indian nations are not conquered.

For Further Reading

The field of American Indian women's history is still wide open, and there are few book-length treatises of Indian women's historical roles. Especially lacking are studies of native women in the twentieth century. Historical overviews of women in American Indian societies that provide some discussion of twentieth-century developments include *The Hidden Half: Studies of Plains Indian Women* (Washington, D.C., 1983), edited by Patricia Albers and Beatrice Medicine; *Women in American Indian Society* (New York, 1992), by Rayna Green; *Women and Power in Native North America* (Norman, 1995), edited by Laura Klein and Lillian Ackerman; and, *Negotiators of Change: Historical Perspectives on Native American Women* (New York, 1995), edited by Nancy Shoemaker.

Life histories and autobiographies provide excellent examinations of the issues that shape the lives of American Indian women. Among these works are *Life Lived Like a Story: Life Stories of Three Yukon Native Elders* (Lincoln, 1992), by Julie Cruikshank; *Yaqui Women: Contemporary Life Histories* (Lincoln, 1978), by Jane Holden Kelly; and *Apache Mothers and Daughters: Four Generations of a Family* (Norman, 1992), by Ruth McDonald Boyer and Narcissus Duffy Grayton. Mary Crow Dog, with Richard Erdoes, discusses the American Indian Movement and her life in *Lakota Woman* (New York, 1990) while Wilma Mankiller, with Michael Wallis, tells her life story in *Mankiller: A Chief and Her People* (New York, 1993). Mark St. Pierre accounts the life of a Lakota woman early in the century in *Madonna Swan: A Lakota Woman's Story* (Norman, 1991).

Literature and poetry by Native American women accentuate their roles and concerns in modern society. Rayna Green's edited collection, *That's What She Said: Contemporary Poetry and Fiction by Native American Women* (Bloomington, Ind., 1984), and a new anthology, *Reinventing the Enemy's Language: Contemporary Native Women's Writings of North America* (New York, 1997), serve as a good introduction to Indian women writers. *Love Medicine* (New York, 1984), by Louise Erdrich; *Storyteller* (New York, 1981) by Leslie Marmon Silko; and Luci Tapahonso's *Sáanii Dahataał: The Women Are Singing: Poems and Stories* (Tucson, 1993) are just a few of the many literary works by American Indian women.

Appendix

Major Dates in U.S. and American Indian History

The following dates suggest the scale and complexity of American Indian history by listing events that are generally overlooked in standard texts. We have slighted treaties and policy statements in favor of tribal migrations, epidemics, and other events which have generally gone unreported. We have also included dates from all parts of the United States. By emphasizing the geographical sweep of Indian history we remind readers again that the story of Native people is more than the record of their contact with Europeans, and that events did not move simply from east to west.

ca. 1400   Navajo and Apache ancestors migrate south into Arizona and New Mexico

ca. 1500   Iroquois Confederacy forms

1520   First epidemics (smallpox, influenza, malaria) in Mesoamerica

1535   Cartier in St. Lawrence Valley; early barter for furs and metal tools; French transmit contagious diseases to Northeast

1540   Coronado in New Mexico, DeSoto in Southeast; destruction and plunder of Rio Grande pueblos, southeastern towns

1585   Spanish establish St. Augustine in Florida to protect territorial claims and support trade with Indians; English settle at Roanoke

1598   Oñate enters New Mexico to establish Spanish colony

1607
Jamestown

1609   Champlain, with Indian allies, engages in battle with Mohawks in northern Vermont

1616–19   Major plague epidemic in New England

1620
Plymouth
Colony

1622   Opechancanaugh leads Virginia uprising against Jamestown Settlement

1624   Dutch Ft. Orange (later Albany) established as fur trade outpost on Hudson River

1637   English destroy Pequot villages

1643   Kieft's war, lower Hudson valley and New York tribes decimated

1649   Iroquois warriors destroy Huron villages

1670   Hudson's Bay Co. chartered by Charles II

1675–76   Metacom (King Philip) leads New England tribes against English; Nathaniel Bacon leads Virginia settlers in established destruction of Chesapeake tribal power

1680   Pueblos revolt and Spaniards retreat from New Mexico

1685
Penn establishes
Pennsylvania

1701   Iroquois Confederacy establishes peace agreements with France and Great Britain

1715   Yamassee War

ca.1725   Crows separate from Hidatsas to form separate Plains hunting society

1729–31   Destruction of the Natchez by French based in New Orleans

1730   First California Indian missions established

1732
Georgia colony
founded

1751	Northern Pimans force Spanish retreat from Arizona
1763	Pontiac leads campaign against British authority in aftermath of French defeat in Seven Years' (or French and Indian) War
ca.1770	Cheyennes begin to abandon farming and migrate out of Great Lakes area; Teton Sioux cross Missouri River
1772	Samson Occum publishes first original work in English by an Indian author
1779–81	Major smallpox epidemic, from Mexico to Canada

1783
Treaty of Paris

1787–89	Major documents of U.S. Indian policy adopted: Northwest Ordinance, U.S. Constitution, early treaties with eastern tribes
1790	Defeat of American troops under Gen. Harmar; Ohio Indian Confederacy defends border with United States at Ohio river
1791	Defeat of Gen. St. Clair by Ohio tribes
1794	U.S. troops defeat Ohio tribes at Fallen Timbers
1799	Founding of Sitka, Alaska
1799	Handsome Lake religion begins among the Seneca

1800
Jefferson
elected president

1810–13	Tecumseh and Tenskwatawa attempt to hold Indiana and establish intertribal army

1812–15
War of 1812

1819
Erie Canal opens

	1825	Treaty at Prairie du Chien (Wis.) with Sioux and other "western" tribes
1828 Andrew Jackson elected president	1828	*Cherokee Phoenix,* tribal newspaper, begins publication
	1830s	Forced removal of Great Lakes and Southeastern tribes to Oklahoma
	1837	Smallpox epidemic on plains virtually wipes out Mandan and Hidatsa villages
1846 Mexican War		
	1847–49	Opening of Oregon Trail and California gold strikes bring wagon trains
	1851	U.S. negotiates Ft. Laramie Treaty which establishes tribal boundaries on plains, right of way for emigrants; Isaac Stephens negotiates treaties with Northwest Coast tribes
1857 *Dred Scott* decision	1857	Publication of John Rollin Ridge's *The Life and Adventures of Joaquin Murrietta,* first novel written by an Indian
	1862	Santee Sioux resistance led by Little Crow
1863 Emancipation Proclamation	1863	Sand Creek massacre of Cheyennes by Colorado volunteers
	1868	Red Cloud defeats U.S. troops; Bozeman Trail forts abandoned and new treaty negotiated at Ft. Laramie
1869 Transcontinental railroad completed		
	1871	Congressional resolution ends treaty making
	1876	Sioux and Cheyenne defeat Seventh Cavalry at Little Big Horn
	1887	Dawes Severalty Act mandates eventual breakup of all reservations into individual homesteads
	ca. 1889	Ghost Dance Religion spreads from Nevada to Plains

	1890	Wounded Knee Massacre at Pine Ridge reservation, South Dakota
1898 Spanish American War		
	1903	Supreme Court in *Lone Wolf* v. *Hitchcock* rules Congress has power to abrogate treaties with Indian tribes
	1911	Founding of Society of American Indians
1917–1918 United States in WW I		
	1918	Native American Church incorporated in Oklahoma
	1924	Congress imposes U.S. citizenship on Indians who lack it
	1928	Meriam Report exposes reservation suffering
1932 FDR elected president		
	1934	Indian Reorganization Act passed to end allotment and allow formation of modern tribal governments
	1935	Indian Arts and Crafts Board established
1941–1945 United States in WW II		
	1944	National Congress of American Indians established
	1946	Indian Claims Commission established to settle all outstanding land claims
1952 Eisenhower elected president	1952	Public Law 280 allows for state criminal jurisdiction over reservations in certain states
	1953	House Concurrent Resolution 108 passed, launching campaign to "terminate" federal role in Indian affairs

| 1961 | American Indian Chicago Conference calls for greater Indian self-determination; National Indian Youth Council founded |

1963
Martin Luther King
gives "I Have a
Dream" Speech in
Washington, D.C.

| 1964 | American Indian Historical Society inaugurates The Indian School |

1965
Escalation of war
in Vietnam

| 1966 | Rough Rock Demonstration School (Navajo Nation) opens, provides influential example of local control and bilingual-bicultural education |

| 1968 | American Indian Movement founded in Minneapolis; Indian Civil Rights Act passed |

| 1969 | Navajo Community College, first tribally controlled college, offers initial classes; start of Alcatraz Island occupation; N. Scott Momaday wins Pulitzer Prize for *House Made of Dawn;* Vine Deloria, Jr. publishes *Custer Died for Your Sins* |

| 1971 | Taos Pueblo regains control of Blue Lake; Alcatraz occupation ends |

| 1971 | Alaska Native Claims Settlement Act |

| 1972 | Newberry Library establishes Indian history center, with D'Arcy McNickle chosen as first director; Trail of Broken Treaties; occupation of BIA offices in Washington, D.C. |

1973
Watergate
hearings

| 1973 | Wounded Knee occupation; Restoration of Menominee reservation |
| 1974 | "Boldt decision" supports Indian fishing rights in Pacific Northwest |

| 1975 | American Indian Self-Determination and Education Assistance Act |

	1978	Establishment of Federal Acknowledgment Branch encourages formal federal recognition of more Indian communities; Indian Child Welfare Act and Indian Religious Freedom Act approved; U.S. Supreme Court issues decisions in *Oliphant* v. *Suquamish Indian Tribe* and *Santa Clara* v. *Martinez*
1980 Ronald Reagan elected president	1980	Penobscot and Passamaquoddy Indian communities in Maine achieve settlement of land claims
	1984	Louise Erdrich publishes *Love Medicine*
	1985	Wilma Mankiller becomes Principal Chief of Cherokee Nation in Oklahoma
1986 *Challenger* space shuttle disaster		
	1988	Indian Gaming Regulatory Act
	1990	Native American Graves Protection and Repatriation Act
	1991	Custer Battlefield National Monument renamed Little Bighorn Battlefield National Monument
1992 Bill Clinton elected president	1992	Mashantucket Pequots negotiate compact with Connecticut to build Foxwoods Casino
	1993	Ada Deer named Assistant Secretary of the Interior for Indian Affairs
	1994	George Gustav Heye Center of the National Museum of the American Indian opens in New York City
	1997	Confrontations occur in Arizona, New Mexico, and other states over construction and operation of Indian casinos

Index

Note: For ease of reference on maps, towns have been located with a modern-day state abbreviation. References to illustrations are indicated by an
"*i*" following the page number. References to maps are indicated by an "*m*"
following the page number.

284

Indians in American History: An Introduction, Second Edition
Developmental and Copy Editor: Andrew J. Davidson
Production Editor and Text Designer: Lucy Herz
Proofreader: Claudia Siler
Maps: Jim Bier and Jane Domier
Index: Fred Leise
Cover Design: DePinto Graphic Design
Printer: McNaughton & Gunn, Inc.